Vernon Lee

Baldwin

Being Dialogues on Views and Aspirations

Vernon Lee

Baldwin
Being Dialogues on Views and Aspirations

ISBN/EAN: 9783337180737

Printed in Europe, USA, Canada, Australia, Japan

Cover: Foto ©Thomas Meinert / pixelio.de

More available books at **www.hansebooks.com**

BALDWIN:

BEING

DIALOGUES ON VIEWS AND ASPIRATIONS.

BY

VERNON LEE

AUTHOR OF "STUDIES OF THE 18TH CENTURY IN ITALY,"
"EUPHORION," "MISS BROWN," ETC.

"*A man is a method, a progressive arrangement, a selecting principle, gathering his like to him wherever he goes.*"—EMERSON

"*And if I contradict myself, why, I contradict myself.*"—WALT WHITMAN

London
T FISHER UNWIN
26 PATERNOSTER SQUARE
1886

TO MY BROTHER,

EUGENE LEE HAMILTON,

I DEDICATE

THIS BOOK OF VIEWS AND ASPIRATIONS,

GRATEFUL FOR ALL HE HAS DONE

IN FORMING MY OWN.

TABLE OF CONTENTS.

	PAGE
OF BALDWIN, INTRODUCTORY	1
THE RESPONSIBILITIES OF UNBELIEF	15
THE CONSOLATIONS OF BELIEF	75
OF HONOUR AND EVOLUTION	127
OF NOVELS	185
THE VALUE OF THE IDEAL	247
OF DOUBTS AND PESSIMISM	309

INTRODUCTION.

INTRODUCTION.

It would grieve me that any reader should question the real existence of my friend Baldwin; yet I confess also that I should be sorry were any one to believe too implicitly therein. There is, in a hitherto unspecified part of this world, a borderland between fact and fancy; and in this borderland my friend has a very actual habitation. I dread misapprehension, and crave permission for a few words on this point. Ask yourself, my patient or impatient reader, how much you actually know of your own nearest and dearest; nay, of the nearest and dearest of all —of yourself. The question is one over which a judicious person might reasonably go mad, or die, without coming nearer to a complete solution. But this much of certainty would be acquired by the way, that the something to which we give the name of our friends is a creature somehow mysteriously born of ourselves and of them; a creature which exists not really in the exterior and concrete world, but in our mind, or, if you prefer, in that particular borderland of fact and fancy. I do not care to commit myself to stating on which side, nearer or farther, of that strip of borderland, lies the exact dwelling-place of the chief speaker in the following Dialogues. To any over-inquisitive person I would make this answer: Tell me precisely how much of yourself is real or imaginary; and you shall have the corresponding information respecting my friend Baldwin.

To be brief, Baldwin exists; and it matters not whether in the kingdom of the subjective or in that of the objective. What is more important, is of his mode of existence. If, as is usually the case, and as I distinctly request, this introductory chapter be read the last of all, the reader will not require to be told that the existence of Baldwin has been, so far as the Past is concerned, equally uneventful and eccentric. He has, in good sooth (and this may lead some to consider him as a denizen of the subjective world), lived a life of exclusively mental experiences, never doing or being done to, but merely receiving a series of impressions and responding thereunto by a series of opinions. These opinions, if you have read the book, you will sufficiently understand: there remains only to explain the circumstances which conduced to their formation; in other words, to say something of Baldwin's impressions.

This rather abstract personage, to whom life has been scarcely more than a string of abstract experiences and resultant ideas, has two further peculiarities, that complete, so to speak, his abstract personality—the something rather negative about him. The accident of education, carried on exclusively at home and in exceptional solitude, has placed this not very feminine man to some measure at a woman's standpoint, devoid of all discipline and tradition, full of irregularities and individualities. And the accident of family circumstances, carrying him from country to country, has made this very English Briton see questions of all sorts through variously tinted cosmopolitan glasses. Indeed, since I have mentioned the subject of nationality, I may say that one of my friend's eccentricities and weaknesses consists in a secret satisfaction at the fact of having been born upon French soil, and a corresponding slight dissatisfaction at being unable to prove the existence in his nature of some strain or other of French blood.

Of my friend Baldwin's actual education and early life I am unable to give any very definite account. I see that they were vague, casual; and that, so far as life is concerned, the various periods of existence, in the sense in which they were symbolized by mediæval artists as Pueritia reading a grammar book, Adolescentia holding a hawk, and so forth, were rather out of sequence or jumbled up in his case. He was a commonplace child, a sentimental boy, a harshly philosophic youth; and is now, close upon what the Poet defined as the "mezzo del cammin di nostra vita" rejected by some as over-sceptical and subjective, by others as densely dogmatic and utilitarian. We have met, he and I, every now and then, turning up when least we expected to see one another, at various periods of our lives. My earliest recollections of Baldwin are of a time when the streets of Rome were periodically strewn with yellow sand, into which the multitude flopped on bent knees, putting out index and little finger against the evil eye, whenever there passed the golden coach of the Holiness of Our Sovereign Pius IX.; when we children woke up and rubbed our eyes one foggy autumn morning with (for such is the nature of children) a slightly delicious horror at the thought that Monti and Tognetti were having their heads cut off, like Browning's Franceschini, at the Bocca della Verità. Baldwin and I, and another lad who, while we have gone off on the endless hunt for ideas (A good day's sport? asked a friend of mine lately of two men with guns on an umbrian road—So, so, only two mushrooms), has seized hold of that more satisfactory though unruly creature, beauty; Baldwin and this other lad and myself used, at that time, to wander along those long muddy roads bordered with arum and shaded with carub, now all built over in streets, then the haunt of solitary cardinals taking their stroll, employing our leisure in digging out of the gutters bits of porphyry and serpentine, which to us represented all antiquity; of an evening we indulged in learned disputes over Dr.

Smith's Smaller Classical Dictionary. Later I met Baldwin again, a decided failure in all that the world calls education, but possessed by a frenzy of enthusiasm, nay, rather madness, for all things musical, especially of the eighteenth century, with which he contrived to infect me, but completely and seriously, with the later result, to myself and literature, which some readers perhaps know. We had a music master in common, Baldwin and I; an old man nearly ninety, chosen by my friend mainly in the vain hope that he might bridge over that fearful gulf separating the eighteenth century from these degenerate days; and whom he adored less like a human being than a precious relic, getting sonnets written by his acquaintances and placing upon the old gentleman's piano large nosegays, which the receiver, I suspect, regarded principally in the light of their being damp. Baldwin was at this time eighteen. He read Goethe and Lessing all day long, descanted upon the wisdom of the Greeks in avoiding the sight of pain and considering illness as a proof of bad taste and a reason to be cut; and believed firmly that all moral qualities were contained in the Beautiful; and that if there were any which the Beautiful did not contain, there was probably something Morbid about them. That word *morbid* was Baldwin's favourite expression; and it was wonderful to see how freely and with what terrible effect he flung it about in his conversation. When next my friend's path suddenly crossed mine, he never mentioned Goethe, nor the Antique, nor eighteenth century music, and manifested impatience when they were alluded to; he was comparatively uncommunicative, and excessively pessimistic. I suspected him of being miserably unhappy, and afterwards discovered that he was struggling hopelessly with certain ideas that were surrounded by a kind of blackness: Death, Sin, Pain, Justice. How he emerged from this, some of the following Dialogues are designed to show. Such is, roughly, the history of my friend Baldwin. Such it is, at least, in so far as an outsider can show it. But a letter which I received from him within the last year seems in a manner to fill up these bare outlines, or at least to show what sort of colour there might be within them. "It comes home to me," he wrote from a small Italian village where he was passing a few days—"it comes home to me, on returning here, how large is the part which this microscopic place has played for me. My life seems hanging, flakewise, like the wool of a sheep, on every stone and bramble; it is the only place which has been to me a home, in the sense of long and close intimacy, and, so to speak, possession; for Rome, Florence, Paris, are things with which one cannot feel intimate, which may possess us, but which we never possess. Also, I think that this sense of so much of my life being represented here is due in part to the fact that nothing new has ever come to me here, that I have merely chewed the cud of any novelty of the winter;

that this place has, instead of producing change, merely registered it. Chewed the cud of my thoughts, mind you, in virtual solitude—the enforced solitude of the four broiling months for which I was pent up in this valley; chewed the cud of my thoughts and feelings as one might do while walking up and down a piece of prison garden; and observed, taken a vivid interest in every detail, much upon the principle of Saintine's *Picciola*. I speak with no disrespect or want of love. Narrow and fatally imprisoning as this place was, and much as I often chafed at the thought of all that lay beyond these eternal green mountains, from the scarce known England, the vaguely remembered Germany, the faintly imagined far-off regions, down to the little country town twelve miles off—despite all this nostalgic craving to get away, I certainly loved the place. It is indeed the only place I have possessed in absolute familiarity, excepting perhaps T——, in my childhood; the only place where I have been obliged to take an interest in everything, or rather within whose limitations I have had to find everything. I can remember something similar in my childish years at T——: the complete intimacy with every turn, every path; the interest in the fern growing on certain walls, in the scarlet mushroom on a particular bank skirting a beech wood; the historical mania and fancies evoked by a few scraps, a tower, an old piece of wall, a graven hand on a milestone. I can remember all this, and the effort to construct myself a universe out of this tiny spot. The same happened, with a more mature myself, greater wants and richer surroundings, here; the same making out of this place my microcosm of the world. The constant going over the same ground, the necessity among all these things, which were old to me, of finding something new; of squeezing some sort of excitement out of this exhausted place, most certainly taught me to see, and in great measure to imagine, to feel, acutely. The smallest trifles gained a value: the particular curve of the hill here, the particular effect of a clump of trees there; the trunk of an olive; the stones in the water; the tips of the cypresses and their beautiful compactly fibrous greyish boles; the feathery tuft of fennel in an old wall; the runnel of water below it, plastering down the grass;—all such trifles became subjects of constant observation, interest, and pleasure. And each path represented a new combination of such specific little impressions, and hence possessed a sort of almost dramatic value by being able to produce a given set of feelings. As with nature, so with associations. I had to make up the Past out of this place. Hence an extraordinary interest in all things local (just as when, as a child, I used to make the schoolmistress of T—— tell me, over and over again about the *Vehmgericht*, the *Wends*, the *Frisians*, all the various legends of the place)—chronicles, documents, traditions, folklore. A dear old friend, a local antiquary, would sit by the hour telling me about Latins and Longobards, and lend me large folios of documents. The little I know of the Middle Ages I learned by thinking over all these little Apennine towns and villages. And when the eighteenth century craze was on me, I got hold of it, quarried for it, here; fixing my mind upon the little villeggiatura houses with sundials, escutcheons, and long flights of steps, seeing Lindoros and Lucindas on the twisted iron balconies, musing even over the old stiff chairs and tables in the villa anterooms. These visions, the strange imaginative fumes raised by myself, still hang about the place. I remember the interest in a destroyed feudal village, which had disappeared off the earth's face, leaving its name, its association of feudal hunts, *San Mamerto a Cerbaiola*, to the chestnut woods on a certain hill. Even now, I cannot see, or think of, the two square grey towers of Pieve a Gioviano, three miles off, rising in the evening light against the solemn background of mountains, the wide river washing round them, without the feeling coming over me that those towers penetrate somehow into the Middle Ages; that their bells, tolling above the river roar, among the hill echoes, have in them the voice of the centuries swinging, as it were, from the Present to the Past and back again. This is the real, the existing, and this is the intensity which restriction within so limited a space produced concerning it. Similarly with the purely imaginary. I cannot but think that a certain intensity, almost broodingness, not much in keeping with an impressionable, and in a sense abstract, unreal, fickle character like mine, was due in a measure to the months of solitude in such a place as this. The very spots where my day-dreams arose bring them back to me: a certain wall on the hillside, leaning upon which and looking down upon the oleanders and tawny honeysuckles in the garden below, and the deep green ravine below that, my mind went a Brocken ride after the Witches of Lodrone, the Lady of Monza, the strange Bonvisi woman of Lucca. Again, a certain lane between high-lying cornfields and vine trellises, haunted, as with the smell of its wild rose and privet, by the thought of Charles the Bold and Louis XI. and Joan of Arc; just as the damp autumnal paths beneath the sycamores of a certain villa bring home to me strains of eighteenth century music, Consuelo visions of singers and poets and composers, Pacchierotti, Farinelli, Porpora, Metastasio. And I remember the struggle in my mind of horror and reason on reading first of the wickedness of the Renaissance, as connected with the simmering, shimmering cornfields, the smell of the green standing hemp, the rush and flash of the river among the reeds. It has done much towards making me, this little place. But making me what? The usual story: many ingredients, much fussing, and a result how out of all keeping! A creature troubled with the desire to create, yet able only to criticize; consumed (which is worse) with the desire to affirm, yet condemned to deny; a life spent in being repelled by the exaggerations of one's friends, and attracted by the seeming moderation of one's enemies, in taking exception in the midst of assent: scepticism in a nature that desires to believe and rely, intellectual isolation for a man who loves to be borne along by the current—an unsatisfactory state of affairs, yet to me the only one conceivable."

A negative being, in many respects, my friend Baldwin, as you have already been told; and negative perhaps all the more that, as you see, there is much which is positive in his nature. An illusive, shimmering personality, seemingly full of contradictions, yet, at the same time, almost repulsively cut and dried. Negative, self-contradictory, abstract, as becomes an inhabitant of the country which lies, as I have observed, upon the boundaries of fact and fancy.

My own relations towards him? Remember what I have just remarked above. They are absolutely indefinable. I am the pupil of Baldwin, the thing made by him, or he is my master, yet made by me; choose and understand, for I cannot. I agree in all his ideas; yet I can place myself at the point of view of some of his opponents. I have felt like Vere, I often feel like Rheinhardt, I respect Agatha, I do not utterly despise Marcel, I love and am dazzled by the beautiful transcendentalist Olivia; yet I agree with Baldwin, and, agreeing, I sometimes dislike him. If I am pushed into a logical corner and compelled to confess the truth, I have to admit the identity between my own ideas and Baldwin's; nay, short of all such, being pushed to extremities, I often internally jubilate and swell with pride at the fact. And yet, Baldwin and I are distinct; he does not understand me quite; he stands outside me; he is not I. No, dear friend Baldwin, better far than I and wiser, but perhaps a little less human, you are not myself; you are my mentor, my teacher, my power of being taught; and you live, dear abstract friend, on the borderland between fact and fancy.

Florence,
November, 1885.

THE RESPONSIBILITIES OF
UNBELIEF.

THE RESPONSIBILITIES OF UNBELIEF:

A CONVERSATION OF THREE RATIONALISTS.

"And finally," asked Vere, "what do you think is likely to have been the result of Monsignore's wonderful sermon?"

He had gone to meet his two friends in the late summer afternoon; and as they walked slowly towards the old farm on the brink of the common, they had been giving him an account of the sermon which they had just been to hear; a sermon probably intended to overcome the last scruples of one Protestant in particular, a lady on a visit to the neighbouring Catholic Earl, but ostensibly delivered for the benefit of Protestants in general, that is to say, of as many countryfolk and stray visitors as could be collected in the chapel of Rother Castle.

"The result," answered Rheinhardt, with that indefinable cosmopolitan accent, neither French nor German, which completed the sort of eighteenth century citizen of the world character of the great *publiciste;* "the result," answered Rheinhardt, "is that Baldwin and I have spent a most delightful and instructive afternoon; and that you would have done so too, Vere, if you had not scornfully decided that no Catholicism more recent than that of St. Theresa was worthy of the attention of the real æsthetic pessimist."

Vere laughed.

"What I want to know is, whether you suppose that Monsignore has succeeded in making another convert?"

"I think he must have succeeded," answered Baldwin; "he had evidently brought that soul to the very brink of the ditch which separates Protestantism from Catholicism; his object was to make the passage quite insensible, to fill up the ditch, so that its presence could not be perceived. He tried to make it appear to Protestant listeners that Catholicism was not all the sort of foreign, illiberal, frog-eating, Guy-Fawkesy bugbear of their fancy; but, on the contrary, the simple, obvious, liberal, modern, eminently English form of belief which they had thought they had got (but in their hearts must have felt that they had not) in Protestantism; and I really never saw anything more ingenious than the way in which, without ever mentioning the words Catholicism or Protestantism, Monsignore contrived to leave the impression that a really sincere Protestant is already more than half a Catholic. I assure you that, if it had not been for the sixpenny chromolithographs of the Passion, the bleeding wooden Christs, the Madonnas in muslin frocks and spangles, and all the pious tawdriness which makes Rother Castle Chapel look like some awful Belgian or Bavarian church, I might almost have believed, for the moment, that the lady in question would do very wisely to turn Catholic."

"I wonder whether she will?" mused Vere, as they walked slowly across the yielding turf of the common, which seemed in its yellow greenness to be saturated with the gleams of sunshine, breaking ever and anon through the film of white cloud against which stood out the dark and massive outline of the pine clumps, the ghostlike array of the larches, and the pale-blue undulation of the distant downs.

"She may or she may not," answered Rheinhardt; "that is no concern of mine, any more than what becomes of the actors after an amusing comedy. What is it to us unbelievers whether one more mediocrity be lost by Protestantism and gained by Catholicism? Tis merely the juggler's apple being transferred from the right hand to the left; we may amuse ourselves watching it dancing up and down, and from side to side, and wondering where it will reappear next—that's all."

Vere was fully accustomed, after their three weeks' solitude together, correcting proofs and composing lectures in this south country farm, to Rheinhardt's optimistic Voltairian levity, his sheer incapacity of conceiving that religion could be a reality to any one, his tendency to regard abstract discussion merely as a delightful exercise for the aristocracy of the intellect, quite apart from any effect upon the thoughts or condition of the less gifted majority. He admired and pitied Rheinhardt, and let himself be amused by his kindly sceptical narrowmindedness.

"Poor woman!" replied Vere, "it does seem a little hard that her soul should be merely an apple to be juggled with for the amusement of Professor Rheinhardt. But, after all, I agree with you that it is of no consequence to us whether she turn Catholic or remain Protestant. The matter concerns only herself, and all is right as long as she settle down in the faith best adapted to her individual spiritual wants. There ought to be as many different religions as there are different sorts of character—religions and irreligions, of course; for I think you, Rheinhardt, would have been miserable had you lived before the invention of Voltairianism. The happiness of some souls appears to consist in a sense of vigour and self-reliance, a power of censuring one's self and one's neighbours, and Protestantism, as austere and Calvinistic and democratic as possible, is the right religion for them. But there are others whose highest spiritual well-being consists in a complete stripping off of all personality, a complete letting themselves passively swing up and down by a force greater than themselves; and such people ought, I think, to turn Catholic."

Rheinhardt looked at Vere with a droll expression of semi-paternal contempt. "My dear Vere," he asked, "is it possible that you, at your age, can still believe in such nonsense? Ladies, I admit, may require for their complete happiness to abandon their conscience occasionally into the hands of some saintly person; but do you mean to say that a man in the possession of all his faculties, with plenty to do in the world, with a library of good books, some intelligent friends, a good digestion, and a good theatre when he has a mind to go there—do you mean to tell me that such a man can ever be troubled by the wants of his soul?"

"Such a man as that certainly would not," answered Vere, "because the name of such a man would be Hans Rheinhardt." And shading his eyes from the yellow gleams of sunshine, Vere stopped to look at a sight which came upon him as something quite unexpected and fairylike. Beyond the blush and gold (coppery and lilac and tawny tints united by the faint undergrowing green) of the seeding grasses and flowering rushes, was a patch of sunlit common-ground of pale, luminous brown, like that of a sunlit brook-bed, fretted and frosted with the grey and rustiness of moss and gorse, specks of green grass and tufts of purple heather merged in that permeating golden brown. The light seemed to emanate from the soil, and in it were visible, clear at many yards' distance, the delicate outlines of minute sprays and twigs, connected by a network of shining cobwebs, in which moved flies and bees diaphanous and luminous like the rest, and whose faint, all-overish hum seemed to carry out in sound the visible pattern of that sun-steeped piece of ground.

"It is very odd," remarked Baldwin, as Rheinhardt. who found effects of light as unnecessary to his happiness as spiritual beliefs, impatiently hurried them out of their contemplation; "it is very odd that neither of you seem to consider that the lady's conversion can concern anybody except herself; Rheinhardt looks upon it as a mere piece of juggling; you, Vere, seem to regard it in a kind of æsthetic light, as if the woman ought to choose a religion upon the same principle upon which she would choose a bonnet—namely, to get something comfortable and becoming."

"Surely," interrupted Vere, "the individual soul may be permitted to seek for peace wherever there is most chance of finding it?"

"I don't see at all why the individual soul should have a right to seek for peace regardless of the interests of society at large, any more than why the individual body should have a right to satisfy its cravings regardless of the effect on the rest of mankind," retorted Baldwin. "You cry out against this latter theory as the height of immorality, because it strikes at the root of all respect for mine and thine;

but don't you see that your assumed right to gratify your soul undermines, what is quite as important, all feeling of true and false ? The soul is a nobler thing than the body ; you will answer, but why is it nobler ? Merely because it has greater powers for good and evil, greater duties and responsibilities ; and for that very reason it ought to have less right to indulge itself at the expense of what belongs not to it, but to mankind. Truth——"

"Upon my word," put in Rheinhardt, "I don't know which is the greater plague, the old-fashioned nuisance called a soul, or the new-fangled bore called mankind." And he pushed open the gate of the farm-garden, where the cats rolled lazily in the neatly gravelled paths, and the hens ran cackling among the lettuces and the screens of red-flowered beans. When they entered the little farm-parlour, with its deep chimney recess, curtained with faded chintz, and its bright array of geraniums and fuchsias on the window-ledge, they found that their landlady had prepared their tea, and covered the table with all manner of home-baked cakes and fruit, jugs of freshly cut roses, and sweet peas. "It is quite extraordinary," remarked Rheinhardt, as he poured out the tea, " that a man of your intelligence, Baldwin, should go on obstinately supposing that it can matter a jot what opinions are held by people to whom opinions can never be anything vital, but are merely so many half-understood formulæ ; much less that it can matter whether such people believe in one kind of myth rather than in another. Of course it matters to a man like Monsignore, who, quite apart from any material advantage which every additional believer brings to the Church of which he is a dignitary, is fully persuaded that the probable reward for Protestants are brimstone and flames, which his Evangelical opponents doubtless consider as the special lot of Papists. But what advantage is it to us if this particular mediocrity of a great lady refuses to be converted to the belief in a rather greater number of unintelligible dogmas? Science and philosophy can only gain infinitely by being limited strictly to the really intelligent classes; the less all others presume to think, the better——"

"Come now," objected Vere, "you are not going to tell me that thought is the privilege of a class, my dear Rheinhardt."

"Thought," answered Rheinhardt, "is the privilege of those who are capable of thinking."

"There is thinking and thinking," corrected Baldwin; "every man is neither able nor required to think out new truths; but every man is required, at least once in his life, to take some decision which depends upon his having at least understood some of the truths which have been discovered by his betters; and every man is required, and that constantly, to think out individual problems of conduct, for which he will be fit just in proportion as he is in the habit of seeing and striving to see things in their true light. The problems which he has before him may be trifling and may require only a trifling amount of intellect; but of such problems consists the vast bulk of the world's life, and upon their correct decision depends much of the world's improvement."

"The world's improvement," answered Rheinhardt, "depends upon everything being done by the person best fitted to do it, the material roads and material machinery being made by the men who have the strongest physical muscles and the best physical eyes; and the intellectual roads being cut, and the intellectual machinery constructed by the men who have the best intellectual muscle and sight. Therefore, with reference to conversions (for I see Baldwin can't get over the possible conversion of that particular lady), it appears to me that the only thing that can possibly concern us in them, is, that these conversions should not endanger the liberty of thought of those who can think, and this being gained (which it is, thoroughly, nowadays), that they should not interfere with the limitation of thought to those whose it is by rights. That religious belief is the best which is most conducive to complete intellectual emancipation."

"But that is exactly why I am sorry that Monsignore should make any converts!" cried Baldwin.

"And for that reason," continued Rheinhardt, fixing his eyes on Baldwin with obvious enjoyment of the paradox, "I think that we ought to hope that Monsignore may succed in converting not only this great lady, but as many ladies, great and small, as the world contains. I beg, therefore, to drink to the success of Monsignore, and of all his accomplished, zealous, and fascinating fellow-workers!" And Rheinhardt drank off his cup of tea with mock solemnity.

"Paradoxical as usual, our eighteenth century philosopher," laughed Vere, lighting his pipe.

"Not paradoxical in the very least, my dear Vere. Look around you, and compare the degree of emancipation of really thinking minds in Catholic and in Protestant countries: in the first it is complete—confession, celibacy of clergy, monasticism, Transubstantiation, Papal infallibility, Lourdes water, and bits of semi-saintly bones in glass jars, as I have seen them in Paris convents, being too much for the patience of an honest and intelligent man who reads his Voltaire and his Renan. With your Protestant your case is different, be he German or English; the Reformation has got rid of all the things which would stink too manifestly in his nostrils; and he is just able to swallow (in an intellectual wafer which prevents his tasting it) the amount of nonsense, the absorption of which is rewarded by a decent social position, or perhaps by a good living or a professorship; meanwhile he may nibble at Darwinism, positivism, materialism, be quite the man of advanced thought; for, even if he be fully persuaded that the world was not created in six days, and consider

Buddha and Socrates as quite as divine as Christ, he will yet perceive that the lower classes absolutely require to be taught that Eve was made out of Adam's rib, and that Jael was most humane in driving that particular nail. Hence, while in Catholic countries intellectual life goes on freely among a set of men who have thoroughly barricaded themselves from all priestly influence, and who go on to the walls merely to pour a certain amount of flaming resin of scepticism on to clerical besiegers; in Protestant countries no one knows exactly what he thinks or what he may say; time is lost, conscience is sophisticated, brains are wasted, and a man is bored to death by having to discuss matters which were despatched when Bayle wrote his Dictionary. And this merely because a parcel of men of the sixteenth century, without any scientific reasons for doubt and up to the ears in theology, chose to find that certain Romish dogmas and practices were intolerable to their reason and conscience; and therefore invented that disastrous *modus vivendi* with Semitic and Mediæval notions which we call Protestantism. And then we men of the nineteenth century are expected to hold Luther and Calvin centenaries, to make fine speeches and write enthusiastic passages about them, and cry 'Long live religious toleration!' No, no; give me the Council of Trent, the Bull Unigonitus, Loyola, Lainez, and Pascal's Jesuits; give me Lourdes water and silver ex-votos, and slices of the Pope's slipper, and

Capuchins and Trappists; give me Monsignor Russell, because in so doing you are giving me Voltaire and Diderot, and Michelet and Auguste Comte!"

"But," put in Vere, "you seem, by your own account (for you know I don't regard Catholicism as you do, and I don't think it matters what a man believes as long as his belief suffices to his soul, to be buying the total emancipation of a few minds at the expense of the slavery and degradation of an enormous number of men. If Catholicism is so bad that no one who has the option will compromise with it, have you a right to prescribe it to the majority of mankind?"

"Progress, my dear Vere, exists only in the minority. The majority may receive an improved position, but it cannot improve itself; so secure the freedom of the minority before thinking of anything else."

"That is all very well," answered Baldwin, who had been leaning upon the table, eagerly following Rheinhardt's words, and watching for an opportunity of interrupting him; "that's all very well as long as you go upon the supposition that the only thing of value in this world is scientific truth, and the only improvement which can be wished is the increased destruction of error. But there is something more valuable than scientific truth, and that is, the temper which cannot abet falsehood; there is something which it is more urgent to demolish and cart off than mere error, and that is, all the bad moral habits, the habit of relying on other folk's judgment, the habit of not sifting the evil from the good, the habit of liking oneself to be moved instead of moving oneself, the habit of sanctifying low things with high names; all the habits of spiritual sloth, spiritual sybaritism, spiritual irresponsibility. In this is the real degradation, the real danger. And Protestantism, which you call a *modus vivendi* with falsehood, merely because the men of the sixteenth century rose up against only as much error as they themselves could discern, Protestantism meant the refusal to abet falsehood and foulness, the effort to see, to disentangle good from bad, to replace mysticism by morality; it meant moral and intellectual activity, and completeness and manliness. It meant that in the sixteenth century; and say what you will, it means that still nowadays. The men who arose against the Papacy in the time of Luther are naturally not the men who would still be mere Protestants in the days of Comte, and Darwin, and Spencer; as they preceded and dragged on their inferiors then, so they would seek to precede and drag on their inferiors now; they would be, what they were, pioneers of truth, clearers away of error. But those are Protestants nowadays—that is to say, possess a religion expunged of the more irrational notions and demoralizing institutions of the Middle Ages, a religion less mythological and more ethical—

those men possess this saner, cleaner, more modern religion who, but for the Reformation, would still be morally starving, and from starvation contracting all the loathsome moral diseases and degrading moral palsies which we observe in their Catholic forefathers before Luther, in their Catholic contemporaries of Spain, and Italy, and France. The Reformation may have done nothing for the thinking minority, it may even, as Rheinhardt insists, have made that minority smaller; but to the small minority the Reformation gave a vast majority, which is not, as in Catholic countries, separated from it by an unbridgeable gulf. The number of completely emancipated minds may be less in Protestant countries; but behind them is a large number of minds which are yet far from being utterly cramped and maimed and impotent, which have not gone very far on the right road, but have never gone at all on the wrong one; minds possessing at least rudimentary habits of inquiry, of discrimination, of secular morality, and which, little by little, may be influenced, improved, enfranchised, by those who are more fully developed and more completely free. This is what Protestantism has done for us; and the highest thing that we can do, is to follow in the steps of those first Protestants, to clear away what appears to be error in our eyes as they cleared away what appeared to be error in theirs."

"The Reformation," persisted Rheinhardt, calmly, "was a piece of intellectual socialism. It consisted in dividing truth so that each man might have a little scrap of it for himself, and in preventing all increase by abolishing all large intellectual capital."

"I have never doubted," remarked Vere, "that the Reformation was, for all the paradoxes of this Voltairian of ours, a most necessary and useful revolution. It swept away—and this is what I most regret—the last shreds of Pagan purple, the last half-withered flowers of Pagan fancy, out of Christianity, and left it a whitewashed utilitarian thing—a Methodist chapel, well ventilated and well warmed, but singularly like a railway waiting-room or a warehouse. But of course such a consideration can have no weight. Protestantism (excuse my confusion of metaphors) may be called the spiritual enfranchisement of the servile classes; it turned, as Baldwin says, a herd of slaves and serfs into well-to-do artizans and shopkeepers. I think, therefore, that Protestantism was an unmitigated blessing for what Rheinhardt calls the intellectual proletariat, for the people who neither increase intellectual wealth nor enjoy intellectual luxury. There is something as beautiful in the rough cleanness of belief of a Scotch or Swiss artizan as there is in a well-scoured deal table and a spotless homespun napkin; and I often have felt, talking with certain French, Italian, and Austrian peasants, that, spiritually, they live in something between a drain and a cellar. So that, if I were a great landed proprietor, or a great manufacturer, or any other sort of modern leader of men, I should certainly feel bound to put every obstacle in the way of a conversion of my tenants and operatives by a man like Monsignore; I should feel as if they were going to sell their solid and well-drained cottages in order to live in mere mud cabins without drains and without chimneys. But when it comes to the upper classes, to those who have a certain secured intellectual life, the case would be different." And Vere puffed away at his pipe, as if he had settled the question.

"Really," cried Baldwin, "I don't see at all why you should be indifferent to the aristocracy of intellect (as Rheinhardt calls it), living in what you describe as a spiritual dwelling partaking of the cellar and the drain."

"I am not indifferent," answered Vere, "but I see that a certain standard of intellectual and moral wealth having now been attained, there is not the faintest chance of a man living in a cellar or a drain. Given a certain amount of intelligence and culture, which one may nearly always assume among our educated classes, our spiritual dwellings are sure to be quite healthy enough; and I can't see, therefore, why each man should not be permitted to build his house to please his fancy, and fill it with whatever things may give him most pleasure; let it be Greek or mediæval, according to his taste; let him become Catholic or Protestant, let him follow Swedenborg, or Buddha, or Comte, or Dr. Pusey, or Professor Huxley;

or let him make up a religion for himself, or have none at all, as he likes : he is doing no harm to anybody, and no one has any right to interfere with him. Oh, I know you, Baldwin! you would be for forcing your way into a man's spiritual house and insisting (with a troop of positivistic policemen and sanitary inspectors at your heels) that every room must have a given number of cubic feet of air and a given number of windows, and that wall-papers must be made to wash, flowers be carefully restricted to the hothouse, and that an even temperature, never rising much above the moral and intellectual freezing-point, should be kept up. Now, I happen to consider that this visit of yours, although most benevolent, would be a quite unjustifiable intrusion; and that you would not have the smallest right to tear down the curtains of a man who enjoys a subdued light, still less to pitch his flowers and incense burners out of his bedroom window. Joking apart, I think there is no greater mistake than to interfere with the beliefs of people belonging to a class which has secured quite enough spiritual freedom ; let them satisfy their own nature, and remember that the imaginative and emotional wants, the spiritual enjoyments of each man, are different from those of his neighbour——"

"That is exactly my view," put in Rheinhardt, "let the imbeciles keep out of my way, and I certainly won't get into theirs. Let us enjoy our own intellectual ambrosia, and leave them to their beer and porridge, which they think every bit as nice," and Rheinhardt threw his cigarette into the fire.

"I understand," said Baldwin, overlooking Rheinhardt's remark, and addressing himself directly to Vere, "according to you the class which professes the highest intellectual life, has, like the governing social body, a right and an obligation to interfere in the spiritual mode of life of such classes as might, if left to themselves, become a public nuisance."

"That is rather a hard way of putting it," answered Vere, "but such in the main is my principle."

"You wish your lower classes to be Protestant for the same reason that you would wish your lower classes to live in sanitary-regulation houses, because a condition of spiritual darkness and dirt would produce nasty spiritual diseases, which might spread to your upper class, and would at all events fill the streets with sights and smells quite unendurable to your upper class, which is of course as æsthetical as it is humane. The unfortunate hardworking creatures who save us from manual labour must be looked after and taught how to be decent, spiritually as well as physically, both for their own sake and for ours. So far I completely follow your ideas. But I confess my inability to follow, in the sense of understanding the justifiableness, the rest of your theory. From your manner of speaking, and your allusion to men building their spiritual homes to suit their fancy, and excluding the light and scenting the air as they please, I presume that in your opinion a man who has inherited the means of living in leisure, untroubled by the necessity of earning his bread or of liberating his conscience (his ancestors having given their labour and their blood for that), need think of nothing beyond making his life as agreeable as possible to himself."

"I wonder, Baldwin, you can be so grotesque as to suppose that I am an advocate of anything of the sort," interrupted Vere, rather angrily.

"Why not?" asked Rheinhardt, "'tis the height of wisdom; and for that reason, indeed, cannot be your idea, Vere."

"You are not an advocate of this theory when applied by fashionable numskulls, certainly, my dear Vere. Of the men who think of nothing but enjoying themselves by eating dinners at a guinea a head, sitting up till six in the morning in ball-rooms or playing cards at the club, driving four-in-hand and having mistresses or wives dressed out by Worth, and collections of bad pictures and apocryphal *bric-à-brac;* of such men, or rather beings, you have as bad an opinion as myself. Indeed, I dare say you have a considerably worse one than I have, because I am always ready to admit that the poor devils whom we revile as the corrupt of the world, are in reality acting for the best according to their lights, being totally unable to conceive of a higher mode of existence or a more glorious destiny. But the case changes when a man's leisure consists not merely in his no longer being required to earn his bread, but in no longer requiring to free his mind from the painful restrictions and necessities of former days; when his inherited wealth consists not merely in estates and cash, but in intellect and knowledge. What are we to think of this new sort of favourite of fortune, if he employ that intellectual leisure and those intellectual riches merely in feeding his mind with exotic spiritual dainties (among which, even as with the more material epicure, rottenness constitutes a great attraction); in playing games of chance with his own beliefs and emotions; in bedecking himself and attitudinizing in the picturesque rags and tags of effete modes of feeling and antiquated modes of thought, because he enjoys making himself look interesting, and enjoys writing sonnet sketches of his poor maimed and crippled soul decked out in becoming purple, and grey and saffron and sad green of paganism, and asceticism, and Baudelairism, and Schopenhauerism. What shall we say of the man who does this, while nine-tenths of his fellow-men are slaving at mechanical labour; who refuses to employ his leisure and his powers in doing that other kind of work without which mankind cannot exist, the work of sowing and grinding the grain which must make the spiritual bread of the world? To me it seems as if this man were but a subtler and less conscious robber; keeping in barren mortmain as the clergy before the Revolution kept the fruitful acres of

France, that which ought to keep and strengthen and support a thousand morally starving and anæmic wretches."

"What!" interrupted Rheinhardt, "a man is not to enjoy his own intellectual advantages, but must consider himself the steward of all the confounded imbeciles, the *prolétaires* and paupers of the intellectual world! This is Socialism, my good Baldwin, of the rankest and most intolerable description!"

"It may be Socialism to you, Rheinhardt, and it may be a private, pet Socialism of my own; but it has nothing to do with what other folks call Socialism, which defeats not only its own, but still more my own object. Understand me rightly—all progress (and I think you will have to agree with me), all diminution of misery and increase of happiness is in direct proportion to the utilization of the various sorts of capital—physical, intellectual, and moral: land, money, muscles, brains, hearts, which we possess; and the more we put our capital to profit, the more do we enable the putting to profit of such capital as has lain dormant; hence progress must increase at a constantly greater ratio. For instance, think of all the energies of mind, and heart, and hand, which must have been wasted in the cast-civilizations and in the feudal system; think of all the precious qualities which must be wasted nowadays owing to the still imperfect exchange of individuals among the various classes of society, which may keep a man with a great financial endowment making bad tables and chairs, and a man with a genius for carpentering ruining his partners with imbecile speculation."

"That is very true," remarked Vere; "but," he added, not perhaps without a touch of satisfaction in his voice, as if unconsciouly pleased at any want of connection in Baldwin's ideas, " I don't see that these remarks, however interesting, have much to do with your onslaught on the poor mortals who venture to retain doubts, and habits, and love of old faiths which your philosophy happens to condemn."

"They have everything to do with each other, since one is but the other's logical consequence. Rheinhardt has just called me a Socialist; well, I don't think you would get many Socialists to agree in my belief that all progress depends upon the existence of a class quite above all necessity of manual labour and business routine, which, while the majority of men are keeping the world going by supplying its most pressing bodily wants, may separate the true from the false, and gradually substitute higher aims and enjoyments for lower ones; in short, do the work of improvement, if not by actually discovering new truth, or even by promulgating it, at least by storing it ready for need."

"All improvement must come from the minority," remarked Rheinhardt, "since improvement means the development of special and rare advantages."

"In short," went on Baldwin, "I hope for a fair

division of labour between the upper and lower classes, the one working for the other, and neither idle. Of course this is but a distant ideal, itself possible only as the result of infinite progress; still, it is clear that we are tending that way. At present the great proportion of what we call upper classes are quite incapable of any work that could not be performed by the lower; their leisure is, and must be, mere idleness. But, as I said just now, within the upper classes there is an upper class; the men who can originate, or at least appreciate, thought; the nucleus of my real upper class of the future. These have not merely leisure, but also the faculties to render it profitable; and their leisure, as I said before, means not only that they have been saved the trouble of supplying bodily wants, but also, which is much more important, that they have been saved the trouble of ridding themselves of so many erroneous modes of thought which are still heaped up in the path of the inferior classes. This is the class of men whom you, Vere, say we have no right to interfere with; who, as we may be sure that they won't elect to live in cellars and drains, ought to be permitted to build their spiritual dwellings in accordance with their own fancy, and to fill them with whatsoever mental and moral *bric-à-brac* and stage property may give them most pleasure, turn them into little pleasure palaces of the *Imitation of Christ*, the *Positive Philosophy*, or the *Fleurs du Mal* style of spiritual decoration. With the unfortunate rich numskull, too stupid to do intellectual work, too stupid to know that there is any to do; too helpless to have responsibilities; with him I can have patience, I can even sympathize. But with this other man who has not only leisure and education, but intellect and conscience, I have no patience, I have only indignation: and it is to this man that I would say—'What right have you to arrange your spiritual house merely to please your fancy or your laziness? What right have you to curtain out the intellectual light from eyes which are required to see for others as well as for yourself? What right have you to enervate with mystical drugs the moral muscle, which must clean out not your own conscience merely, but the conscience of others? Above all, what right have you to bring up in this spiritual dwelling of your fancy, in this confusing penumbra, and amid these emasculating fumes, those for whose souls you are most responsible, your children; that not only your mind and heart, but theirs, should be mere waste and vanity for all the world?'"

Baldwin had gradually grown earnest and excited; and, what had been at first but an abstract discussion, became, as the thought burned stronger within him, almost a personal attack; in speaking the last words he had risen from his chair, and instinctively fixed his eyes on Vere, where he sat in the dusk of the twilit room.

The latter did not look up; he knocked the ashes

out of his pipe and remained seated, watching the smouldering fire. There was a moment's silence, during which the ticking of the clock and the cackling of the poultry outside were painfully distinct.

"If there is a thing I detest," muttered Rheinhardt, "it is the militant, humanitarian atheist; no priest ever came up to him for spoiling a pleasant chat."

He felt that the discussion had long ceased to be academic; and to him, who enjoyed controversy as a sort of æsthetic pleasure, nothing could be more utterly distasteful than a discussion taken too much in earnest. He suddenly broke the silence by exclaiming—

"Just look what an odd sky!"

The room was by this time getting rapidly dark, so that Rheinhardt, who was at bottom the most sympathizing of men, could feel rather than see the excited face of Baldwin, the gentle and melancholy, but slightly ironical, just a little pained, expression of Vere. In the midst of the duskiness, the window blazed out white and luminous, with the sashbars, the stems and leaves of the flowers, the bushes outside, the distant firs and larches bounding the common sharp and black against a strange white light. He stepped into the garden.

"Do come out," he cried, "and look at this preposterous sunset, it is worthy the attention of æsthetical creatures like you, and Vere may write a fine splash-dash description of it."

The two men rose, and followed Rheinhardt out into the garden, and thence on to the road, which wound behind the stables and hayricks of the old farm. The sun was sinking, hidden behind a thick bank of grey clouds, and below them was a rift of open sky, white, luminous, lustrous, into which gradually emerged the lip of the sun, slowly working its way, a great rayless ball of brilliant white, into this sea of white luminousness; the sky like a liquid, molten sun; the sun like a denser, more lustrous sky, white upon white, metallic sheen upon metallic sheen. And all the while the clouds from whence the sun had descended grew dark, of bluish grey, and all the upper sky of strange darkness; not the blackness of cloud, for it seemed scarce covered with mist film, but a metallic darkness as of burnished blue steel.

"I have never seen anything like it in my life," said Vere, as they stood upon the brow of a hill, overlooking the sea of gently undulating hillocks, steeped in a broad and permeating white light, the mere consciousness of which, as it were, dazzled and dazed. A brilliant light which seemed to suck out of the landscape all its reds and yellows, and with them all life; bleaching the yellowing cornfields and brown heath; but burnishing into demoniac energy of colour the pastures and oak woods, brilliant against the dark sky as if filled with green fire. Along the roadside the poppies, which an ordinary sunset makes into flame, were quite extinguished, like burnt-out embers; the yellow hearts of the daisies were quite lost, merged into their shining white petals. And, striking against the windows of the old black and white chequered farm (a ghastly skeleton in this light), it made them not flare, nay, not redden in the faintest degree, but reflect a brilliant speck of white light. Everything was unsubstantial, yet not as in a mist; nay, rather substantial, but flat, as if cut out of paper and pasted on, the black branches and green leaves, the livid glaring houses, with roofs of dead, scarce perceptible red (as when an iron turning white-hot from red-hot in the stithy, grows also dull and dim). The various ranges of hills projected beyond each other like side-scenes covered with uniform grey; the mass of trees towards the distant downs were bleached white against the white sky, smoke-like, without consistence; while the fields of green barley and ripening wheat trembled, and almost vibrated with a white, white-hot light.

"It looks like the eve of the coming of Antichrist, as described in mediæval hymns," remarked Vere, "the sun, before setting never more to rise, sucking all life out of the earth, leaving it but a mound of livid cinders, barren and crumbling, through which the buried nations will easily break their way when they arise."

"For the matter of that," answered Rheinhardt, "the sun might have taken its departure a good many years ago, if it was waiting for the arrival of Antichrist," and he looked towards Baldwin, as much as to say, that violent discussion was his idea of complete fiendishness. Baldwin indeed had no intention of resuming the subject, conscious as he was of the utter futility of attempting to make either of his friends feel like himself; and sorry also that he should perhaps have hurt Vere, who always appeared to him as a somewhat sickly mind, and deserving of the forbearance with which such people should be treated, especially if too old to be cured. But to Baldwin's surprise, and Rheinhardt's annoyance, Vere himself returned to the subject of their former conversation. As they were slowly walking home, watching the strange whiteness gradually turning into the grey of twilight, he said, as he passed his arm through Baldwin's—

"My dear Baldwin, I see very plainly that you think you may have hurt my feelings, and that you are sorry for it. But don't worry yourself about that, because you haven't really done so. I am, excuse my saying so, sufficiently your elder, not merely in years, I think, but in experience of the world, to understand perfectly that to you everything seems very simple and obvious in this world, and that you haven't had time to find out how difficult it is to know right from wrong. It seems to you that you have written me down, or rather have compelled me to write myself down, a selfish and cowardly wretch; and you are sorry for me now that it should have happened—nay, don't try to deny it. But I know very well that I am nothing of the sort; and I can understand your position sufficiently to understand why you think me so; and also, considering your point of view, to like you all the better for your indignation. But tell me, has it never struck you, whose philosophy consists in checking the waste of all the good and useful things in the world—has it never occurred to you to ask yourself whether you may not, in this instance, be wasting, ruthlessly scattering to the four winds of heaven, something quite as precious as this leisure to think and this power of thought of which you make so much— wasting a certain proportion of the little happiness which mankind has got?"

"I don't see what you are driving at, Vere," answered Baldwin, pushing open the wicket which separated the farmyard from the common.

"The happiness of mankind—that is to say, of the only part of mankind worth taking into account," put in Rheinhardt, with a malicious pleasure in intruding his own jog-trot philosophy among what he considered the highflown nonsense of his two friends—"depends upon its being able to discuss abstract questions without getting red in the face, and telling people that they are vile."

"There is some truth in that also," laughed Vere "but that was not in my mind. What I mean is this," he went on, as they entered the farm parlour once more, now in complete darkness, except where the fire threw a broad red light on to the opposite wall; "has it never occurred to you that instead of increasing the happiness of mankind, as you intend doing by insisting that every one who can should seek for the truth in spiritual matters, you would in reality be diminishing that happiness by destroying beliefs, or half-beliefs, which afford infinite comfort and consolation and delight to a large number of men and women?"

"I have never doubted," answered Baldwin, somewhat bitterly, "that it would be extremely distressing to many souls to find that they must give up the pleasant spiritual warmth and spiritual half-light to which they are accustomed, and go forth into the cold and blearness and fog in order to help their inferiors. I don't doubt that it was very distressing for the French nobles to have their domains confiscated in the Revolution; and for the poor, elegant, chivalric planters to have their negroes emancipated for them. Still, such distressing things have to be done occasionally."

"You misunderstand me again," answered Vere, "and you might know better than to continue fancying that I am a kind of spiritual æsthete or sybarite——"

Rheinhardt, who had lit the lamp, could not refrain from raising his eyebrows and ejaculating an incredulous "Oh!" at this remark, for Vere represented to him the very perfection of that kind of æsthetic and spiritual vague craving upon which he was wont to descant as a specially English quality.

"Be that as it may," continued Vere, " my meaning is simply this. The world which surrounds us is not everything; the faculties with which we perceive it enter for just as large a share into our life; and this action is as much a reality as is a stone or a bench outside us. The world exists around us in a certain definite way, and with certain definite necessities, which we may find out by trying, as we find out that the stick plunged in water is not crooked, as it looks to our eye, and that the sun which seems to go round our earth does nothing of the sort; in the really existing universe, the objective universe, there is death and inevitable decay, and there is, as it seems to you and me and Rheinhardt, a cruel and conscienceless will, or no will at all, and, as an end to all our efforts, there is annihilation. But besides the outwardly existing, there is the inwardly existing, our faculties which act in a given way, reconstructing this outward world; and in this universe thus reconstructed by our mind and our conscience there is no real death, no evil will or indifferent omnipotence; above all, there is no annihilation. It is false, you will say; but is it false if according to the laws of our sight, the stick plunged in the water is crooked? Would it not rather be false were we, because experience has taught us that the stick is straight, to cease to see it as crooked?"

"I see," put in Rheinhardt, who loved metaphysics as he loved a French comedy; "and the fact that all have faculties which make us see sticks which are straight as crooked when plunged in the water, is an obvious proof that somewhere or other there must exist a world in which all straight sticks really do become crooked when held under water. The theory is not new, but it has the charm of eternal freshness."

"Be quiet, Rheinhardt!" cried Baldwin.

"The subjective universe," answered Vere, with a smile at Rheinhardt's absurdity, "is not equally true with the objective universe; but in many cases it is much more beautiful and consoling. In short, what I mean is this: since at the bottom of the Pandora's box which has been given to mankind, and out of which have issued so many cruel truths, there exists the faculty of disbelieving in some of them, of trusting in good where there is only evil, in imagining sympathy where there is indifference, and justice where there is injustice, of hoping where there is room only to despair—since this inestimable faculty of self-delusion exists, why not let mankind enjoy it, why wish to waste, to rob them of this, their most precious birthright?"

"Because," answered Baldwin, "increasing truth is the law of increasing good; because if we elect to believe that which we wish instead of believing that which is, we are deliberately degrading our nature, rendering it less excellent and useful, instead of more so, than it was; and because by being too cowardly to admit that which is, we are incapacitating ourselves, misleading and weakening others, in the great battle to make the kingdom of that which is into the kingdom of that which should be."

"I leave you to fight out your objective and subjective worlds," said Rheinhardt, taking up a book and settling himself by the lamp, "and, by the way, here is a hero, by name John Inglesant, who is also wondering about the what is and what should be, and who, for my part, I most decidedly consider as belonging to the kingdom of what should *not* be, namely, Boredom."

Vere was silent for a moment. "Every one," he said, "is not called upon to battle in life. Many are sent in, to whom it might be merely a tolerably happy journey. What right have we to insist upon telling these things which will poison their happiness and which will not, perhaps, make them any the more useful? You were speaking about the education of children; and this, which to you is a source of bitterness and reproach, has been to me the subject of much doubt and indecision. And I have come to the conclusion that I have no right to take it for granted that my children will necessarily be put in such positions as to require their knowing the things of which I, alas! have had the bitter certainty; that should such a position be awaiting them, disbelief in all the beautiful and consoling fictions of religion will come but too soon, and that I have no right to make such disbelief come any earlier."

"In short, you deliberately teach your children things in which you disbelieve?"

Vere hesitated. "I teach them nothing; their mother is a firm believer, and I leave the children's religious instruction entirely in her hands. I have never," he added, with some pride, "made the slightest attempt to undermine my wife's belief, and shall not act differently towards my children."

Baldwin fixed his eyes searchingly upon Vere.

"Have you ever really cared much about your wife, Vere?" he asked.

"Well, I married her for love; and I think that even now I care more for her than for any one else in the world. Why do you ask?"

"Because," answered Baldwin, "it is perfectly inconceivable to me that, if you really love your wife as I should love a wife if I took one, not as my mere squaw, or odalisque, or as the mother of my children, but, as you say, more than any one else in the world, you can endure that there should exist a subject, the greatest and most solemn in all the world, upon which you and your wife keep your thoughts and feelings secret from each other."

"I have friends, men, with whom I can discuss it."

"And you can bear to be able to open your whole soul to a friend, while keeping it closed to the person whom you say you love best in the world? You can bear to feel that to your highest thoughts and hopes and fears there is a response in a man, like me, scarcely more than a stranger to you, while there is only blindness and dumbness in this woman who is constantly by your side, and to whom you are more than the whole world? Do you consider this as complete union with another, this deliberate silence and indifference, this growing and changing and maturing of your own mind, while you see her mind cramped and maimed by beliefs which you have long cast behind you? This divorce of your minds, which I can understand only towards a mistress, a creature for whom your mind does not exist, how can you reconcile it to your idea of the love of a husband to a wife?"

"I love my wife, and I respect her belief."

"You may abet her belief, Vere, but if, as you say, you consider it mere error and falsehood, you cannot respect it."

"I respect my wife's happiness, then, and my children's happiness; and for that reason I refrain from laying rough hands upon illusions which are part of that happiness. Accident has brought us into contact with what you and I call truth—I have been shorn of my belief; I am emancipated, free, superior—all the things which a thorough rationalist is in the eyes of rationalists; but," and Vere turned round upon Baldwin with a look of pity and bitterness—"I have not yet attained to the perfection of being a hypocrite, a sophist to myself, of daring to pretend to my own soul that this belief of ours, this truth, is not bitter and abominable, arid and icy to our hearts."

Rheinhardt looked up from his book with a curious expression of wonder. "But, my dear friend," he said, very quietly, "why should the truth be abominable to you? A certain number of years employed as honourably and happily as possible, and after that, what preceded this life of yours; what more would you wish, and what evil is there in this that you should shrink from teaching it to your children, instead of telling them of a Heaven which we cannot conceive otherwise than as utterly monotonous and insipid, a delightful life despoiled of all that gives a little delight and nobility to our earthly life; and of a Hell which required the united efforts of all the crazy and blood-thirsty maniacs of the Middle Ages to invent it. I am not afraid of death; why should you be?"

"You misunderstand me," answered Vere; "heaven knows I am not afraid of death—nay, more than once it has seemed to me that to lie down and feel my soul, like my body, grow gradually numb and number, till it was chilled out of all consciousness, would be the greatest of joys. The horror of the idea of annihilation is, I think, to all save Claudios, the horror, not of our own annihilation, but of the annihilation of others; this Schopenhauer overlooked, as you do, Rheinhardt, when he comfortably argued that after all we should not know whether we were being annihilated or not, that as long as we ourselves are awake we cannot realize sleep, and that we need only say to ourselves, 'Well, I shall sleep, be unconscious, never wake.' In this there is no horror. But Schopenhauer did not understand, having no heart, that death is the one who robs us, who takes away the beloved, leaves us with empty arms. Eurydice, melting away into mist, sorrows at most for Orpheus; once dissolved, there is for her no more grief; it is for him, left alone, who has had to look on, to lose without possibility of struggle, for whom emptiness only remains. The worst of death is not the annihilation of ourselves; oh no, that is nothing; no, nor even the blank numbness of seeing the irremediable loss; it is the sickening, gasping terror, coming by sudden unexpected starts, of foreseeing that which will inevitably be. Poets have said a great deal, especially Leopardi, of Love and Death being, brothers, of the desire of the one coming along with the presence of the other; it may be so. But this much is certain, that whatever may be said of the brothership of Love and Death, Love, in its larger and nobler sense, is the Wizard who has evoked for us the *fata morgana* of an after life; it is love who has taught the world, for its happiness, that there is not an endless ocean beyond this life, an ocean without shores, dark, silent, whose waters steam up in black vapours to the black heavens, a rolling chaos of disintegrated thoughts and feelings, all separate, all isolated, heaving up and down in the shapeless eternal flood. It is love who has taught us that what has been begun here will not for ever be interrupted, nor what has been ill-done for ever remain unatoned; that the affection once kindled will never cease, that the sin committed can be wiped out, and the good conceived can be achieved; that the seed sown in life will yet bloom and fructify in death, that it will not have been cast too late upon an evil soil, and the blossom of promise will not for ever have been nipped, the half-ripe fruit not for ever have fallen from the tree; that all within which is good and happy, and for ever struggling here, virtue, genius, will be free to act hereafter; that the creatures thrust asunder in the world, vainly trying to clasp one another in the crowd for ever pushing them apart, may unite for ever. All this is the wonderful phantasmagoria of love; love has given it to mankind. What right have we to sweep it away; we—" and Vere turned reproachfully towards Baldwin—"who have perhaps never loved, and never felt the want of such a belief?"

Baldwin was silent for a moment, then answered, as he struck a shower of sparks out of the dull red embers.

"I have never actually had such a belief, but I have experienced what it is to want it. I was brought up without any religious faith, with only a few general notions of right and wrong, and when I first began to read and to think for myself, my ideas naturally moved in a rationalistic, nay, a materialistic path, so that when in the course of my boyish readings I came upon disputes about an after life, it seemed to me quite impossible to conceive what people could dispute about. When I was very young I became engrossed in artistic and archæological subjects; it seemed to me that the only worthy interest in life was the beautiful; and, in my Olympian narrowness of sympathy, people who worried themselves about other questions seemed to me poor morbid mediæval wretches; you see, I led a life of great solitude, and great, though narrow happiness, shut up among books, and reading only such of them as favoured my perfect serenity of mind. But little by little I got to know other men, and to know somewhat more of the world; then things began gradually to change. I began to perceive the frightful dissonances in the world, the horrible false notes, the abominable harmonies of good and evil; and to meet all this I had only this kind of negative materialism, which could not suffice to give me peace of mind, but which entirely precluded my accepting any kind of theory of spiritual compensation and ultimate justice; I grew uneasy, and then unhappy. Just at that moment it so happened that I lost a friend of mine to whom I was considerably attached, whose life had been quite singularly unfortunate, indeed, appeared to be growing a little happier only a few months before his death. It was the first time that death came near me, and close before my eyes. It gave me a frightful moral shock, not so much perhaps the loss of that particular individual to myself, as the sense of the complete extinction of his personality, gone like the snuffed-out flame or the spent foam of the sea, gone completely, nowhere, leaving no trace, occupying no other place, become the past, the past for which we can do nothing." Baldwin paused for a moment, as if it had all returned to him with painful reality, then continued, in a very quiet, subdued tone—"I remember, as it were yesterday, a crisis, a sort of dreadful vision which came to me in those weeks of acute, moral sickness following my friend's death; a vision of the full sense of the words *never again;* I had not realized before the interminableness of time, the infinity of negation. For a moment there came home to me as in a flash the consciousness of the unceasing waves of time which roll and die away, and rise again and furl again, and which, could we wait for ever, watch for all eternity upon their banks, would never disclose that which we have lost. Separation, after all, is a soft word; it means a gulf, a gulf of centuries perhaps, but a gulf which has a limit, another shore, a bottom; and it is the mercy of our nature that we feel thus, that our consciousness cannot bear the strain of realizing absolute negation, that there lurks in our mind and heart a vague sense of limit; that we feel as if we might wait, wearily indeed, but wait for an end of the negation. And yet I knew that it was not so."

Rheinhardt had put down his book for a moment, and listened, with a puzzled and wondering look. That people should be haunted by thoughts like these seemed to him almost as incomprehensible as that the dead should arise and join in a ghastly dance round the grave-stones; nor would this latter phenomenon have seemed to him much the more disgusting of the two; so, after a minute, he settled down again and pulled out of his pocket a volume of Aristophanes.

"You have felt all this, Baldwin," said Vere, "and you would nevertheless deliberately inflict such pain upon others? You have felt all the misery of disbelief in a future life, and you are surprised that I should be unwilling to meddle with the belief of my wife and children?"

"I am surprised at your not being almost involuntarily forced into communicating what you know to be the truth; surprised that, in your mind, there should not be an imperious sense that truth must out. Moreover, I think that the responsibility of holding back truth is always greater than any man can calculate, or any man, could he know the full consequences thereof, could support. We have been speaking of the moral discomfort attendant upon a disbelief in a future life; a moral discomfort, which, say what we may, is nowadays only momentary, does not outlive our first grief at death, for we moderns have not a very vital belief in a future state. Well, we ought also to think of what was the state of things when such a belief thoroughly existed, when what you call the phantasmagoria of love was a reality. Bring up to your memory the way in which the mystics of the Middle Ages, and, indeed, the mystics of all times, have spoken of life—as a journey during which the soul must neither plough nor sow, but walk on, the eyes fixed upon Heaven, despising the earth which it left barren and bitter as when it came. "Servate tanquam peregrinum et hospitem super terram, ad quem nihil spectat de mundi negotiis," that is what the *Imitation* bids us to. Ask yourself which is the more conducive to men making the world endurable to others and themselves, to men weighing their wishes and thoughts, and bridling their desires, and putting out all their strength for good : the notion that there is a place beyond the grave where all is perfect, where all sloth and unkindness, and repented folly and selfishness may be expiated and retrieved ; or the notion that whatever excellence there can be, man must make with his own hands, that whatever good may be done, whatever may be felt, repaired, atoned for, must be done, felt, repaired, and atoned for in this world. Even were I logically convinced of the existence of a future life, I should be bound to admit the enervating effect thereof on our sense of responsibility and power of action ; I should regret the terrible moral tonic of the knowledge that whatever of good I may do must be done at once, whatever of evil I have done be effaced at once also. But let this be; and answer me, Vere, do you believe that a single individual has a right to hide from others that which he believes to be the truth? Do you seriously consider that a man is doing right in destroying, for the sake of the supposed happiness of his children, the spark of truth which happens to be in his power, and which belongs neither to him, nor to his children, but to the whole world? Can you assert that it is honest on your part, in order to save your children the pain of knowing that they will not meet you, or their mother, or their dead friends again in Heaven, to refuse to give them that truth for which your ancestors have paid with their blood and their liberty, and which your children are bound to hand on to their children, in order that this little spark of truth may grow into a fire which shall warm and light the whole world?"

"There is something more at stake than the mere happiness or unhappiness of my children," answered Vere; "at all events than such happiness as they might get from belief in an after life. There is the happiness, the safety of their conscience."

"Do you think you can save their conscience by sacrificing your own?"

"I should not be sacrificing my conscience were I doing that which I felt bound to do, Baldwin. Would you have me teach my children that this world, which they regard as the kingdom of a just and loving God, whose supremest desire is the innocence and happiness of his creatures, is in reality the battlefield or the playground of physical forces, without thought or conscience; nay, much worse, is the creation either of a principle of good perpetually allying itself to a principle of evil, or of a dreadful unity which permits and furthers good and evil alike? What would you think of me were I to tell my children that all that they had learned of God and Christ is falsehood; and that the true gods of the world are the serenely heartless, the foully bloodthirsty gods of early Greece, of Phœnicia, and Asia Minor? You would certainly think me a bad father. Yet this old mythology represents with marvellous accuracy the purely scientific view of the world, the impression given by the mere contemplation of Nature, with its conflicting and caballing divinities, good and bad, black and white, resisting and assisting one another, beneficent and wicked, pure and filthy by turns. The chaos, the confusion, the utter irresponsibility, which struck the framers of old myths, is still there. All these stories seem to us very foolish and very horrible: an omniscient, omnipotent Zeus, threatened by a mysterious, impersonal Fate, looming dimly behind him; a Helios who ripens the crops and ripens the pestilence; a Cybele for ever begetting and suckling and mutilating; we laugh at all this. But with what do we replace it? And if we look at our prosaic modern nature, as is shown us by science, can we accuse the chaotic and vicious fancy of those early explainers of it? Do we not see in this nature bounty and cruelty greater than that of any early gods, combats more blind than any Titan's battles, marriages of good and evil more hideous than any incests of the old divinities, monster births of excellence and baseness more foul than any Centaur or Minotaur; and do we not see the great gods of the universe sitting and eating the flesh of men, not unconsciously, but consciously, serenely, and without rebuke?"

"That's a curious observation of yours," put in Rheinhardt; "but it would appear as if there had here been a difference between the two great races; that with the Semitic the feeling of right and wrong, of what ought or ought not to be in the abstract, entirely overshadows mere direct perception, scientific perception of Nature, and considerable phenomena, not with respect to their necessity, but with reference to their ethical propriety; while, as you remark, the Aryan race——"

But Rheinhardt's generalizations were altogether wasted upon his two friends.

"Such is Nature," pursued Vere, with impetuosity; "and in it you scientific minds bid us to seek for moral peace and moral safety. How can we aspire, as to the ideal of moral goodness, to that which produces evil—ineffable, inevitable evil? How measure our moral selves against this standard; how blush before this unblushing god? How dare we look for consolation where our moral sense, if enlightened, must force us to detest and to despise? Where, then, shall we seek the law, the rule by which to govern our lives? And the horror of horrors lies in this—that we are forced to conceive as evil all that which is at variance with the decrees of Nature, of this same Nature which is for ever committing evil greater than any of us could commit; herein, that we cannot rebel. As long as Nature meant the Devil, it might be opposed; but we know that for us there can be no good save in obeying Nature—obeying that which is not good in itself; it has, as if with intentional malice, forced us to bend, to walk in its ways; if we refuse solidarity with it, we are sucked into a worse evil still. The sight of individual misfortune can never bring home this horrible anomaly as does a study of the way in which whole peoples have been sacrificed first to sin, then to expiation; of the manner in which every rebellion against this evil-polluted nature, every attempt of man to separate himself, to live by a rule of purity of his own, has been turned into a source of new abominations. Am I to show all this to my children, and say to them: Only Nature is good; and Nature is the evilest thing that we can conceive, since it forces to do evil and then punishes. Would a belief in Ashtaroth or Moloch not be as moral as this one?"

Baldwin waited till Vere had come to an end.

"I can quite understand all that you feel, because I have felt it myself," he said, unshaken by his friend's vehemence. "I was telling you of the terrible depression which gradually came over me as I perceived what the world really was; and which, for a couple of years, at least, made me live in constant moral anguish, especially after the death of that friend of mine had, as I told you, brought home to me how the disbelief in a future life took away the last possibility of believing in a just and merciful Providence. I revolved in my mind every possible scheme for conciliating the evil inherent in the world with our desire for good. Christianity, Buddhism, Positivism—they all assumed to quiet our conscience with the same hollow lie; Positivism saying that the time would come when Nature and good would be synonymous; Christianity reminding us that man may have but a moment wherein to be righteous, while God has all eternity; always the same answer, the evil permitted or planned in the past is to be compensated by the good in the future, agony suffered to be repaid in happiness, either to the worn-out, broken soul in another world, or to the old, worn-out humanity in this. Such answers made me but the more wretched by their obvious futility: how efface the indelible, and can God Himself undo the accomplished, cancel that which has been committed and suffered? Can the God of religion with His after death Paradise joys, efface the reality of the agonies endured upon earth? Can the

Inconceivable of Positivism efface with the happiness of the men of the twentieth century the misery of the men of the nineteenth? Can good cause evil in the same individual,—the warmth and honour of the old man cancel the starvation and cold and despair of the youth? Can evil suffered be blotted out, and evil committed be erased? Forgiven perhaps; but effaced, taken from out of the register of the things that have been, never. This plea of the future, whether in this world or another, what is it but a half-hour which the mercy of man gives to his God wherein to repent and amend and retrieve; a half-hour of centuries indeed, but a half-hour none the less in eternity, and to expiate the evil done in a lifetime of infinitude?"

"What is the use of going on like that?" asked Rheinhardt; "why cannot you two be satisfied with the infinite wickedness of mankind, without adding thereunto the wickedness of Nature? As Wolfram von Eschenbach remarked already six centuries ago: —'Ihr nöthight Gott nichts ab durch Zorn'—try and reform man, but leave God alone. But in truth all such talk is a mere kind of rhetorical exercise, brought into fashion by Schopenhauer, who would have been horrified at the waste of time and words for which he is responsible."

"We shall certainly not make Nature repent and reform by falling foul of her," answered Vere; "but at all events, by protesting against evil, however inevitable, we shall prevent ourselves being degraded into passive acceptance of it."

"I was going to say," went on Baldwin, "that I went through all these phases of moral wretchedness. And while they lasted, the temptation to have done with them, to free myself by a kind of intellectual suicide, was constantly pursuing me; it seemed as if every person I spoke with, every book that I opened, kept repeating to me:—'Disbelieve in your reason, and believe in your heart; that which may be impossible to your logic, may yet be possible to God's goodness.' It seemed to me as if I would give everything to be permitted to lay down my evil convictions, to shut my intellectual eyes, to fall into spiritual sleep, to dream—to be permitted to dream those beautiful dreams which consoled other men, and never again to wake up to the dreadful reality. But I saw that to do so would be mean and cowardly; I forced myself to keep awake in that spiritual cold, to see things plainly, and trudge quietly forward upon that bleak and hideous road. Instead of letting myself believe, I forced myself to doubt and examine all the more; I forced myself to study all the subjects which seemed as if they must make my certainty of evil only stronger and stronger. I instinctively hated science, because science had destroyed my belief in justice and mercy; I forced myself, for a while, to read only scientific books. Well, I was rewarded. Little by little it dawned upon me that all my misery had originated in a total misconception of the relative positions of Nature and of man; I began to perceive that the distinction between right and wrong conduct had arisen in the course of the evolution of mankind, that right and wrong meant only that which was conducive or detrimental to the increasing happiness of humanity, that they were referable only to human beings in their various relations with one another; that it was impossible to explain them, except with reference to human society, and that to ask for moral aims and moral methods of mere physical forces, which had no moral qualities, and which were not subject to social relations, or to ask for them of any Will hidden behind those forces, and who was equally independent of those human and social necessities which alone accounted for a distinction between right and wrong, was simply to expect one set of phenomena from objects which could only present a wholly different set of phenomena; to expect sound to be recognized by the eye, and light and colour to be perceived by the ear. In short, I understood that man was dissatisfied and angry with Nature, only because he had accustomed himself to think of Nature as only another man like himself, liable to human necessities, placed in human circumstances, and capable, therefore, of human virtues and vices, and that I had been in reality no wiser than the fool who flew into a rage with the echo, or the child who strikes the table against which it has hurt itself."

"I see," said Vere, bitterly, "your moral cravings were satisfied by discovering that Nature was not immoral, because Nature had never heard of morality. It appears not to have struck you that this utterly neutral character of Nature, this placid indifference to right and wrong, left man in a dreadful moral solitude; and might make him doubt whether, since morality did not exist for Nature, it need exist at all; whether, among all these blind physical forces, he too might not be a mere blind physical force."

"On the contrary," answered Baldwin, "when I came to understand why morality was not a necessity for Nature, I also understood why morality was a necessity for man; the rule of the road, the rule that each coachman must take a particular side of the street with reference to other coachmen, could certainly not exist before the existence of streets and of carriages being driven along them; but without that rule of the road, gradually established by the practice of drivers, one carriage would merely smash into another, and the thoroughfare be hopelessly blocked. Thus it has been with morality. Rules of the road are unnecessary where there are neither roads nor carriages; and morality would be unnecessary, indeed inconceivable, where there are no human interests in collision. Morality, I now feel persuaded, is the exclusive and essential qualification of the movements of an assemblage of men, as distinguished from an assemblage of stones, or plants, or beasts, the qualification of man's relation, not with unsentient things, but with sentient creatures. Why go into details? You know that the school of philosophy to which I adhere has traced all the distinctions of right and wrong to the perceptions, enforced upon man by mankind, and upon mankind by man, of the difference between such courses as are conducive to the higher development and greater happiness of men, and such other courses as are conducive only to their degradation and extinction. Such a belief, so far from leaving me in moral solitude, and making me doubt of my own moral nature, brings home to me that I am but a drop in the great moral flood called progress; that my own morality is but a result of the morality of millions of other creatures who have preceded me and surround me now; that my morality is an essential contribution to the morality of millions of creatures who will come after me; that on all sides, the more society develops, there is a constantly increasing intricacy of moral connection between the present, the past, and the future. If I refuse to pass on in the ranks of good, there will be so much the less havoc made in the ranks of evil; if I fall, those on either side of me will be less united and less vigorous to resist, those following after me will stumble; I must therefore keep in my place, be borne along by the current mass of moral life, instead of being passed over and trampled by it."

Vere did not answer. He looked vaguely towards the window, at the ghostly billows of the downs, dark blue, bleak, unsubstantial under the bright cold windy sky. The wind had risen, and went moaning round the farm, piping shrilly in all its chinks and crannies, and making a noise as of distant waters in the firs of the common. Suddenly in the midst of the silence within doors, there came from the adjoining room a monotonous trickle or dribble of childish voice, going on breathless, then halting suddenly exhausted, but with uniform regularity.

"It is Willie reading the Bible to his grandmother," remarked Rheinhardt; "the old lady is left alone at home with him on Sunday evenings, while her husband goes to the village. It is a curious accompaniment to your and Baldwin's pessimistic groanings and utilitarian jubilations."

"I think," remarked Baldwin, after a moment's fruitless listening to catch the words from next door, "I think in some matters we unbelievers might take a lesson from our neighbours. I was very much struck to-day, while listening to Monsignore's sermon, with the thought that that man feels it his duty to teach others what he believes to be the truth, and that we do not."

"It is a priest's profession to preach, my dear Baldwin," put in Rheinhardt; "he lives by it, lives off his own preaching and off the preaching of all the other priests that live now or ever have lived."

"We unbelievers—I should rather say we believers in the believable"—answered Baldwin, "should all of us be, in a fashion, priests. You say that Monsignore lives off his own preaching and the preaching of all

Catholic priests that ever have been—well; and do we not live spiritually, do we not feed our souls upon the truth which we ourselves can find, upon the truth which generations of men have accumulated for us? If, in the course of time, there be no more priests in the world, I mean in the old sense, it will be that every man will be a priest for his own family, and every man of genius a priest for the whole of mankind. What I was thinking of just now is this—that this Monsignore, whom we consider a sort of clever deluded fool, and this old country woman, whose thoughts scarcely go beyond her village, are impressed with the sense of the responsibility incurred by the possession of what they consider superior truth—the responsibility of not keeping that truth to themselves, but participating it to others; and that herein they both of them assume a position far wiser, far more honest, far nobler, than do we unbelievers, who say, 'What does it matter if others know only error, as long as ourselves know truth?'"

"You forget," answered Rheinhardt, "that both Monsignore and our landlady are probably persuaded that unless they share their spiritual knowledge with their neighbours, they will be responsible for the souls of those neighbours. And if you remember what may, in the opinion of the orthodox, happen to the souls of such persons as have been slightly neglected in their religious education, I think you will admit that there is plenty to feel responsible about."

"You mean that there is nothing for us to feel responsible about. Not so. Whatever may happen to the souls of our fellows will indeed not happen in an after world, nor will they suffer in a physical hell of Dante, or enjoy themselves in a physical Paradise of Mahomet. But there is nevertheless, for the souls which we know, for the souls which look up to us for instruction and assistance, a hell. A hell of moral doubt and despair and degradation, a hell where there is fire enough to scorch the most callous, and ice enough to numb the warmest, and mud to clog and bedraggle the most noble among us. Yes. There is a hell in the moral world, and there is heaven, and there is God; the heaven of satisfied conscience, the God of our own aspirations; and from this heaven, from the sight of this God, it is in our power to exclude those most beloved to us. Shut them out because we have not the courage to see them shiver and wince one moment in the cold and the light of truth; shut them out and leave them to wander in a world of phantoms, upon the volcano crust of that hell of moral disbelief, unaware of its existence or aware too late, too suddenly of the crater opening beneath their feet. That old woman in the next room is teaching, feels bound to teach, her child the things which she looks upon as truth. And shall a man like you, Vere, refuse to teach your children what you know to be true? Will you leave them to believe that the world and man and God, the past and future and present, are wholly different from what they really are; or else, to discover, unaided, with slow anguish or sudden despair, that all is different from what they thought, that there is falsehood where they relied on truth, and evil where they looked up to good; till falsehood and evil shall seem everywhere and truth and good nowhere? You spoke of the moral happiness and safety of your children; will you let that consist in falsehood, and depend upon the duration of error; will you let your children run the risk of losing their old faith, without helping them to find a new one? Will you waste so much of their happiness for themselves, and of their usefulness for the world?"

Vere did not answer; he remained as if absorbed in thought, nervously tearing the petals off a rose which stood in the glass before him.

"Do please leave that flower alone, Vere," remonstrated Rheinhardt; "that is just the way that all you pessimists behave—pulling to pieces the few pleasant things which Nature or man has succeeded in making, because the world is not as satisfactory as it might be. Such a nice rose, that was, the very apple of our landlady's eye, who picked it merely to afford you a pleasant surprise for supper; and you have merely made a mess of it on the tablecloth. That's what comes of thinking too much about responsibilities. One doesn't see the mischief one's fingers are up to."

And Rheinhardt, who was a tidy man, rose, and

carefully swept the pink petals and the yellow seeds off the table into his hand, and thence transferred them into a little earthenware jar full of dry rose leaves, which he kept in true eighteenth-century style, on his writing table.

"That is the difference of our philosophies," he remarked, with satisfaction; "you tear to pieces the few roses that are given us, and we pick up their leaves, and get the pleasant scent of them even when withered."

"The definition is not bad," put in Baldwin, throwing a bundle of faggots on the fire, and making it crackle and flare up lustily, flooding the room with ruddy light.

Vere turned away his face from the glow, and looked once more, vaguely and wistfully, into the bleak blueness of common and downs lying chill and dim in the moonlight.

"What you have been saying, Baldwin," he at last remarked, "may perhaps be true. It may be that it would be wise to teach my children the things which I believe to be true. But you see I love my children a great deal; and—. Well, I mean that I have not the heart to assume the responsibility of such a decision."

"You shirk your responsibilities," answered Baldwin, "and in doing so you take upon yourself the heaviest responsibility of any."

THE CONSOLATIONS OF BELIEF.

THE CONSOLATIONS OF BELIEF.

> "*Y a-t-il de véritables athées?*
> *Oui; s'il y a de véritables Chrétiens.*"—Diderot.

THE summer evening was turning into night, merging in delicate twilight grey the houses of the harbour, the shipping all round, the oozy sandbanks where the boats lay embedded at low water. From the town, its big square belfry looming in the dusk, came the first yellow reflections across the water, and the distant sound of the Rappel drums and bugles. Agatha, who had been silently watching the sailors going and coming on the wharf, the cranes slowly swinging upwards with their clutched bales, the ooze of high water lazily trickling from the green, clammy walls, turned suddenly to Baldwin as he paced up and down the lonely deck.

"I want to speak to you," she said.

He had not taken much notice of that stubborn-looking Scotch girl whom he had met the previous day travelling homewards with his friends; she had been silent, depressed, and almost morose that whole afternoon, and he had thought, if he had thought about it at all, that the sense that this long, first journey having come to a close, of the confusion of new impressions, stolidly received at the moment, but now overwhelming, was the cause of her depression.

"I want to speak to you," repeated Agatha, without giving him time to answer, "because I have been thinking all day long about what you said in the cathedral—do you remember?—about religion being a waste of energy, because there is no God with whom it could bring us into connection. Of course it's possible that you may not really have believed what you were saying, though I don't understand how people can say things they don't believe. But I want to know whether that is the case, or whether you seriously think in that way."

Baldwin stopped and leaned against the side of the boat.

"People do very often say things which they don't believe, especially on such subjects; and I don't find it as impossible as you do to realize their doing so. But I don't think there is much danger of it with me."

"Then you seriously think that there is no God?"

"I do not think that at all. I did not say there was no God; I merely said there was no God with whom religion can bring us into contact."

"Oh yes," burst out Agatha, contemptuously, "I know the sort of thing. You believe that there is a god who is really in everything and virtually in nothing; you believe that there is a god who is in the steam of a kettle, and the brain of a convict, and the virus of smallpox, and the chlorophyl of the leaves—a god who is the cosmos and all it contains—a deaf, blind, inconscient, overallish god, whose qualities are gravitation and expansion and so forth, who is much the same sort of thing as electricity, or heat, or light, and who can be approached, not by prayer, but by chemical analysis. I know the sort of god you mean."

"You think that you know him," corrected Baldwin, quietly.

"Well, perhaps I don't know him as exactly as you do, because I have not studied chemistry, and dynamics, and physics, and all those things which reveal what he is. But I know what he is not; I know that he has no mind and has no heart; I know that he is no god. I feel that I am repeating blasphemies in saying these things which you think, and I know that I shall hear more blasphemies if I continue speaking with you on the subject. But I must talk about it all the same—I must talk about it, although I dare say you will consider me absurd and childish, and forward, and disagreeable, because I think you must be very unhappy with such beliefs as those."

"I don't think I am particularly unhappy," answered Baldwin, "and, supposing I were unhappy, I don't see how that could affect my belief. I believe things

—at least I try to do so—not because they make me happy or unhappy, but because they appear to me to be true."

"But you wilfully refuse to see one half of the evidence; you wilfully choose to hear only one side of the argument. It is no use saying that you do not; if you did not, you would not believe what you do. Now, I know that in people like you—in materialists or atheists, or whatever you may choose to call yourselves—all this may often be the result of a sort of self-importance which inclines you to think that the more painful path must be the path of duty. You disbelievers are the very same men who in former days would have been religious fanatics: you desire martyrdom, you take a pleasure in tormenting yourselves, and, just as people used formerly to wear hair shirts and to drink brackish water because they wanted to feel that they were saints, so you choose to believe all the things that cost you most pain, that do most violence to your feelings, because you also are vain and morbid, and wish to feel yourselves better than other men; and so you force yourselves to think that there is no good save yourselves in the universe, and that there is no God outside it: things which are cruel and abominable to believe, just in proportion as they are false to God's nature and your own, and which you take a satisfaction in believing, just in proportion as they are cruel and abominable."

Baldwin did not answer. Agatha had surprised him;

she was not, as he had imagined, merely an amiable and self-sufficient young quixot, parroting the stale arguments of some fashionable Broad Church preacher.

"You think that very noble on your part, I have no doubt," went on Agatha, "just as those anchorites of former time, and those Indian ascetics, thought it noble to torture their bodies. I think it is merely repulsive and contemptible, and I, personally, don't feel any compassion for you: if you deliberately go out of your way to court suffering, why then suffer. But in suffering you are diminishing the amount of good which it has pleased God to put into the world; you are running counter to His will; you are laying wanton hands upon His work—and to see that makes me indignant."

"I thought Christianity taught mankind to hate the sufferings of others for the sake of those others."

"I am not a Christian; I do not care what may be taught or may not be taught. I believe in God, and in the goodness of God's will—that is all. I don't think God would be offended merely by your doubting His existence; but He is offended because you refuse to see the goodness which He has made manifest in order that men and women may be happy."

And Baldwin saw Agatha's eyes fixed solemnly on him in the dusk.

"You are indignant with me because, by being wilfully unhappy in my belief, you suppose me to be frustrating God's will," he answered; "but what if I am not unhappy?"

"That is impossible. Oh," added the girl, with fierce contempt, "I don't mean to say that a kind of happiness may not be compatible with such a belief as yours. A sheep is happy nibbling the grass, a cat is happy lying in the sun, or a dog running about in the fields; and we have all of us sufficient of the animal in our nature to experience some sort of happiness so long as we have what would satisfy the mere animal, or the scarcely higher creature which seeks bare comfort, not in actual food or in actual physical warmth, but in worldly prosperity or worldly consideration. But supposing you be something better than that, supposing you have a mind and a heart, do not your mind and your heart require something which is to them as breathable air and food and space to move in are to the mere body—a spiritual atmosphere in which you can see and live, and which is the all-pervading goodness of God?"

"I do not feel such a want;" said Baldwin; "I feel, like you, a desire, a want, that the world be full of justice and forethought and charity; but I do not imagine that this justice and forethought and charity are to be those of God: I desire them of man."

"The justice and forethought and charity of man!" cried Agatha—"what can they be—what could they be—even at the best? Individual, impotent, finite things. Man can set right, at the very best, only the smallest speck of wrong ; only that tiny speck which is near enough to his weak eyes, to his weak hands ; he can love only those that he knows, and how many are they? Nay, only those whom his imperfect understanding, his limited sympathies, permit him to understand. Take the very noblest, and wisest, and most loving of men—how narrow is his power of separating the good from the evil, of making allowance, of justly weighing—why, he can understand only those who are made like himself. But God, who has made all, knows all, loves in each and every one whatever microscopic good there may exist, invisible to other men's eyes ; He, in whose hands is all good and all evil, can not merely destroy all evil, but can create all good ; He can bring in the right hand as much good as He can remove evil with the left. He, who is everywhere and all-seeing, can come always at the right time, can always help and console at the moment that help and consolation is wanted, can always revive with the consciousness of His love at the instant that want of love is letting us freeze or stifle to death. The knowledge that such love surrounds not only ourselves, but all men, surrounds those whom we see down-trodden and suffering without being able to help them—the knowledge of this love, is happiness, and the absence of this knowledge is misery."

Baldwin listened to Agatha with a patience and a reverence which his friends, who complained of his uncompromising and impatient spirit of dispute, would have been surprised to witness. The fact was, it seemed to Baldwin that there was as much ground for reverence and gentleness towards this strange, quixotic girl, who had cast off every orthodox faith to make herself a faith which mirrored only her own nature, as there was reason for contemptuous impatience with men who, while able and accustomed to think, repeated nevertheless, from moral laziness or pusillanimity, the threadbare arguments of others.

"I perfectly agree with you, Miss Stuart," he said, "that a conviction such as you describe is an element of happiness in the life of a man or a woman. But an element of happiness may be none the less fallacious and none the less mischievous. The persuasion of a conceited man that he is the admired of all beholders is so great an element of happiness in his life that without it his life would be unendurable; yet the persuasion is utterly unfounded, and the man has no right to it. You will say that this is a grotesque instance—well, let us take one from the very class of subject about which we are discussing. In the Middle Ages some of the noblest and purest-minded men and women, like St. Catherine of Siena, and nearly all the mystical saints, firmly believed that the hysterical fits induced by fasting and want of sleep and maceration—pitiable and disgusting prostrations of body and mind—were participations in the life of God. This belief compensated them for every imaginable evil and hardship, this delusion of superhuman happiness where there was only a degrading disease, enabled them to go cheerfully through lives which were almost unendurable, and which were noble and even useful. You cannot say that the happiness was not true, or that the belief on which it rested was not false. How can you be certain that this belief of yours, which you describe as so enormous an element of happiness in your life, which you say would make such a difference in mine, is not a delusion like St. Catherine's or St. Francis's belief in ecstasy?"

Agatha looked round her for a moment. Something in the hour and the light, a poignancy in the sense that an eventful time in her young life was fading into the past with this fading away of this last day of her first long journey, brought home to Agatha, even more strongly than before, a dull pain, which she misnamed indignation to her resolute spirit, at the moral blindness of this man.

"The belief of St. Francis and of St. Catherine," she answered, with a little Scotch contempt for saints, "was, for all their virtues, due to mere diseased vanity, and appealed to a morbid, degrading craving for excitement: they wanted to be God, they did not want to know God's goodness. Besides, it was a survival, in people whom it disgraced, of superstitions which they accepted along with the spiritual truths of their religion."

"That is what you think, and I think," replied Baldwin, "but it would have seemed a monstrous blasphemy to the people of those days. Does it not occur to you that this belief in the goodness of God, which affords you so much happiness—happiness less acute, I am inclined to think, than that of the saints, conscious of their power of ecstasy, but also less selfish and nobler—does it not strike you that this belief also may be the expression of a mere desire of your nature, the survival from some phase of belief which you have in the main left behind you?"

Agatha shook her head.

"In the first place," she answered, looking up in the pale blue overhead, where the earliest stars seemed struggling to the surface, and watching the swallows whirring about the rigging of the ship, and dipping across the deck, "you are mistaken in supposing that I accept any religion as those saints, superior as they were to me, could not help doing in their day. I was brought up among devout believers, and I was, for a long time, a devout believer myself. I loved religion; it came naturally to me, and was my greatest pleasure. When I was a child I used to cut out angels of tissue paper with crowns of gilt foil, and to lie dreaming of heaven for hours under the bushes in the garden; after that I liked nothing so much as reading religious books and scribbling verses about God and Christ. But then one day, while reading some book on the Fall and the Redemption, it suddenly came home to me how terrible, how wicked it was of God to have brought sin and death into the world to avenge so trifling a disobedience, such as every boy and girl commit by the dozen; and then to let His own Son offer Himself up to be insulted and martyred, and to wash out the memory of His wrath only in innocent blood. And then it came home to me also how incredible it seemed of a good God to condemn so many men and women to eternal torture; and I began to disbelieve. It was most cruel to me to have to wrench myself from my belief, to give up Christ and the angels in heaven, to bring it all down to human proportions, to find myself quite alone, without any mediator to help and encourage me, in the awful presence of God. Oh, you can't think how horrible it was: all the poetry and cheerfulness and security seemed to have gone out of life. But still I went on doubting and disbelieving; and now I accept no one's belief but my own—nothing except what my heart tells me is true. So you see that I am able to tear myself from beliefs which I love; and that you have no right to suppose that my present faith is either a mere concession to my wishes, or a lazy survival of the doctrines of other folk."

Baldwin smiled at this deeply religious nature persuading itself so seriously that it was strong-minded and sceptical.

"I see," he said, gently, "that you started with the belief in a good and loving God; and that as soon as you saw in the orthodox religion notions about God which did not square with your belief in His goodness and lovingness, you forthwith broke with orthodoxy. But this merely proves to me that I was quite right in suggesting that your belief was, what you scornfully defined the belief in ecstasy of St. Catherine and St. Francis, a survival of a traditional creed and an expression of personal desires. You have dropped some portion of the orthodox creed; but you have not dropped what corresponds to this faith in visions and trances, since you have not dropped what was to you the delightful part of your belief."

"I did not drop what is vital in all religion, what is necessary for spiritual life, what is proven to every mind which does not wilfully refuse the evidence of the whole universe. No! I have not dropped that," cried Agatha, indignantly: "but what right have you to compare the delusion of those half-crazy monks and nuns, taking their own fever visions for God's presence, and their own hysteric ravings for God's voice — what right have you to compare such things with the testimony of all nature proclaiming the goodness of God? Look there," she went on, passionately, pointing at the port where the boat lay awaiting the tide, where the whitewash of the houses on the wharves glared a lurid white beneath their huddled roofs, the light in windows and doorways still struggling, yellow and uncertain, with the fading twilight, the chimney stacks black against the pale sky delicately streaked with smoke-like cloud-wreaths, upon which the rigging and pennons of the boats appeared clear and thread-like, while the gurgoyles and pinnacles and lit-up clock alone remained distinguishable from the dark mass of the cathedral belfry. All was marvellously subdued and delicate and peaceful: the whirr of the swallows and the distant song of the children playing in the twilight mingling with the drowsy lapping of the waves against the ship and the wharf side, as the subtle curls of smoke from the old town mingled with the grey mists streaking the sky.

"Look there," went on Agatha, "does not everything on this beautiful evening speak to you of the goodness of God? does not the very sense of the purity and peacefulness of the sky and the water— does not the knowledge of the great green rolling country, with its orchards and cornfields, and rows of poplars, and lily-grown canals behind us, of the great grey, misty sea before us, mean the sense, the knowledge of the goodness of God? Do you not feel it even in the very perception of the lovely tints of the sky, of the reflections on the water, of the breeze and the swallow's sound? And does not the remembrance of all the hundreds of men and women and children who are resting from their day's work in yonder town, and the strong wish which you feel that they may be peaceful and happy all their lives —does not all this say, as clearly as all your various sensations and thoughts say, that there is a yourself, that there is a God, and that He is Love?"

"I follow your argument," answered Baldwin. "These things are beautiful and noble, they make us happy, they represent so much happiness; and the God who has made them thus must therefore be good and loving. But let us look a little closer at the things around us—let us try and realize what exists beneath this beautiful scene. This water, which looks so lovely with its black wavy surface broken by the long yellow reflections—what do you suppose it really is?—a wash of filth and of death, a drain-and-shambles-polluted slime, which sends up fever to poison into weakness a proportion of those men and women, to poison into death a proportion of those children whom you suppose to be happily resting after their day's work. That fertile country behind us, with the fields and farms and orchards, does it not suggest to you all the overwork, the ignorance, the sordid avarice of the people who cultivate it? As to the sea, which happens to be so calm at present, what is it except an enormous watery charnel-house, where not only the bones of uncountable dead men, but the hopes and honour and happiness of even a vaster number of living men and women, lie buried? This seems to you far-fetched—well, then, try for one instant to realize all that is at this moment going on in that little sleepy city; try for a moment to guess at the amount of cruelty and falsehood and bestial foulness which exists even among those comparatively few men and women; try to bring home to yourself merely one-twentieth of the misery, the bodily and mental agony, the bodily and mental starvation, and corruption, and dying inch by inch of its inhabitants; try and conceive the condition of merely one dying man, or sick child, or polluted woman among the many in those few houses opposite, and tell me whether you still think that the things which surround us at this moment bear to us the assurance that the God who made them is a God all love."

Agatha gave a slight shudder and did not answer for a moment.

"Everything in the world is not good," she said, after a pause, "but everything in the world is for the best. We cannot even conceive existence without this amount of evil; without it we might be happier, but we should be happy merely like well-provided domestic animals; if there were no temptation, no degradation, no despair, there could be no purity, no aspiration, no charity, no self-sacrifice, no justice. Tell me, can you conceive a world less bad than this?"

"I cannot—I, being part and parcel of this world, taking all my notions of possible and impossible from its already established arrangements; I, with the limitations imposed upon me by this world, certainly could not. But the God of whom you speak is not merely all good, He is all powerful. He is met by no limitations, since all limitations are imposed by Himself. You cannot say of Him, 'He put into the world as much happiness as was possible,' for the words possible and impossibility have no meaning in relation to Omnipotence."

"I do not know why God has permitted what evil there is in the world," said Agatha, with eager thoughtfulness—" no one can, on account of those very limitations of our nature of which you speak. And I know, oh, I know but too well, that there is evil, terrible, hopeless evil in the world. I know it; and the thought of it would overwhelm me, were it not that I know that God has no limitations like ours, that He is all good and all just, and has the whole of time, the whole of space, wherein to compensate for this evil of the world; that if a man or a woman, nay, the humblest of His creatures, is doomed to suffer in the few hours of this life, that suffering will be washed out by the floods of happiness which will be poured forth in eternity. Oh, yes herein lies the blessedness of the belief in God's goodness; herein, that every time we see some creature disinherited, hopelessly and cruelly, of happiness, of health, or freedom, or love, in this world, and that we feel that we are powerless to help; that every time we look upon a city like this one, and picture to ourselves all the vice and degradation and misery in it which we can only shudder at in impotence, the thought comes to console us that all these things shall be set right, all this evil turned to good, and that God has Infinitude and Eternity wherein to do it."

"But," objected Baldwin, "what assurance have you, who have rejected as mere human utterances the words of promise handed down by the Church—you, who accept only your own convictions—that there is for any of these creatures, higher and lower, for the dog tied down for hours while disembowelled by the physiologist, or for the man wasting away from hereditary disease which has carried off, one by one, all his beloved ones, for the stag rushing along with the teeth of the hounds already upon him, and for the woman hounded by society from one stage of infamy and misery to another, till she sinks down a mere mass of bodily and moral disease—what assurance have you that when death releases them from their miseries, death does not also put an end to all possibilities of compensation and justice? when, on the contrary, everything fresh that we learn respecting the physical basis of mind and character, the physical constituents of identity, renders it daily more difficult to conceive the survival of the soul when separated from the body of which it seems uncommonly like a a function, or a combination of functions? An orthodox believer, who accepts the teaching of the Church as the word of God, settles the matter by a reference to the creed, as I might settle a question of my future financial condition by a reference to my father's or grandfather's will at Doctors Commons;

but you cannot say, I know there will be an after life, because I possess a written promise to that effect."

"I know that all the things which science is teaching make it very difficult for us to understand by what means and in what manner our soul will survive our body," answered Agatha, composedly; " we do not know, and have no need to know. Our conviction rests elsewhere. We possess a document by which a future life is promised to us more solemnly and certainly than by any lawyer's parchment; for the promise that all evil will be compensated hereafter is written and sealed deep in our heart, and, if we look into that, and seriously contemplate that mysterious writ, we must recognize that God's own hand has traced it."

"There is indeed in our consciousness," said Baldwin, " a difficulty of conceiving annihilation, something analogous, I fancy, to our mechanical difficulty of seeing our own back; and there is also a strong instinctive desire for the preservation of our life and of our property, among which latter the life of those beloved of us is certainly the most valuable. This horror of annihilation and this difficulty of conceiving it, both of them peculiarities explicable by reference to our mere present condition, naturally combined and produced, in the absence of any scientific facts which rendered such a conception difficult, a hope, a belief in a future existence, which it is quite possible may have become almost hereditary in us. Your God-written promise is thus easily reduced to a mere wish for a prolongation of consciousness, grown to a certainty for sheer want of being contradicted."

Had it been less dark Baldwin might have seen a sort of convulsion pass over Agatha's quiet and earnest face.

"Had such a belief been a delusion," she burst out, after a moment, "do you think that God would have permitted it to rise up in our heart? Is it not more consonant with all we know of His wisdom and goodness to suppose that He caused these blind instincts of our nature to unite into such significance, to reveal what our reason could not grasp, than to imagine that He is a callous bungler, or a cruel liar, deluding us with belief in the impossible?"

"Your certainty, then, of the existence of a future life depends upon your conviction of the goodness of God?"

"Yes; God cannot let us perish after such a life as this; God cannot bid us hope for what He is not going to give."

"You found your belief in a future life upon your certainty of the goodness of God?" repeated Baldwin.

"I do," interrupted Agatha; "are there not moral facts revealed to the heart as well as intellectual facts revealed to the reason?"

"But you forget that this very future life had been postulated by you to vindicate God's goodness," he went on. "The opportunity of compensating for the evil of this world is thus made finally to rest upon that very incompatibility with evil, whose existence it was intended to prove. Is this too complicated? Well, then, in plainer terms, belief in the goodness of God depends upon belief in immortality, and belief in immortality depends upon belief in the goodness of God. Does this strike you as a satisfactory argument?"

Baldwin smiled rather bitterly; he was an impatient man, and even with a girl like Agatha he felt just a little out of patience.

"Why not?" answered Agatha, defiantly. "Is not the goodness of God a fact sufficiently important to account for all things?"

"The goodness of God," replied Baldwin, drily, "that is to say, the goodness of all-wise Omnipotence, does not seem to me a sufficient explanation for the evil which He has inflicted upon His creatures. The moral character of God is so fearfully compromised in your eyes by all the foulness and misery which He has admitted into His scheme of things, that you require to rehabilitate Him, to save Him from condemnation by your own conscience, the supposition of another state of existence in which He will compensate for the injustice and cruelty with which He has treated us in this one. But what right have you to suppose that the God who does not shrink from inflicting unnecessary evil—for God is bound by no necessity—must feel bound to repair it? What right have you to expect the absolute justice and kindness, which would plan a future life, from the Being who has shown the absolute injustice and cruelty which He has worked into this one? Oh no! the God who has created evil is not the God from whom we may expect compensation—the Unjust is not the one from whom we may await final justice."

Agatha was silent. The night was hot and windless, the sky overcast with a dark film. The town, all save the brilliant eye of the cathedral clock, was hidden in darkness; only close by, the wharf was distinguishable by the flicker of its lanterns; and dark figures hovered about in the glow of the furnaces of engines, which belched out, ever and anon, great masses of thick flame-reddened smoke, drowning all voices with their constant whirr and grind and tremendous pant. A kind of terror came over Agatha; the light seemed to be dying out of her soul as out of the heavens, leaving only lurid gleams like those all round them. But she struggled bravely against this horror.

"But evil," she said, "is not really of God; it exists, but it is foreign to Him. Evil, physical and moral, are against nature; nature is for ever trying to cast out evil, punishing the existence of crime and foulness; and nature is but the expression of God's will."

"Evil is not contrary to nature," answered Baldwin—and his words had a horrible fascination to Agatha, mingling as they did with all the unearthly sounds of the wharf—"evil is not contrary to nature; it is contrary, or partially contrary, only to certain processes of nature upon which depend our life and happiness. But do you suppose there are no other processes in nature than these which are for our benefit? The movement which disorganizes is as natural as the movement which organizes; the process which means pain and death is as natural, as easy, as much a part of the whole, as the process which means pleasure and life. It so happens that out of these various processes, some have made us; that does not mean that they are one whit more natural than those which may unmake us; it means merely that they happen to have been the stronger; but the weaker are in nature also. Disease follows upon putrescence, but putrescence and disease are as much products of nature as are the health in ourselves to which they are opposed. However much we may get the better of these hostile powers of nature, however much we may in future secure ourselves from sickness, famine, earthquake, and all the destructive powers of nature, we shall not diminish the fact that those powers, or at all events the elements thereof, exist within nature, even as the vanquished malefactor, bound hand and foot, reduced to harmlessness, exists in nature, is its product as well as the policeman who has got the better of him? Nay, these evil powers of nature, these which we choose to call against nature because they are against us, are not by any means hostile even to those processes which befriend us; they work together. Destruction helps preservation, life lives off death; not only does the survival of this civilization depend upon the destruction of that one, even as the survival of one particular race of animals depends upon the destruction of another particular race of animals, but the bodily and moral health, the material prosperity of one part of the community depends upon the dying out, the annihilation of another part of the community. It is useless to say that it is the less endowed giving way to the better endowed, or the minority to the majority; the very fact of being worse endowed or of constituting a minority is, inasmuch as it entails this destruction, a sufficiently positive evil. The crimes of nature are not unnatural, neither are the crimes of man. Unnatural in what sense? Unnatural when nature, with countless meshes, drags generations and races of men into it, compels them, with the irresistible force of inborn constitution and surrounding circumstances, to be corrupt and cruel; unnatural because crime is punished by the same necessity of nature by which it is created? because Nature hounds up all mankind against the tyrant which she has produced, or tears to pieces with disease the profligate of her own making? In proportion as the world improves, so does justice triumph, and good; but the injustice and evil over which it triumphs is as much a product of nature as itself. But mark, this which improves is human justice; man improves, but nature, fate, do not. The cases when the innocent man is crushed by the hand of guilty mankind are becoming rarer; but not one whit the rarer become the cases when the wretch is condemned to misery, to sickness, to sin, by the unjust hand of Fate. Nature remains as callous and as impartial as in the days of Nero; and nature, you say, is the expression of God's will."

Agatha had listened not so much with patience as with a kind of stupefaction. But she roused herself and said, when Baldwin had ended—

"You argue according to your reason, according to the appearance of things in your reason's light. But your reason is the work of God; and who can be so bold as to say, upon the authority of this created reason, that its judgments may not be mere error, its ideas of good and evil mere delusions? Be this as it may, God, although He has given us reason which may be fallible, has given us a heart whose words must, must be true. If evil is not, as may perhaps be the case when things are seen unwarped by our judgment, then God requires not to compensate; and if evil really is, then God, who has permitted us to know of such things as goodness and justice, will show that He is all good and all just: He will compensate hereafter."

The men had come on deck, and were beginning, with strange nautical chants and shouts, and amid the roar and whizz of the engine, to take in the cables.

"If, according to your first suggestion, our reason deludes us into supposing that there is evil, and our senses, I must add, to carry out your thought, delude us in telling us that there is pain, why then," answered Baldwin, "I can only say that of all the evils which may be laid at the door of the First Great Cause, none is so monstrous as to have thus created His creatures that what is really good and therefore joy, should be to them evil and suffering; none is so base as to oblige them to have falsehood, and to make the universe in which they live nothing but one vast lie. If, on the other hand, our senses and our reason may be trusted, if there is pain, and if there is evil, why then that pain, that evil, can never, never be compensated. For compensation is a vain word when applied to the Almighty. We may compensate for what the necessity of our nature, the force of circumstances, or our own imperfection has made us do; I may testify, by going out of my way to make my victim happy, that I had no intention of hurting him, or that such an intention no longer exists for me save as a shame in the past. But how can He compensate who made necessity instead of being made by it? How can He compensate who was ever-present, almighty, and omniscient? What ignorance of consequences misled Him, who established all relations of cause and effect? Therefore I say that the Almighty God can plead no extenuating circumstances, that He is responsible for every millionth of a vibration of pain in this universe, and that all the æons of bliss which He might offer as compensation could not buy off one tittle of that responsibility. The Omnipotent and Omniscient has willed evil, and the moral sense which He has made to arise in His creatures must judge Him and hold Him guilty."

"Agatha! Baldwin!" cried the voices of their friends through the darkness, "are you on deck? Why we thought you must have gone ashore and lost your way in the town, and that we should have to leave without you. Do you know that it is not at all proper for you two people to sit up on deck while your friends think you are lost?"

Agatha rose to meet her friends, while ropes thumped back from the wharf to the deck, and the first dull throb of movement ran through the boat.

"We shall have a beautiful calm night," said Baldwin, looking up to where the clouds were breaking and the rising moon sending a first broad beam of silver on to the water: "it seems a pity that our theological discussion should be broken into just in the middle; but we will resume it, if you be not too tired, to-morrow morning. Good-night, Miss Stuart."

"Good-night," answered Agatha, coldly. But she

stopped suddenly, and, stretching out her hand, said, in a curious tone, agitated and yet solemn, " I don't suppose any longer that you do it from mere perversity ; I think you could not—oh no, you could not think as you do of God from free choice. And God will not be angry with you, because you must be too unhappy ; He must be merely grieved, since even I am merely grieved—and perhaps, perhaps some day He may persuade you of His goodness."

For a moment, as he stood watching the moonlit ripple in the wake of the boat, and the port lights gradually fading away, Baldwin thought he was very prosaic and brutal.

II.

The next morning, when Agatha came on deck, she found Baldwin leaning over the side of the ship, looking out on a scene very different from that which they had left the night before. The sea had disappeared, and the river was already narrowing, and exchanging its green marshes for low banks, ghastly with low black sheds and coal cinders, with here or there a tall factory chimney spectral in the grey mist: a desolate sight, these masses of thick livid water, curdling in huge folds beneath the wind, and reddened here and there into a strange tawniness by the fitful, yellow gleams from out of the leaden clouds—grey water and grey banks, and grey gusty sky as far as you could see up and down its great snake-like bends, a gaunt tree or two dim in the mist below, a faint forest of masts and chimneys in the smoke-cloud higher up; the red, distended sail of some big barge, rocking on the waving surface of the river, carrying out, as it were, the pattern of the reddish sun-gleams on the muddy grey water.

"I have been thinking all night of what you told me yesterday evening," said Agatha to Baldwin, "and the more I think about it the more horrible and incredible it seems to me that a human soul should live in such a nightmare of wickedness as that—should endure the pollution of a belief such as yours. Oh, it is much worse than any physical horror of which one can read, than any story of travellers dying all alone of thirst and agony among the ice or the burning sand, than any torture of being shut in a charnel-house and feeling the slimy creatures creeping on to one's living flesh from the corpses all round; it is worse than being tied up, alive, with a dead body, this horror of living, a soul which knows good and evil, in the tangle of a world where evil is as natural as good, to know oneself to have been made by a power of injustice and cruelty, to know that all the good there is in the world, and in oneself, all the good which one strives after, and all the good which one can attain, is kneaded up with evil; that the Being to obey whose laws is one's sole notion of good, that the God who has taught us the difference of right and wrong, who is our sole standard of righteousness, to please whom is our highest virtue, is more callous and cruel and unjust than the wickedest of mankind. Oh, the fate of the worm who works his way in the slime is noble compared with yours, if you believe such things! But you cannot believe them! you could not have believed them for one moment!"

"My dear Miss Stuart," answered Baldwin, with a half-touched, half-admiring smile at the girl's fervour, "I am very sorry you should have been making yourself unhappy about me. Had our conversation not been interrupted last night I would have made it plain that I really do not deserve any commiseration; nay, perhaps even that I am happier in my opinions than most people. I was going to explain to you that I do not in the least believe that the First Cause is either unjust, or callous, or cruel."

"You do not?" exclaimed Agatha, joyfully; but added indignantly, after a moment, "then why, why did you pretend to believe the horrible things which you did?"

"I did not pretend to believe anything which I do not believe," answered Baldwin, quietly. "Indeed I made no full-length confession of faith at all—nay, have patience; I know what you are going to say. I merely answered your arguments. You said that the whole world proclaimed the lovingness of God, and I pointed out to you that if the constitution of the universe was the proof of God's nature, it was quite as easy to prove that He is entirely cruel and unjust as that He is all loving and righteous. You then said that He would set everything right in a future life; and, when I asked for your reasons for a belief in a future life, you returned to your original statement that God was all good, and insisted that, since He was all good, we must absolutely believe in a future state where He would compensate for the evil of this world. Then I told you that in my opinion Omnipotence could not have the benefit of compensation, and that, moreover, the very fact of there being evil to compensate in the world militated against the notion of the Creator of this evil caring to compensate it. That is all I said."

"But do you, or do you not believe all these things?" cried Agatha, impatient with such subtleties. "Do you believe that God is good, or do you believe that God is bad?"

"I do not believe either," he answered, gravely, and turning round to look in her puzzled face.

"Then you do not believe in God at all; you are a real, complete atheist," she said, disappointed and contemptuous; "that is a very easy solution of the difficulty; but I never understood how a man with any reasoning faculties could be a real atheist."

"Nor could I; and although at one period, when I had gone through the same argument with myself that I went through with you last night, I tried, out of sheer moral and intellectual despair, to believe myself a thorough atheist, I never could succeed. No, I am not an atheist: to be an atheist, a real atheist, means simply to disbelieve in the existence of a God ; well——"

"Well, if there *is* a God, He *must* be either good or bad," cried Agatha.

Baldwin shook his head. "Look at this river," he said, pointing to the huge mass of heaving, wind-worried water, with its metallic grey lustre where it caught the light ; its strange, unearthly opalescent films under the sides of the big anchored ships, and the smoke-encrusted piles of the wharves—" look at this river: if I ask you whether you believe in its existence, you will certainly answer yes. But if I ask you whether this river, which is at once so hideous and so beautiful, which rises and sinks with the tide as if for our benefit ; which occasionally overflows, destroying property and leaving pestilence ; which lets hundreds of wretches dishonour and make miserable their families by drowning their responsibilities instead of bearing them ; which, on the other hand, permits our poorest classes to live on corn from Russia, and vegetables from the South, and fruits and spices from the East and the tropics, as the Tiber never permitted any Roman emperors—if I asked you whether the river is just or unjust, kind or cruel, whether it loves men or hates men, what would you answer? You would laugh, and ask me whether I expect you to have the beliefs of an educated woman of the nineteenth century, or of a fetish-worshipping savage——"

"The cases are not at all parallel," interrupted Agatha.

" Pardon me, the cases are parallel—the First Cause, the inscrutable something behind all law and all phenomenon, moves and upheaves itself (and with it the world) in such a way that we men and women are sometimes benefited and sometimes injured ; bringing us, as this river does to the city, power and a wealth of joy to our lives, or overwhelming them with sin and misery as this river drowns or poisons its banks with its waters and its slime. We know of the First Cause, of God, only this much—that through it things are such as they are, for good and ill, and this much is not one whit more than we know of the river ; we have no more right to say that the good of the world is due to God's kindness, and its evil to His wickedness, than we have a right to ascribe the benefits and injuries done us by the Thames to some venerable weed-bearded river-god, stretching his huge limbs beneath this water."

"That is absurd," cried Agatha, indignantly. "We know that the river does us good and harm unconsciously, without any such thinking and feeling as are requisite for a knowledge of good and evil ; we know that a river is a river."

"And we know that God is God ; I understand.

But tell me, how do you know that a river has no consciousness, that it cannot think or feel, that it can have no knowledge of good and evil? You know it because a river is not a human being, because it has not the body, the brain, the physical necessities and social relations of man; because you can conceive no reason why this river, which is not a man, and which does not associate with men, should resemble mankind in soul, when it does not resemble mankind in body. But tell me, do you know of the First Cause that He is a human being? Do you believe that He has the body, the brain, the physical necessities and social relations of man? You do not know it; and, moreover, you do know that such a supposition is as absolutely irreconcilable with your notion of a First Cause as the supposition of this Thames having limbs and a head and a beard is irreconcilable with your visual perception of this mass of muddy water."

"I know," answered Agatha, fervently, "that God has made the universe and man, that God has made man's soul; and I know, therefore, that the instincts which He has placed in the heart of man are His instincts."

"Who tells you that God has made the universe and man and man's faculties? Who tells you that He has placed any particular faculties in man's soul, Miss Stuart? You have been told these things by your father and mother, who have learned them from their parents; it is a tradition, a mere guess or fancy handed down, for want of a better explanation, from generation to generation. But where is your evidence? Here is the universe and ourselves, and a certain number of phenomena which account for the universe and for ourselves, which account, within a certain limit, for each other. Beyond that limit we find no further explanation; and here our mind, which cannot conceive an effect without a cause, places God—a first great hidden cause, behind which we forbid our reason to seek any further, since we should merely multiply thereby the unknown and the unknowable. The original cause of all phenomena—that is all that we have a right to define God. But that this cause should imply will, scheme, plan, consciousness, is merely attributing to the Unknown the qualities of the known—attributing to God the modes of existence and of action of man. God has made man, God has placed instincts in man—is God made in man's image that you should say that He makes or plans or designs? The sun is nearer to us than God; we can see, feel his influence directly, we can study his properties and habits; and the sun we no longer endow with a will, with motives and plans; but of God, who is beyond the boundary of the directly or indirectly knowable, of God, who is merely a surmise, a phantasm created by the necessity of our reason, which may or may not have a corresponding reality, we assert attributes which are intelligible only of creatures identical with ourselves. You spoke just now of God's having placed moral instincts within us—taking for granted that the mode of connection between us and the First Cause was a mere copy of the connection between man and what he manipulates—as being a proof that He must have what He is able to give. Do you suppose, then, that God has got carnal necessities, since He, if He has made us, has implanted them also in His creatures?"

Agatha seemed to think for a moment. "I am willing to believe," she said, "that the necessities of our body are not the direct work of God; that they may be the physical results of a physical evolution, which I am far from denying. Thus God need possess none of these. But the moral necessities of our nature are explicable by no such physical evolution; hence they come direct from God, and if God has given them, He must possess them."

Baldwin smiled. "Your theory is very ingenious," he said, "but I fancy it is not without its parallel in the old mystical speculators about God and the universe. Unfortunately, I don't think it will hold water for various reasons. One is, that it continues to suppose that the relations of the First Cause and its effects are identical with the relations between man and his works. They say that the moral necessities of our nature cannot be accounted for in the same manner as the physical ones; but upon these physical necessities depend our mental necessities, upon which, in their turn, depend the moral ones; so that since, as we daily see more and more plainly, a difference in the structure of our brain, of our nervous system and perceptive organs, would necessitate a difference in our mental conceptions, this physical difference would surely also imply a difference in those moral notions which are based upon, nay, perfectly interwoven with, our intellectual notions."

"All that is very well. But there are other moral notions which cannot be thus explained. Our reason may tell us what is beneficial to our neighbours, but our reason cannot tell us that we ought to benefit them. The physical constitution of man does not explain this; it comes to man not from within, but from without."

"I perfectly agree with you. Our moral instincts are not explicable by mere physical or mere mental evolution; they come not merely from within, but from without. But you forget that besides the exterior world pressing upon and moulding our body, and our body pressing upon and moulding our mind, there is something more which coerces and modifies our instincts; you forget that there is something outside man which is not God, but mankind."

"Oh," said Agatha, contemptuously, "I had forgotten that. The old eighteenth century argument, warmed up in our days, that man and mankind will choose virtue from self-interest, always seems to me so shallow, so idiotic, that I can never realize that any one really believes in it."

"No one does believe in it, as it happens. The eighteenth century, in this matter as in so many other questions connected with evolution, guessed where the truth lay, but failed to see the truth itself. No one imagines nowadays that man respects his neighbour's welfare from an egoistic calculation which, in many cases, would be utterly mistaken: what we believe is that mankind sees its own proximate interest sufficiently to make the position of any individual who endangers it so insupportable, that the individual is speedily deterred from his intentions, or as speedily exterminated; and that as the individuals whose mode of life is most favourable to the welfare of the majority have a greater chance of surviving and leaving descendants, a certain habit of conforming to the general standard of proper behaviour becomes hereditary in the race, producing, every now and then, an accumulation of itself, an individual more than usually sensitive to the common welfare, who adds some new idea of right and wrong to the little stock already existing; some man who surprises his neighbours by applying their rules of self-restraint and benefit to some larger section of living beings; some man who says: These negroes, despite their blackness, feel the same physical and moral pain as yourselves; in this respect they are exactly like the white men whom you neither sell nor lash; so why should you sell and lash them?—a notion which seems quite crazily far-fetched, till one day the whole of that man's nation are, so to speak, born with it, and wonder how any one could ever have done without. No; certainly morality is not a result of mere physical or mere intellectual development; it requires that man should be brought into relation with man; it is, indeed, the gradually established mode of relation between man and man, the unconsciously established rule of social movement involving least effort and waste, even as the logical instinct is the habit of thinking of things in such relations with one another as involve least mental trouble and error. And this being the case, it seems to me, as I said before, that it is not only wholly unnecessary to suppose that God has instilled into us moral instincts whose origin can be otherwise accounted for, but, moreover, that as the Godhead, inasmuch as the First and Absolute Cause, can be subject to no necessities and liable to no relations, it is wholly unwarranted to attribute to Him the possession of such moral instincts, which would be as utterly uncalled-for in Him as would all social virtues in Robinson Crusoe, had he been born of the rocks and waves of his island, and never met his man Friday."

"I understand," said Agatha; "you do not call yourself an atheist; oh no, that would be blundering, unscientific, impolite, old-fashioned. You admit that there is a God—a God somewhere or other, doubtless doing something or other, a God by all means. But you spunge out His God-like qualities—you spunge out the God-like from all the world. Everything is but an accident, and of these accidents God is the earliest and man's soul the latest. You say this satisfies you—well, after extirpating divinity from God and from the world, you have perhaps extirpated it from yourself—you, your universe, and your First Cause are all of a piece." And Agatha leaned against the sides of the boat, looking back upon the hull of a large vessel stranded in the mud, a black and melancholy carcass in the lurid grey light, whose green and slimy ribs were slowly being broken up for firewood. It seemed to her as if the whole belief of mankind was such a thing as this, a noble wreck which had weathered many a storm, and was now falling ignominiously in the mud beneath the workmen's tools. "You have got rid of the terrors which beset our mind," she said, "but what have you left? You have made our spiritual life more easy to live, but who would care to live it? There is for you no goodness in God, no goodness in man; nay, there is no goodness itself; it is the mere sea slum, the mere land-making deposit of life, a sort of mud that happens to harden and carry weight, instead, like vice, of letting you sink in and stick. What master shall man serve?"

"You make me remember," answered Baldwin, "some thoughts which came into my mind only yesterday, reading the announcement, posted upon the cathedral door, of the centenary of some saintly person who is styled 'the servant of God.' If God is the maker and master of the universe, why then every man, do he what he may, good or bad, is His unconscious servant, since he is doing what God has pre-established; if, on the other hand, God is the principle of good, why then only a few of those men obeying His orders are really His servants; He is misleading the rest. If the whole world is but an emanation of the will of the sovereign good, the incitement to do evil must emanate also from Him, and resistance to the will of the sovereign good must surely be evil. You see how soon the principle of God being identical with righteousness leads us, if logically applied as it was logically applied by certain mediæval mystics, to the obliteration of all distinction between good and evil; nay, to the principle of men like Molinos, that man must not refuse to sin. What do you say to this manner of serving God?"

"You have no right to attribute such abominable theories to me. I say that to do good is to serve God; and the knowledge that God is being served is our highest inducement to doing good."

"You mean," answered Baldwin, gently, "that I have no right to suppose that you will be as rigidly logical as poor Molinos; it's by relaxing this logical severity that religion has for ever been saving itself from falling into immorality. But tell me, how can you define what *is* good—which, among the innumerable actions that God, supposing Him to be, as you do, a conscious creator, has made inevitable to us, are those in whose performance we are really serving Him? If you think over the matter you will find yourself reduced to define the good actions as those which are conducive to the greatest well-being of mankind. You will find yourself reduced, in choosing among the thousand God-ordained actions, to the use of that purely human and utilitarian standard of right and wrong which you despise. You say that I am for expunging the divine not only out of God, but out of man. But tell me, does it not seem to you, when you consider the number of purely indifferent or absolutely unrighteous actions forced upon us by Nature or God—that this element which you call the divine, this element of respect for man's collective and increasing welfare, this law of righteousness—ought to be called, not the divine element in man, but the human element in the Godhead?"

Agatha did not answer. The gaunt black-chimneyed factories, the gaping warehouses at whose feet were moored the heavy barges, the wood of distant masts and funnels, the whole grimy and hideous and yet grand and solemn array of the docks and wharves seemed to pass before her like a dream; her thoughts were whirling like the water at the boat's keel, and she tried to seize hold of a thought which she knew must be present, as vainly as she attempted to identify one particular bit of driftwood among those which danced in their wake.

"Why should you therefore imagine that I am unhappy in my belief?" he went on; "because I think that the First Cause is an unknowable something of which we have no right to suppose any human qualities, any attitude towards ourselves, any consciousness of our existence, any sense of right and wrong, because I think that morality is a necessity grown out of social life, that the only duties of man are towards the mortal creatures of the present and the future, and the highest possible conception of mankind is the man who enlarges the sphere of its moral obligations—why should you think me unhappy?"

"Because," answered Agatha—"because, for one thing, you isolate your noblest man from all companionship; instead of walking with God you make Him walk and suffer in solitude, in solitude proportionate to His nobility."

"And do you then suppose that the noblest men can ever be consoled for the injustice which they endure? Do you suppose that to a just mind the fancied companionship of God can ever truly compensate for the sense of the injustice of the world? To the good evil can never lose its bitterness. Heroism is not that which suffers only physically, not feeling the shafts in its side because the heavens have opened rosy above, and the angels are singing all around. The consciousness of God's approval would be but a drug deadening our noblest sensibilities if it could make us indifferent to man's injustice, a mere moral chloral, or moral opium. The real martyr sees no heavens open, hears no angels sing, feels only the smart of his wounds, the dreariness and darkness and isolation, feels that he is abandoned to fight the battle with evil, unseen, unpraised, unrewarded, suffers in anguish and desolation, suffers for a good which does not exist as active principle of the world, for a good which lets him perish. It is the infinite pathos and grandeur of Christ that he dies, not like some Dorothea of the stage martyrdoms, with angels singing and strewing flowers; not like Sebastian, with a crown of glory descending on his head; but alone, scoffed at, and crying out in the darkness that he has been abandoned by the God for whom he suffers."

"But it is not given to us all to be the best and noblest, to make the great sacrifices from which we are certain that great good will come," objected Agatha: "most of us I mean—of those who do really care enough about right and wrong to be pained by the victory of wrong over right—most of us are condemned to lead mere humdrum lives of small, partial, unsatisfactory, often useless sacrifice, condemned to look on at their own and other men and women's lives being overwhelmed or slowly eaten away by the flood of misfortune. Most of us are given no solid ground of present and of future upon which to build up an edifice of good; we live in marshes whose dykes are for ever giving way, on mountain sides which are for ever crumbling, in the beds of torrents which have swept away our friends, which must fatally, inevitably, sweep away ourselves. And if there is no God to lead us on to more solid ground hereafter, or to look down, visible as the sun looking down upon the grime and squalor of this town; why, then, what remains for us but to pray that the dyke may give way at once, that the rubble on the hillside may slip beneath our feet, that the river may rise and wash us away?"

Baldwin was silent for a moment.

"I do not see why we should do that," he answered. "You speak of living in a river bed and praying that the flood may overwhelm us. Let me tell you about a real river bed which I know, in an Apennine valley where I have spent a good part of my life. When the water subsides in early summer it leaves a tract of shingle and river sand. The shingle, all the summer long, is reddened and yellowed with I know not what very delicate and lovely stone-flower, whose seeds are brought there by the inundation; and the little patch of sand and mud, separated from the swirling blue river by a few inches of barren stones, has been laid hold of by some peasant of the neighbourhood, who digs and hoes it up as soon as the river has gone down, and plants it with beans, oats, sometimes a little wheat and hemp among the red-berried river brambles. All summer long the sun pours down upon it, making the shingle into burning metal; the river flows by, but too low to wet or refresh it, so that morning and evening the peasant comes down into the river bed to water the drooping, withering plants. Sometimes, in the course of the summer, the river suddenly rises, killing the plants with a layer of ooze and sand, or else a violent downpour—one of those cataracts of rain which fill the whole valley with a wind-shaken curtain of water—washes the roots out of the soil, and whirls them down the river; and always, in the autumn, comes the flood; the river, swelling, swirls, a great tossing, foaming mass of reddish water, higher and higher round the bank of shingle, eating its way with every moment, dashing to and fro like long grass the branches of the red-berried willows and ashes on its surface, till at last the whole river, a great curly red flood, passes across the island, covers it, eddying and jerking up its foam, not so much in anger, it would seem, as in triumph. And then, when the flood has sunk, the island reappears, and what was once a garden, a field, is a mere barren expanse of round stones and sand and slime, like any other in the river. But during those few weeks of constant watering and weeding and tilling, of constant struggle with the river and the sun, that bank of stones in the river bed has been green with its hardly planted crops; so that, if they are swept away before the ripening time, they have at least been sweet to see in their greenness. And even if the peasant should lose courage, and think it is not worth while to hoe and plant and water morning and evening, and lop and protect with boughs from the sun these few green things which may never bear fruit or grain, which will be washed away by the autumn floods, even then God—for why not call nature by that name?—does not lose heart, and for those short weeks which the river gives in peace He makes the pale purple and yellow stone-flowers rise out of the shingle, and the short sweet herbs out of the sand; and the bees and butterflies, and things of shorter life than those weeks, come and are happy. And to be pleased that the shingle should be made sweet and fruitful, between the floods of June and the floods of September, this seems to me more wise and noble than to say: 'I have no solid present or solid future on which to build,' and to pray that the water may overwhelm you."

"All that is very well, said Agatha, after a pause, "and it sounds very beautiful. But our lives are not always mere clean sand-banks in a clear river, which may easily be beautified and made fertile; they are more often things like those banks," and she pointed to the soft, wet strand, encrusted with coal ash, and fringed with loathsome shiny ooze, which the grey water lapped as the boat made its way slowly among the shipping and the wharves. "And how, if you no longer believe in God—in a God who loves us—can you endure the horrible eating away of the good by the evil—the horrible waste of happiness, the horrible purposelessness of suffering?"

"I endure the purposelessness of so much unnecessary pain, of so much fruitless action," answered Baldwin, "because I do not seek in things any universal purpose. Things are the results from a cause; and it is only when these results from a cause are accidentally or purposely combined that they become, accidentally or purposely, means unto an end. The old habit of making Nature or God in the semblance of man, persists in our habitual, almost instinctive, tendency to see in the ways of the universe the mere magnified picture of the ways of man: to chide that earth and spar which drifts unconscious and aimless on the ocean. It drifts not because its broken and rotting fragments, if brought by the current near to other drifts and kneaded together with them by sea-slime and froth, may form the beginning of an island—for this may never happen: the current may disperse it for ever and ever, and the waves may drift it for ever. It drifts because the crumbling earth, the shattered mouldering wood, were one day fetched, licked out into the ocean by the tide. That is all. Pain, passion, struggle—all things which are because other things were before them—used to a purpose only by the accident of fate, or by the great accident of man's will. What is there in this to rebel against?"

"We must rebel," cried Agatha, "we must rebel

against pain, against ruin and disappointment, scattered all over the world to bear no fruit, or only the fruit of worse misery."

"You must rebel? Well, so I thought once. I was a pessimist, indignant with all the wastefulness and wanton loss of the world, angry with God. Now I would as soon be angry with, indignant at, the table corner against which I hit myself. You have been saying that such a belief as mine is too intolerable to be endured; that it leaves man isolated with evil, with no master to serve, no father to look up to. But in reality this belief is yours, and not mine; it is your belief whenever you let your mind think and judge, whenever you ask yourself how the arrangements of this world tally with your conscience—nay, don't interrupt me. I once believed in such a God as yours, as you once believed in such a God as that of the Bible; and, as you were miserable in the belief that God had doomed man to disobey and to die, that He had required the sacrifice of His own innocent Son to atone for the guilt which He had abetted; so I, also, was miserable in the belief in an Almighty First Cause who had implanted in His creatures instincts of right and wrong which His whole repartition of the fate of those creatures was perpetually violating. I did not, like you, relinquish my belief because it pained me. I went on suffering. No human wickedness or injustice could possibly have filled my mind with such gloom as did the notion of this fearful contradiction; no human guilt could have taken away my hope as did the contemplation of this Divine imperfection. Indeed, my only consolation lay in the perception of the way in which the creature gradually rose superior to the Creator, rose so much, indeed, as to be unable, in his greater justice and mercy, to conceive the indifference and iniquity of his Maker; refusing to believe in it, trying to explain away as a good man would refuse to credit, would explain away some crime too foreign to his nature to seem real. The righteousness of man, nay, rather his very incapacity of believing in the evil of God, was my only comfort during the daily increasing conviction of the callousness and cruelty of God. It seemed to me as if I saw, mysteriously, a new Satan, a rebel angel of good, raising his banners against the Jehovah of Evil; a creature, like Frankenstein's image, a terrible new kind of monster, more noble than its base maker. These were the things I felt; and they are the things which, in your heart of hearts, whenever you let your reason shed light on the subject, you feel also, vainly trying to arrange matters by appeals to your own ignorance, by theories of compensation which will not hold water, by notions of a future life for which you have no ground, by saying to yourself, 'I know that God is good' when you feel that He is bad. You think that your belief is sustaining and consoling; but what you take for your belief is merely a reflection of your desire, what you take for certainty is merely hope. Your real belief, if you have one, the real scheme of things which your reason must present to you, is that you are the creature of a God who has shown you the difference between right and wrong, and who, at the same time, is forcing you to do wrong, and is doing wrong Himself. This is your belief, and not mine. And can you still wonder if I consider that I am a happier man for believing that morality has no meaning, no *raison d'être*, no use, except where human beings are brought into relation with each other; that it cannot, therefore, be expected of any save human beings; and for having thus been liberated myself from the frightful incubus of a Creator who establishes morality and violates and forces to its violation? Do you think I am to be commiserated, or rather to be envied?"

The ship was rapidly approaching the wharf. The sun had made its way through the fog; it was shining bright from a pale blue rift in the heavy smoke-clouds, burnishing the surface of the thick livid water into steel-like lustre, making the coal in the barges, the coal refuse along the wharves, glitter like blue jet, and drowning the distant lines of roofs, the tall chimneys and towers, in a delicate smoke-like blue haze. A blind man with an accordion had somehow come on to deck, and was squeezing the long, melancholy notes of a march out of his instrument, while the steam let off from the engine screeched a series of hoarse screeches; and the vessel throbbed with a dull roar as it turned towards the quay, splashing the water in its slow movement.

A strange melancholy, almost like a physical ache, came over Agatha.

"Do you still think I am deserving of compassion Miss Stuart?" repeated Baldwin.

"I think you are deserving of envy," answered Agatha, coldly, looking vaguely about her, at the blue of the sky, the grime of the land, and the bluish grey of the water. "I think you are deserving of envy. But I prefer to believe in the goodness of God."

OF HONOUR AND EVOLUTION.

OF HONOUR AND EVOLUTION.

BALDWIN had noticed a change in Michael since their last meeting five months before, when the young man had talked evolution by the hour in his Oxford rooms, and had displayed his chemical instruments with the pleasure of a schoolboy.

'You don't seem to have enjoyed your Sunday in the country, my dear Michael," he remarked, as they walked across the high-lying cornfields which separated the railway line from the country house where they had met the previous day. "I thought you would have been so pleased to meet the Professor—you who are so science-mad—and you positively snubbed him. By the way, how goes chemistry?"

"Chemistry doesn't go on at all. I have given it up," answered the undergraduate, briefly. "You see, Baldwin," he went on, after a minute, avoiding the other man's eyes, and looking straight before him at the rising ground sparkling with stubble in the sun's last rays, closed in by the round bluish elms, impervious to light, and flat as if cut out of paper against the pale evening sky—" I dare say it will make you laugh, as it would have made me laugh a few months ago, but I feel I have lost all pleasure in science ever since. I have found out something about vivisection."

Baldwin looked up with a look of surprise, but did not speak.

" Of course," went on Michael, " I had often heard of vivisection in a vague sort of way; and I knew that one of my aunts made herself ridiculous going on about it. I thought it was one of the fads of faddy people, or I thought nothing at all. But this spring, when Ruskin gave up the Slade Professorship, and every one was talking about vivisection in consequence, I thought I ought to know something about it, and I borrowed some of my aunt's pamphlets on the subject. Of course they were rather rubbishy as literature, and had a deal of sentimentality and piety, and the 'Faithful Dog' and 'Merciful Creator' sort of thing. But they contained facts, hundreds of quotations, title, and date and page, on the subject ; and they induced me to open the various physiological treatises and hand books and periodicals from which these quotations had been taken. And the result has been that I feel as if I could never take any pleasure in science again—as if all science were dishonoured."

Baldwin had been listening very attentively.

"Why all science?" he asked. "Why, if you are disgusted with the one science which inflicts pain on living creatures, should you, therefore, be disgusted with the other sciences, which deal only with gases, and earths, and plants, and historical facts, and so forth?"

"Science endeavours to discover the manner in which things happen, the circumstances which determine their happening in that manner; and the whole of every science consists in observing facts (however carelessly at first), having ideas, observing facts again; a perpetual round of seeing, thinking, and seeing again. Do you grant me that?"

"Certainly: go on," answered Baldwin.

"Well, then, all sciences are identical in their speculative dealing with facts, and differ only in the different mode of obtaining the facts; the intellectual method is the same, the physical method various. Some sciences seek their facts by the mere observation of real phenomena, in the past or present; by the mere watching of how bees build hives, or how races supplant each other; but others require for the obtaining of their facts that the objects of their inquiry be subjected not merely to observation, as in reading a chronicle or watching an ant-hill, but also to experiment; that is to say, to the artificial producing of circumstances which will expose that which the ordinary course of events does not leave bare. In these more physically analytical sciences, we must get at the constituent parts the result of whose properties and functions have attracted our inquiries; we must undo the mechanism to understand the action; we must seek for the reason of a movement or the trace of an action by placing the objects of our examination in conditions differing from those of every-day experience. The chemist, by means of complicated machinery, by the action and reaction of a thousand substances, must divide his earths and fluids and gases into their component elements, and reunite these into new compounds; the geologist must lay bare the strata of rock and soil, examine by the microscope the broken fragments, seeking in this the trace of fire, in that of water; the botanist must cut up his plants, examining their different organs, and subject them to strange processes of artificial fertilization and crossing. Now what is the fact-collecting and theory-testing process for the man who studies the properties and functions, not of gases and minerals or of plants, but of animals and animal man? What is, for the physiologist, the experimental process corresponding completely to the experimental processes of chemist or botanist?"

"Evidently," replied Baldwin, "the opening of the body, or the subjection of its organs to given conditions."

"Yes; but if the physiologist places on his table a corpse, opens it, examines its contents, subjects it to various chemical or mechanical conditions, and argues from the structure the manner of the functions, the parallel between this *modus operandi* and those of the other men of science is not, as yet correct. The chemist has his gases just as they exist in the laboratory of Nature; the geologist has his inorganic masses just as Nature has left them; the botanist has his unsentient plants, growing as they grow in the field. But the physiologist, so far, has only the corpse; he has the living thing without its life, the sentient thing without its sensation; the organism with its functions stopped, the vast organic laboratory with its chemistry suspended. Visibly he has not in his domain that which corresponds to the possessions of his fellow-workers in theirs: where they can test, he can only speculate; where they can see, he can only infer. What more is needed? On his table no longer death, but life; the organism with its processes going on, with its cunning system of concatenated action and reaction, sensation and motion, in full work; no longer the corpse, but, as in the studies of the contemporaries of Celsus, as in the workrooms of the predecessors of Harvey, the living slave, the living felon; as in the laboratories of the more easily satisfied, or less easily gratified, men of science of our own day, the living animal: the strapped-down monkey, the poison-paralyzed dog. This is the equivalent, to the student of the body and its workings, of the gases and minerals of the chemist, of the stratified stones of the geologist, of the plants of the botanist; and the equivalent to this student of organism and functions—of the relations of process to process, of sensation to movement, of the whole animal fabric to the atmosphere, the heat and cold, the electric condition, the drugs of surrounding Nature—the equivalent to the physiologist of that well-nigh complete manipulation, that tested speculation, which to the chemist is passing gases through black-lead, or pouring liquids on to solids; which to the geologist is testing his pounded fragments and placing them under the microscope; which to the botanist is slicing his bulbs and fertilizing his flowers: this physiological equivalent, this complete physiological experimental process, consists in opening the living stomach, removing fragments of the living brain, injecting the living veins with drugs and purulent matter, tying up the living viscera or cutting them out; ulcerating the living tissues, and sending streams of electricity through the living nerves; baking or boiling the living cuticle; watching which way flows in the opened chest the living blood; how shrink and twitch the ripped-up living muscles; how impressions are received, and writhings and yells are ordered, by the uncovered living brain-mass.[1]

[1] Experiments of Prof. Schiff; experiments of Profs. Goltz, Gergens, Tiegel, Schreiber, Ferrier, &c.; experiments of Dr.

Michael paused in obvious emotion; the words had come faster and faster, and as they came, hurried and hoarse, his pale face had flushed painfully. They walked for a few seconds in silence, Michael looking vaguely around him, as if contrasting the things of which he had been speaking with the things all round: the last low lights, grazing the yellow stubble and the tawny corn sheaves, making each wayside dry grass blade or down-laden thistle sparkle like silver, while in the suffused sunset greyness the distant trees were separated into distinct groups, the foremost almost blue and still substantial, the furthest quite white and bodyless, by the layers of bluish haze. The rooks formed black lines across the field, cawing; and from the sky came the twitter of invisible larks.

"This is," resumed Michael, "or rather this would be, if the human subject could be vivisected instead

Burdon Sanderson, of M. Thidy, of Prof. Ludwig, of Dr. Crisp, of Vulpian, and Dr. Savory, &c.; experiments of Magendie, of Dr. Legg, of Profs. Tiedemann, Camelin, Leyden, Golowin, and H. Mayer; experiments of Dr. G. Fischer, of Dr. Radcliffe, of Prof. Hermann; experiments of Bernard, Schiff, and Gavarret; experiments of Bernard, Heidenhain, Cyon, Brown-Séquard; experiments of Profs. Rutherford, Ferrier, Goltz, Schiff, Schreiber, &c. Prof. Paolo Mantegazza, Senator of the kingdom of Italy, has made a whole series of experiments on the perception of pain as such ("Fisiologia del Dolore"). I have given only a few references, taken from Pflüger's *Physiol. Archiv*, Reichert and Du Bois-Reymond's *Archiv*, Fritzsch, and Hitzig's *Archiv*, the *Lancet*, various other medical and physiological journals and magazines, besides special works by individual writers.

of being merely intellectually manipulated by analogy, the physiological equivalent for the unhampered experimentation of the sciences which deal with lifeless things or unsentient; and this is the mechanical process which is called vivisection. Now let us see the mental process by which this mechanical process is governed; the necessities of proof and verification by which this experimentation is distributed and systematized. The various sciences differ solely by their manner of acquiring facts, due to the difference of the materials with which they deal; but they agree exactly in the manner in which such facts are intellectually dealt with, because the laws of evidence are in every science the same. Hence in physiology, as in chemistry, mechanics, botany, nay, even history, a man does not always know exactly that for which he seeks. He seeks knowledge in this or that direction; and, as the chemist, or physicist, or botanist, or historian, turns to his instruments, his gases and metals, his plants, or his chronicles and statistics, to see whether his mental eyes may see some facts or groups of facts (and hence some law) unperceived by his predecessors; so also the physiologist turns very often to his live subjects, and does something to their circulation, or nerves, or brain, and waits for what results may appear and what ideas may suggest themselves, at least as often, or rather far oftener, than he goes intending to find the confirmation of some preconceived idea. And again, like every other man of science, the physiologist has often a vague inkling of something somewhere; and, on the principle which made Cook or Vancouver set sail not knowing for what coasts, he also does something to an animal, and watches whether some effect will not manifest itself in some particular set of organs, which happens to be the guessed-at unknown Polynesia of his mind. Moreover, as the physicist or chemist has to repeat his experiment, as the arithmetician must prove his calculation, as the historian must collate his sources, so also must the physiologist try once, twice, and thrice, and again under slightly different conditions, his experiments upon his living subject, doing the thing over again on the original animal, or taking a series of successors, lest some individual peculiarity have disturbed the natural course of things. And then, in order that the observation may profit to science and to the observer, it must, just like an observation on expansion of gases, on the mutation of consonants, or on the finances of France under Louis XVI., be published. Again, just as the assertion of the chemist concerning the property of an element, of the philologist upon a phonetic change, of the historian upon some point of past events, cannot be accepted and registered as a scientific certainty until the vast majority of the other chemists, or philologists, or historians, have each separately gone over the chemical process, compared the phonetic conditions, or collated the historical documents; so also the alleged discoveries, be it no matter how trifling, of the physiologist, must submit to the same intellectual necessity; and his experiment must be repeated and re-repeated, his observations tested by all the other men who have any knowledge of the matter. Furthermore, as in every other science, so also in physiology, different scientific observers and thinkers will conceive different reasons, will seek in a new set of observations, in a new set of experiments, an explanation more in keeping with their general conception of phenomena; which new explanation will again require the test of universal repetition of experiment. And, as in every other science, so in physiology likewise, the student cannot be expected to accept upon mere authority the facts which are to form the basis of his own further discoveries: as the young chemist must be shown the material processes of which he reads; as the young philologist must be given examples of languages and dialects; as the young historian must have access to chronicles and State Papers; so also the young physiologist must be taught how to perform, or must witness the performance by his teacher, of at least a certain number of the experiments which have been the basis of alleged facts. As, therefore, physiology is a science, its mode of obtaining, testing, publishing, disputing, and demonstrating its facts must be intellectually similar to that of other sciences; and, indeed, there are daily published all over the world books and pamphlets describing the experiment which Professor A., B., or C. has made, with or without a theoretic result; and the experiment which Professor D., E., or F. has made to disprove the correctness of Professor A., B., or C.; there is a whole class of periodicals, in pretty well every language, containing accounts of discoveries and refutations thereof, recipes for experiments and counter-experiments; and, finally, numerous handbooks for students, from the most elementary to the most advanced, in which, just as in the handbooks of chemistry or physics, the reader is taught by description and diagram the precise manner in which he is to set about practically to convince himself of the received facts of the science. All these things being the case, physiology being a science with the same intellectual processes of induction and verification as every other, and moreover, like every other, rapidly spreading in the number of its students and the multiplicity of its problems, it becomes evident that the assertion of Professor Ray Lankester, that the number of experiments must increase in almost geometrical proportion as the science enlarges, is merely the equivalent of what might be said of every other science, and so self-evident as to be well-nigh a platitude."

They had come to the little station. The daylight had faded away; the fields were drowned in mist, and the white shafts and arms, the crimson and green lights of the signals along the line, rose fantastic against the blue of the evening. The two men paced up and down the gravelled platform, waiting for the train that should carry them to London.

"So much for the scientific justification," said Michael. "As regards the moral one, what veto can be opposed by an ethical system which accepts nature as a mass of contending and cruel forces, a system which sets up as final aim the preservation of the fittest, that is to say, of the strongest and most fortunate? Christianity may invoke a higher law, but scientific morality cannot condemn the sacrifice which is for the glory of science and the benefit of mankind. I am not a Christian, and never can be one; but I swear to you that since reading those handbooks and magazines and treatises I wish to heaven I could see my way to a moral system different from this moral system which is bound to abet abomination, this moral system sprung from the solidarity of the clean-handed sciences with this foul-handed science of physiology."

"I think you are unreasonable, Michael," began Baldwin.

"Unreasonable?" interrupted the young man. "I dare say I am; reason ought to teach me that vivisection is good, and my whole sickened nature teaches me that it is evil. Stupid? Oh, yes, I know I have grown quite stupid over this matter. It is stupid to talk about it with you. A man should speak against vivisection with silly pietistical old maids, not with men who have ideas and are up to their times; they will only think him a sentimental jackass. Forgive me, Baldwin, for having bored you so long," and Michael laughed a bitter little laugh.

Baldwin shook his head.

"You don't understand me," he said. "I think you are unreasonable, Michael, at present, in your hostility towards all science on account of the sins of a single one; but heaven knows I can sympathize with your unreasonableness. I have passed through it all myself, my dear boy. If any one felt inclined to think you silly and sentimental because of your discovery of the realities of vivisection, how much sillier and more sentimental would such a one think me when I say that this same discovery, when I was your age, made my life black for months, and caused me to pass through a moral struggle as sickening and seemingly hopeless as that of other men who have suddenly come to doubt of the goodness of God! Everything seems very simple and comprehensible now that my mind has long been made up; but I can remember those black days: I could not easily forget them. It so happened that my attention was first drawn to vivisection, which, like most people I had associated with the pricking of a guinea-pig and the inoculation of a cow, while I was very anxious about a friend of mine, much older than

myself, a dear, bright, child-like woman who was
supposed to be dying of consumption. One morning I was allowed to see her for the first time after
a long and dangerous relapse, during which my
thoughts had been constantly with her, lying stiff
and forbidden to move, with ice and salt in her
mouth, silent for days in a darkened room. I remember it so well: the little room with the
southern sunshine in it, and she seated propped
up in her armchair, a table covered with hyacinths
and jonquils and roses, sent by her friends, at her
elbow, looking, after such loss of blood, as white as
her pillows, the bunch of violets I had brought
her lying on her lap; and I holding one of her poor
thin little hands in both mine, and looking into
those childish eyes of hers; she seemed so good, so
child-like, and so helpless. She insisted on knowing
what I had been doing; and, without intending it, I
mentioned, as I mentioned everything to her, that I had
been reading up about vivisection. I felt remorseful
the next second, for such horrible things ought not
to be alluded to before her. But it had done her
no harm. The look came into her eyes which she
had whenever the past was vividly recollected, and
in her childish whisper she told me. . . . How she told
it me God knows; it seemed a sudden thunder-clap,
a revelation from hell that this woman, whom I saw
before me so white and weak and patient, had, in her
girlhood, helped her brother in his work, tied down

the creatures he was disembowelling, prowled with him at nightfall to coax stray dogs to his laboratory. There was an anecdote of a performing poodle they had bought and let off on account of his comic tricks, which made her laugh. I don't know how she told it, or I listened. I know that I was conscious that she was there, weak, bloodless, with a scarcely healed wound in her chest, that a word might bring on another frightful hæmorrhage; and that I must hold my tongue, but that all was black before my eyes, and a taste of copper in my mouth, that everything seemed to reel and darken as I left the house. She had given me some of her delicate yellow roses in return for my violets. When I came home I flung them on the fire, and stood stupidly watching them shrivel and blacken; and yet they seemed to me, at that same moment, the only clean things in this filthy world."

They took a turn or two in silence.

"And then," said Michael, briskly, "you gradually subsided into her belief that vivisection was quite scientifically useless, a mere new-fangled vice, which would soon become obsolete; and you kept quite cheerful, and scientific, and utilitarian, and believed that the great God Evolution would evolve physiology out of its errors? I am not so lucky. I see that Vivisection is, considered from the merely intellectual side, the rational equivalent in physiological science of the experimental processes of other sciences. I am not one of those optimistic persons who most honestly persuade themselves, and attempt to persuade others, that this practice is a scientific mistake, and can lead neither to abstract truth nor to practical benefits; clinging, in their disgust for the doings of man, to an ideal arrangement of God, according to which good could not arise from evil, and Nature would hide her secrets from those who violate and torture her. No, I cannot logically persuade myself that physiologists should be different from chemists, physicists, or any other men of science, in not knowing best the exact value of their various scientific methods, even as a cobbler knows best the value of his various tools, and that they should all cling with fearful tenacity to a method of observation from which nothing can be hoped; neither can I persuade myself, with the best will in the world, that, making allowance for the greatest possible amount of disturbance due to artificial conditions, the experimentation on living animals does not afford much practical knowledge which the dissection of dead bodies could not give. I think, therefore, that physiologists are distinctly the only people who can really estimate the scientific value of vivisection. But for these very reasons, on account of this same unanimous tenacity which persuades me of the intellectual fitness of this practice, I am persuaded also that physiologists, and all those who obtain facts and theories from physiology, are utterly unfit to really estimate the moral legitimacy or illegitimacy of vivisection. Similarly, I am most lamentably persuaded of the fact that (contrary to the good, beautiful poetical belief of Christians and deists) good results may most assuredly be obtained from infamous means; and that, just as very useful and bread-giving money may be obtained by murder, so also very reliable and applicable knowledge may be obtained by vivisection. But just on account of my recognition of this nasty arrangement of things am I impressed with the necessity of rebelling against its nastiness. I know that science requires vivisection, and that scientific morality allows it; and for that very reason I wash my hands of science, I reject scientific morality, I break with this rationalism which rationally abets abomination; and I say 'give me any folly, any superstition which my reason refuses, but which my conscience can accept.'"

"I quite understand your state of mind," answered Baldwin; "I have gone through it myself, and a great many people have gone through it also. This question of vivisection is pretty well unique in the anomaly which it presents, and in the anomalies to which it gives rise, because it consists of two parts, each separately most singular in the history of moral dilemmas; and combining in confusion and contradiction to form a tangle of good and bad most painful and difficult to unravel. The first half of this anomaly compounded of anomalies consists in the fact that, in the question of vivisection, we are dealing with the relations of creatures so separate in their interests, and so unequal in their power, that the victimized party receives no benefit while suffering the whole pain of the sacrifice ; whereas the victimizing party is at once sole culprit, accuser, and judge in the matter. And the second anomalous half of this most anomalous question is, that the evil is not one inherited from more barbarous times, and certain of being abolished by the mere general movement of progress; but is, on the contrary, a thing of modern development and infinite future extension, and that it is entangled by a whole network of scientific solidarity with that same new philosophy which is securing for us not only a more prosperous future, but a more reliable conscience."

Baldwin's voice was drowned by the hurtling din of a train rushing by ; a red flame of light, a jet of reddish vapour suddenly in the distance ; just time enough to perceive the fact that it was not yet there, that the rails were free ; a screech and a rushing wind as from the wing of death, and then, for another second, a red spot again in the distance ; and all was silence, with only the bleating of sheep and cawing of rooks from the neighbouring fields.

"Evolution and evolutional morality," remarked Michael, "have seemed to me, ever since this question of vivisection has come up, just about as God-like as that express. Make a religion out of an express train, and a moral code out of its woes, if you like; I can't."

"My dear Michael," answered Baldwin, "you are just an instance of the results of not bringing evolutional morality sufficiently to bear upon the problem of vivisection."

"I have seen enough of bringing evolutional morality to bear upon it, thank you."

"You don't understand what I mean. Listen. When this system of physiological experimentation, which had been hitherto carried on as one of those mysteries of science into which no layman cares to pry, was suddenly revealed, by the miscarriage of certain technical manuals into the uninitiated circles for which they were not intended, there was an almost universal shock of indignation; an almost universal impulse to examine, to interfere, to check, to forbid; the literature of physiology was dragged from off its placid scientific shelves; the physiological laboratories were broken into by the imagination of the lay public, the reluctant men of science were button-holed by the conscience of England. The sudden scuffle of consciences has now been succeeded by an organized warfare of books, articles, lectures, and societies, which is to it what a year-long campaign might be to the sudden rush to arms of a whole city; but that first movement has existed nevertheless. And though the convulsion of conscience has subsided, and only two distinct parties have remained, to one of which gravitates each straggling opinion, in which is merged each individual struggle, the moral commotion has nevertheless been, and the moral anomaly has not yet been settled. Peace of conscience has indeed been obtained by each party ; by the one which said to physiology, *You may*, and by the other which said, *You may not*. But it is on both sides a false and selfish peace ; a peace obtained at the expense of injustice towards a portion of the heart or a portion of the mind ; at the expense of suppression of some of the instincts, either of justice or of reason, of the individual. For let us examine what are the persons, or rather what are the conditions of mind, constituting each of these parties, after excluding from each the huge fluctuating mass of people incapable of mental or moral struggle, who have joined whichever party appealed to them first, whether because the stories of animal torture unconsciously roused their fears for their own pet beasts, or because the oracular assertion by their doctor that vivisection had discovered the cure for this, that, or the other disease, made them tingle with fear lest they or theirs might ever require the remedy. The party which said to the physiologists *You may*, is also a fusion of two kinds of minds ; first, of those minds completely mutilated by merely scientific interests of the bare possibility of conceiving that the agonies of any number of scientifically-experimented-on animals can be a matter of any consideration; and secondly, of minds which did distinctly participate in the horror of the first disclosures respecting the nature of vivisection, but whom the connection of their sciences—psychology, anthropology, chemistry, with physiology —or the strong instinct of the solidarity of all the sciences, has gradually accustomed and reconciled to the requirements of physiology; minds whom the all-pervading sense that theological systems having been thrown aside, there remains no security for them save in scientific progress, no hope save in the improvement of human conditions, no moral test save the diminution of human misery, has forced to acquiesce in what they recognize as an evil, but persuade themselves to be inevitable and decidedly the lesser of those submitted to their choice. Of the party which said and still says to the physiologists *You shall not*, one half are minds with whose pre-existing indifference or aversion to science, the horror at the sudden disclosures of physiological literature came quite harmonious: artistic minds, to whom Science meant what Art most hates—analysis; and religious minds, of believers or deists, to whom science represented what religion most hates—the reduction of God to physical necessity; of the wonderful to the simple; while the other half of the party, saying "You shall not," are minds hitherto inclined to scientific conceptions, but whom the monstrous things of physiology and their calm support by the whole confraternity of sciences have gradually made sceptical of a scientific philosophy which produced, abetted, and cherished such things; so that the whole party may be said to consist of minds who either lost nothing by quarrelling with science, and of minds which preferred breaking with all science to contracting a solidarity with that which appeared to them abominable. Thus has that first great movement of indignation ended. It has ended in a feud, which means in reality a compromise—a compromise made for the sake of unity of endeavour and peace of mind by the more worthy half of each party with the less worthy. And the moral loss, the loss in the amount of individual moral judgment among our thinking classes, has, I think, been very great. For the battle between those who say to vivisection *Yes*, and those who say to it *No*, while offering a great show of moral weapons and moral entrenchments, and moral loopholes and moral pitfalls, and giving a general impression of great moral vigour, has meant in reality a mere diminution of moral activity; each individual of each party making up for his cowardliness in not venturing to attack his own neighbours when he thought them wrong, in not venturing to fight only for what was really his cause against what was really the opposed cause; by his readiness to attack much which ought to be to him most sacred, while elbowing many things which ought to be to him most abominable. So that, in this question of vivisection, we see repeated that loathsome historical phenomenon of men being willing to burn their intellectual kith and kin because they have enrolled in a crusade beside people whom they ought to have gibbeted; and this from sheer want of the strength of will required to reject the mistakes of either party, to stand alone, and hope that others, equally willing to stand alone, might join to form the nucleus of a group whose object is to accept the good whatever its origin, and to reject the bad whatever its neighbourhood. For, while in this question of vivisection there exist two halves of each party who are always single-minded and who make no compromise—namely, those who, like so many physiologists, simply throw aside any moral restraint; and those who, like the greater part of the religious believers, snap their fingers at scientific progress, two sections who sacrifice nothing in sacrificing respectively moral feelings which they never had, and scientific interests which they have never understood; there exist the balance of each of the two parties who have hitherto simply let themselves be dragged by their intellectual neighbours into either repudiating rationalistic beliefs which they ought to have held, or abetting moral sophisms which they ought to have combated. It is for these persons, and these alone (since all the rest can see only one alternative, and consequently one decision), that the question of vivisection is one of real moral choice; it is these, and these alone, who, being able to weigh the *pros* and the *cons*, to appreciate the sacrifice which must be made, to feel the temptation which must be resisted, can ever finally settle the question. If I were a writer, I would wish to write for those of my intellectual comrades whom belief in scientific methods, in human development, and in evolutional morality seems by the bond of scientific solidarity to be drawing to the admission of the legitimacy of a practice from which their feelings shrink; and, on the other hand, for those whose moral repugnance at an abomination abetted by science is gradually inducing to seek for a philosophic creed in the unintelligible, for a moral code in the arbitrarily stated, and for an ideal future state in the impossible."

Michael smiled.

"You might write your fingers off, Baldwin, before you could persuade your people that vivisection is not merely the pricking of an occasional guinea-pig or the dissection of what is, virtually, thanks to anæsthetics, a corpse. Nervous and fastidious people have an insuperable aversion to believing that vivisection means every manner of horrible mutilation, ulceration, racking with electricity, poisoning by drugs or by excision of excretory organs, baking, flaying, and dissecting of an animal with his motor nerves paralysed, but his sensory nerves horribly excited, most likely by curare, &c. They don't like having their opinions changed and their stomachs turned by the reading of physiological literature."

"That is but too true. But you see there are logical proofs, besides direct evidence from books. First, it is preposterous to suppose that a moral tumult, followed by a moral crusade such as is presented by the anti-vivisection agitation, could arise nowadays and continue for several years, unless there were a very serious and real evil to produce and maintain them. Second, the habit of asserting the moral right to inflict suffering in the service of mankind, after having argued and insisted that vivisection does not entail suffering, proves pretty plainly that those who can argue that they have a right to inflict pain do not believe that there is no pain in the matter. And thirdly, it is not likely that men who, perceiving that vivisection being scientifically and medically valuable to mankind, have persuaded themselves that the service rendered to mankind quite outweighs the iniquity committed to animals, that such men will consider an extraordinary and compromising correctness of statement preferable to an alleviation of human ignorance and misery. Oh, there is no insurmountable difficulty in showing vivisection to be what it really is. But what interests me at present is not the class which tends to abet vivisection because it sympathizes with science and scientific ethics, but the class which, because it abominates vivisection, tends to become alienated from the doctrines of evolution and evolutional morality; because, my dear Michael, I have passed through that danger myself, and I see you gradually coming very near to it. You are, without knowing it, growing a sort of independent retrograde; you will soon take a secret pleasure in every bungle of science; you will soon feel a secret hankering after any mystically established code of right and wrong."

They were interrupted by the arrival of their train. It advanced slowly, casting a blood-like stain on the line before it; a vague moving blackness, enveloped in flameless smoke and vapour, which waved scarlet and orange in the deep blue of the evening sky; an unearthly and terrible magnificence of luridness, like Turner's "Fighting Téméraire." And as it approached that seeming slowness was revealed to be speed, as the great engine, with its seams of crimson and yellow light, its wreaths of luminous vapour, bore forwards, stately, resistless.

"Well, yes," said Michael, when they were seated in the train which was bearing them towards London —"well, yes; perhaps I am growing into an *independent retrograde*, as you are pleased to call it. Perhaps I do long to invoke something higher than mere expediency as a moral standard. I want, in this question of vivisection, to invoke a principle which used to exist before people began to deal in evolutional morality; I want to invoke the principle of pity."

Baldwin shook his head.

"You are mistaken," he answered. "The real horror of vivisection is not, however it may express itself, the horror at something piteous, but the horror at something dishonourable. It is, vaguely formulated as it may be, and strangely confused with ideas of mercy, not the shrinking with which we may contemplate some inevitable or righteously inflicted pain, the pain of the starving poor whom we cannot relieve, the pain of the sick wretches whom we cannot cure, the pain of the hounded criminal whom we cannot let off; it is the shrinking at the idea, not of pain, but of injustice; it is the feeling, not of sympathy with misery, but of indignation against fraud. The code condemning vivisection is the code of honour; and the code of honour is the code of justice, enforced not upon police-watched men by the judge and the hangman, but by the self-scrutinizing conscience on the unhampered will."

"This code of honour," went on Baldwin, "forces us to refrain from a variety of sets of actions wholly apart from the consideration of their ultimate result upon ourselves; actions which, in some circumstances, may be disadvantageous and dangerous, but in other circumstances (such as those of the Renaissance princelets philosophized by Machiavelli, and the seventeenth-century gentry instructed in *direction of the intention* by the Jesuit casuists) may be, on the contrary, safe, advantageous, and delightful to the persons undertaking them. Among such actions which—the back of the police being conveniently turned or the supreme jurisdiction of one class over another being thoroughly recognized—honour, nevertheless, insists upon men and women desisting from, may be mentioned: robbery, which is seizing advantages by force which cannot be resisted by other force; deceit, which is obtaining advantages by telling untruths, which are not resisted by doubt nor retaliated by untruth, but acted on as truths; cheating, which is making another stake all where he can win nothing, while we stake nothing and can win all; and a variety of similar actions, the tendency of which is to increase instead of diminishing the inequality of chances of good and bad. This code of honour, which in our tolerably moralized civilization is often in harmony with the dictates of enlightened selfishness, does yet sometimes appear in opposition to that nobler kind of selfishness, that selfishness immolating self, but immolating also others, which asks for the greatest good for the greater number. The greatest number insisting upon obtaining the greatest good are sometimes liable to receive from the principle of honour a rebuke:—What right have you to the good which you have not earned, and which belongs to others? What right have you to a diminution of the pain mixed up with your pleasure, by a diminution of the pleasure which is mixed up with your neighbour's pain? If this other man, or class, or nation is to lend you, for your benefit, its work, its happiness, its life, how soon will come the day when to this man, or class, or nation, maimed or beggared in your service, you will repay with accumulated interest the good which all this while has ceased to be enjoyed? This says the principle of honour; and this does it say to the men who wish to have for physiology the same unlimited freedom of experiment permitted to other sciences which deal with senseless elements or vegetables."

Michael here interrupted.

"But what becomes of your utilitarian principles?" he asked. "Shall pain not be inflicted on the few, that it may be spared to the many?"

"Yes," answered Baldwin, "if the few are part of the many, and share equally with the others the chance of suffering, and equally with the others the chance of benefitting thereby. No, if the few are separate from the many, if they alone can lose, and they alone cannot win. Otherwise, the many are simply playing with the few a game of loaded dice: the many are really not staking, and are bound to win; the few are really excluded from winning, and are forced to stake. That the few are often deliberately sacrificed to the many is most true: the soldier who slowly dies abandoned on the field of battle is sacrificed to the people at home; but the soldier is originally part of those at home—he, as a child, has eaten the bread, the corn of which would have been trampled, he has been sheltered under the roof which would have been burnt, he has been protected in mind and body by the whole civilization which would have been ruined, had not other men been singled out to fight and die miserably in defence of the country. Nay, when in the course of history we see whole classes and nations temporarily sacrificed for the benefit of others, those classes and nations have yet in the long run benefitted; since, as in the case of the feudal serfs and the negro slaves, the very oppression meant the predominance of the class and race most capable of improvement, which inevitably led to a raising of level even for the temporarily sacrificed class or nation, and of which that sacrificed class or nation would, if let alone, have been incapable; moreover, that very class or nation sacrificed at one historical moment to another class or nation, owed much of whatever advantages itself enjoyed to the sacrifice to it of a class or nation equally inferior. The whole movement is one of taking the good with the bad, being refunded in process of time for the evil to which one is submitting, or refunding some other by one's suffering for the evils often by which one has benefitted. The system is harsh, but it is in the long run equitable: 'You have inherited an incurable disease; but have you not also inherited therewith a certain fortune, a certain intelligence?' 'In this particular case I have inherited a disease, but I have inherited neither fortune nor intelligence—that is unjust.' 'But had you, like your neighbour yonder, inherited at once good health, fortune, and intelligence, would you deem that unjust?' 'No.' 'Then accept your chance in peace.' Thus goes the great lottery. But in reality there is neither so much chance nor so much inequality. We all participate in the good and the bad of our neighbours. Our parents have suffered that we might be prosperous; our children may suffer because we have been prosperous; and moreover, in reality, the suffering is greatly of our own making, or of the making of those who have made for us also our pleasure. The mass of mankind is a sea of constantly shifting atoms: not one but has at one moment been in every place, or will at one moment be brought there. The wave that rises is the water that has just sunk, the water which has just sunk is the wave which will next rise. And when the conscienceless movement of things brings to one man the power of making himself more fortunate by making his neighbour less fortunate; when, after having fed one man into strength and starved another into weakness, it offers to the strong an opportunity of snatching the remaining food of the weak, something interposes and says 'No'—and that something, that further equalizer of insufficiently balanced good and evil, is honour. Now such a condition of fluctuation, of giving and taking, of disimbursing and reimbursing, does not exist where two classes are so utterly separate that the one which suffers does not profit even eventually by the result of its sufferings. The advantages which may accrue from the vivisection of animals are of two sorts: the direct and less important ones being the detail, improvement in medicine; the indirect and more important ones being the advance of knowledge upon questions intimately connected with the great and almost social and religious problems of mind and matter; but those advantages are both of them advantages to mankind, for it is not merely a lie, but a stultification, to pretend that animals will gain anything equivalent to the sufferings of vivisection, by the improvement of veterinary medicine, of the greater kindness of mankind, since it is evident that the remedy for such ignorance or inhumanity as exists is to them much greater than the evil—in short, a case of chopping off the head to cure its aching. These advantages are therefore simply advantages to mankind; advantages bought at the expense of other creatures. And the buying of such advantages for one class at the expense of another is, as I have said, dishonourable."

"But," again interrupted Michael, "there is no rule without exceptions. There are cases where it may be more moral, and therefore more honourable, to lie and even to steal than to let respect for truth or respect for property entail agony on those whom we can help; morality can mean only the right course, and in many an instance the right course may be to do the thing theoretically wrong, but practically right, because the theory has not taken special circumstances into account."

"No," answered Baldwin, "it all sounds plausible enough, and of a higher kind of morality. But morality which is eccentric and dwells in higher isolation is no morality at all. It is most true that life is so complicated and so ill-organized that even with regard to righteous laws, where exceptional cases do occur the law may be in the wrong, the criminal in the right. But we cannot legislate for such exceptions, nor does society ever do so except at its cost. If one of the angels of good had remained shut out of the heavenly fortress, and its holy body were on the point of being trampled by the spirits of evil, the postern of heaven could not be opened, for with that one spirit of good would rush in a thousand devils. Good and evil are unfortunately often mixed, but we cannot let pass the evil in order to obtain the good. Morality, be it remembered, deals with frightfully huge masses, and masses one atom of which being displaced, the whole may crash on to our heads. This has long been tacitly recognized by mankind: thus certain actions, in themselves wholly indifferent, give a woman the opportunity for being unchaste, and as society cannot actually witness the unchaste action, but only these indifferent actions by which it is surrounded, society is forced to punish as unchaste every woman who indulges in these indifferent actions; yet an honest woman may not only honestly commit them, but may even, under certain circumstances, be forced by some serious moral obligation to their committal. This society knows, but being unable to plant a fence round the ditch itself, it is obliged to rail over a larger space of ground, in itself perhaps quite safe, and the laws of honour have to be drawn tighter instead of slacker."

"Do you remember," asked Michael, "that mediæval legend, made into a poem by Hartmann von Aue, about a noble knight, surnamed the poor Henry, who might have been cured of a loathsome disease, and his strong heart and arm given back to Christendom, by means of a bath in the blood of a very insignificant little peasant wench, twelve years old, and of no use to any one? The advocates of vivisection are fond of placing before us a re-edition of this tale, showing that the refusal to sacrifice a few dogs might widow the world of some noble spirit and cheat it of his works; but they draw the conclusion, contrary to that of Hartmann von Aue's poem, that the dishonour would consist not in the accepting, but in refusing the bath of blood for their hero."

"Exactly. This is one of those exceptional cases in favour of which mankind is ever and anon requested, by romance writers and Jesuit casuists, to change its code of honour. Now it is possible that if morality were composed of mere single cases, instead of being

a most compact mass, easily upset by tampering with
one part, that the blood bath of vivisection might be
honourably prescribed for one inestimable Knight
Henry; although I think that the inestimable man
would be cleaner with his leprosy than with that
blood which had washed it off. But as such things as
single cases do not in reality exist for the legislator,
and must be treated, being specialities, only by
attempting special things to prevent their recurrence;
the permission to vivisect three particular dogs to
save one particular man in the exceptional case which
might occur once in a thousand years of that man being
such that the rest, not only of mankind, but of beast-
kind, would suffer by his loss, would mean in reality the
permission to vivisect an unlimited number of beasts
all over the world with no direct object, and merely
because we know that the advance of science will
improve the condition of mankind at large, and of
any stray invaluable man who may be included
among its millions of valueless numskulls and
scoundrels. This would mean by analogy that in
order that one honest woman might not unjustly be
accused of being no better than she should be, all
the weak and fleshly women in Christendom should be
enabled to sin unnoticed and with impunity. For in
reality the admission of the legitimacy of vivisection
means not one operation for one case, but a systematic
torturing of thousands of beasts all over the world
during hundreds of years, in order to obtain whatever

advantages may result therefrom. And when this vivisectional poetic episode is reduced to prose, when the unique Knight Henry, the saviour of the world, is shown to mean all the Toms, Dicks, and Willies of mankind—to diminish some of the physical and moral aches inherent in whose otherwise daily improving lives we are asked to turn into fierce agony the mere physical life which is all that the thousands of beasts to be sacrificed for hundreds of years possess or ever can possess; when we have seen the real state of the case, can we deny that the legalization of vivisection would be the authorization of a huge theft, of a casting of loaded dice—a gigantic magnifying of that act of taking all the profits for ourselves and giving all the risks to another, which in its pettiest and most individual form means to a man indelible dishonour?"

"Honour, dishonour—very fine-sounding words!" exclaimed Michael: "but how much are they worth? Figments, useful enough in their day when only figments had power; effete expressions inherited from a time (answers my historical and sociological friend), when it appears that people committed abominations with much greater impunity than nowadays. This code of honour is scientifically merely a museum curiosity."

"True enough," answered Baldwin; "but it so happens that the standard by which we must judge vivisection has two faces and two names, a very old and a very new one, is a sort of Janus. The old face I have spoken of, and is this, as you consider it, god of other days, called Honour. But there is another face, or rather the same thing presents a younger one seen from the other side. And this newer face is what is called evolutional morality. For the old name and the new mean but one thing. The old code of things to be done and things to be avoided, which used to be considered as a mysterious, inexplicable something, of no particular origin, miraculously given, I suppose, is in truth a now intelligible something, whose reason and origin we understand. As the sudden word of command by which things were created, is now understood as the mere inevitable adjustment and development of physical things, so also this old principle of honour is now comprehensible as the instinct, the ingrained habit due to ages of deliberate choice, of preferring certain sets of motives to certain other ones. For as our physical nature has been evolved by the selection and survival of those physical forms which are in harmony with the greatest number of physical circumstances; so also has our moral nature been evolved by the more and more conscious choice of the motives including consideration for the greatest number of results from our actions, of the motives which, instead of merely enlarging the shapeless and functionless moral polyp-jelly of *ego*, work out, diversify and unify, lick into shape, the complicated moral organism of society, with all its innumerable and wondrously co-ordinated limbs and functions. And thus has evolved itself that which was formerly called *Honour*, and whose other name is natural morality : the preference of justice to expediency. Slowly and with difficulty, indeed ; every single preference of right to desire having been as a touch which has moulded the wonderful instinct into existence ; every single preference of desire to right having been the rude thumbing which obliterates the nascent form ; every single just action making easier a score of just actions, every single unjust decision having begotten a score of future unjust decisions. A very arduous work has been this making of man's conscience, which seems to be at once the greatest requisite and the most crowning perfection of the evolution of society ; for if mere overbalance of pleasure above pain had been the highest goal of our gradual evolution, evolution might have ended with those half-existing things whose happiness is more complete than that of the most noble mind. And the making of man's conscience has been the evolution of a spiritual organism which perceives and chooses justice within ranges ever and ever extending : justice, at first (when the moral sight was a mere titillating all-overishness on the contact of some adjacent thing, and the moral limbs were fastened like those of a limpet to one spot) limited to the mere family, then to the tribe, then to the class and the race; and nowadays, when the times of justice, limited to class and race, are separated from us by barely a century—nay, by barely a score of years—extending to whatever can feel, to whatever can have its poor little portion of happiness exchanged by fraud and violence for misery."

"But Nature," objected Michael, " is not thus just ; she uses as her instruments starvation, pestilence, continuous sacrifice of weaker to stronger ; and Nature having made us, shall we be wiser or mor pharisaical than she ? "

" True enough ; but this Nature of which you speak, what is she, when you tear away the allegorical and mythical rags of religion with which we still mumm up our scientific conceptions? What is this Nature ? contending forces, a chaos which has not made us, but out of which we have gradually emerged. If Nature—that is, the course of continually clashing and reacting events—has been unjust, why should we be unjust, who are not an abstraction formed out of abstract ideas, but living men and women, with eyes and ears to see and hear, and minds to judge and wish and hope and choose; why should we, with our reason and conscience, pretend to take lessons from a mere abstract entity, a mere expression by which we symbolize phenomena? Indeed, we do not ; and had we done so, society would never have existed.

" Hence, when I say that honour rejects vivisection

as an unjust and cheating practice, I mean thereby also that it is contrary to the tendencies of the highest result of our gradual evolution. I mean that by preferring in this case the advantages which our race might gain at the expense of wholesale and profitless agony to another race, we are laying obliterating fingers upon those delicate moral features which have thus slowly and arduously been moulded into shape. For, in the first place, we are deliberately buying our good with the evil of others, and thus running counter to the great moral principle of obtaining advantage only in return for advantage, of being spared pain only by sparing it; of making the actions of men into the transactions of those who barter, lend, and repay, instead of those of men who cheat and rob. And, in the second place, this great movement of moral retrogression consists of a number of minor movements of moral retrogression. For we are making our perception of the evil of others give way to our perception of our own desire: we are letting ourselves slip instead of holding ourselves erect, and thus weakening our moral muscle. We are diminishing our most precious quality, the power of submitting to justice, of foregoing our wishes. And with this weakening of our moral will, goes inevitably the diminution also of our moral perception; for every time that we prefer desire to right, we not only increase the tyranny of covetousness, but, by jostling the one wrong choice with the many right ones which all except an utterly immoral life must contain, we let our soul lose its keenness, its moral scent: it endures foulness, gets pimply, weak, diseased, sometimes loses a limb, and always loses somewhat of its most precious power, of its elasticity, its endurance, its resistance. Moreover, every time that we prefer desire to justice, we are warping not only our moral, but also our intellectual nature. For a man, who is naturally inclined to morality and thoughtful as well, finds in his life numbers of opportunities of eschewing evil, and doing good with either no cost at all to his selfishness, or only so little as merely to enhance the natural pleasure which he takes in virtue; thus he develops for himself a moral nature in which acknowledged evil cannot dwell without constant moral discomfort from its presence; hence if the temptation of some evil choice overcome him, he will, in proportion to his honesty of habits and ideals, be anxious to persuade himself that this choice was not evil, but good; he will persuade himself that what was culpable self-indulgence was wise self-sacrifice, that the mud with which he has bespattered himself while seeking his pleasure is the trace of honourable moral labour; and thus he will, after giving way to a lower motive, listen to a false argument; and strange and lamentable are the sophisms which have ever, from the well-intentioned society-reorganizing Jesuit moralists of the seventeenth century to the honest and humane advocates of the modern vice of vivisection, followed upon a choice in which the desire or the habit of evil has conquered the perception of good.

"I think you will find," went on Baldwin, after a pause, "that this deliberate choice of advantages to mankind, bought by unrequited and cheating infliction of agony upon creatures who cannot participate in the gain while they sustain all the loss, is nearly always followed by a blunting of moral judgment and a stultification of intellectual argument among those who defend this retrogression in the path of moral evolution, this preference of desire to right. The temptation to recognize vivisection as a legitimate practice is to any person imbued with modern scientific views a very great temptation; vivisection means a most valuable instrument, or rather a most valuable short cut, for the attainment of a kind of knowledge, with which are connected not only a great number of problems of body and soul, of present and future life, of moral health and disease, having an almost religious importance to us, who have forsworn our old creeds; but also a kind of knowledge at the same time bearing upon the actual well-being of mankind, upon the diminution of misery, which has become the mission of the men and women who would formerly have wasted their energies in prayers and crusades. It is a practice, therefore, which—to us who are scarcely weaned of our beloved old creeds, and but ill-accustomed as yet to the rude bracingness of a new faith which merely tells us to do right without reward, and endure pain without compensation—still craving for the imaginative stimulant, the almost physically rapturous self-unconsciousness of complete surrender to a single object—to us still so unable to dispense with a superstition—is in reality an ingredient in the heady elixir with which we comfort our chilly souls, in the spiritual cordial of a religion of science and humankind which has replaced the old religion of Christ and His wounds, until the world be fit for the religion of justice. Hence those, and they are among the noblest of us, who have been seeking strength and warmth in this belief, are, when the sense of this horrible ingredient of vivisection comes home to them, tempted by the strongest of all temptations, habit, to gulp down the poisonous moral absinth of acquiescence in injustice together with the strengthening and purifying things with which it has lamentably got mingled. They have not the strength to bear the dreary soul-chilliness which they know they must suffer while carefully analyzing this creed of complete subservience of all good to human progress; they prefer to take it as it is, and they persuade themselves that all its ingredients are good. Thus to a large class of men, not merely physiologists and physicians dependent upon physiology, but a multitude of generous thinkers to whom the idea of a loss to science or to medicine is unendurable, vivisec-

tion has become as much a vicious necessity as any
beastly vice to a swinish sinner ;—a necessity which
it has become necessary to their conscience to make
from a vice into a virtue, or at least to exclude from
any moral analysis. And while they have thus
sophisticated or silenced their own conscience into
acquiescence with evil, their example—the example
of men eager in the cause of good which is agreeable
to them, earnest against evil with which they do not
sympathize, noble with all that nobility which is
inherent in a fine nature and costs it no more than
would vice to a vicious one—the apparently deliberate
sanction of vivisection by these the moral censors of
our day, implies also the blind acquiescence of those
conscientious men and women who feel that they
must accept the decisions on right and wrong of their
intellectual superiors. There stands before the eyes
of the honest mediocrity, which in all such matters
has the casting vote, an irresistible array of sanction
of vivisection by men who are the highest authorities
in the new philosophic morality. But this seeming
strength is mere weakness, this apparently energetic
decision is for the most part mere apathetic acquiescence. The knowledge that vivisection is conducive
to progress of ideas and human welfare ; the sense of
the solidarity of science, of free thought with experi-
mentalism ; the habit of abetting anything which is
modern and due to a modern movement; all this goes
to make up that imposing display of approbation by

which progress, freedom, generous thought are made responsible for a huge act of injustice."

"Yes," interrupted Michael, "but there is also something lower than all this, lower and yet more irresistible and natural: the social habit, the official solidarity, of thinking men, which makes the historian, the philologist, the political man meet the physiologist on terms of familiarity, perhaps of professional comradeship; and which has for results that the clean-handed man, who has been writing of Buddha, or Christ, or the new basis of morality, who has been moralizing back-slums or speaking against Nubian slave-dealers persuades himself that there must be a frightful deal of exaggeration in the stories told about Professor A.'s or Dr. B.'s laboratory, that Professor A. or Dr. B. is the best authority about his own doings, that his own statements about the mere tickling pains he inflicts, and the gallons of anæsthetics which he employs, are surely the most reliable; and finally, that vivisection must be perfectly justifiable and praiseworthy, since it is practised by his colleague and friend, Professor A. or Dr. B., who must be an altogether exemplary man, willing to sacrifice his profession and his fame on the least suspicion of immorality, since he is the necessary colleague and friend of himself, the noble, humane, conscientious writer on ethics or reformer of abuses. This may seem unjust; but let any of us ask his conscience how often he has successfully resisted the desire of believing in the moral cleanness of the hands which he is forced to shake in comradeship, or pleased to squeeze in friendship and admiration; let us ask ourselves whether one of the reasons of most acquiescence in evil has not always been, in all mankind, the reluctance to perceive the foulness and injustice and cruelty mixed up with the greatness of our heroes and our gods.

"As to those moral anomalies, intellectual stultifications, self-contradictions, and fact-garblings to which you alluded, Baldwin, I who am fresh from the polemical literature of vivisection, could give you a fine collection of them, culled from the various papers on the moral bearing of vivisection by notoriously most honourable men and distinguished thinkers, perhaps I may add sincere philanthropists, like Sir J. Paget, Mr. Lowe, Professor Owen, Dr. Carpenter, and Professor Virchow. The argument of Dr. Carpenter, that moral duties exist only towards those possessing moral responsibility, carries as logical conclusion that infants, idiots, and madmen may freely be maltreated, not to speak of their being rendered useful to mankind by undergoing vivisection; the argument of Professor Virchow, that a man may in all morality inflict whatever pain is necessary for his purposes (for vivisection, like all rational crime, restricts pain to the strictly necessary) as long as he does so on creatures which do not belong to some other man, but are his honestly bought chattels, brings the great German thinker into close intellectual cantact with the slave-dealers and slave-owners whom mankind at last pronounced unfit to judge moral questions."

"Yes," said Baldwin; "and there is another favourite argument, largely employed by all the advocates of vivisection, which moralizes this practice by claiming for it the right of being endured which is still enjoyed by a number of barbarous sports and practices inherited from more callous days, sports and practices which it must be the strenuous wish of every thinking and feeling man to see outgrown, as we have outgrown many another nasty habit; and this argument, this legitimizing of a new kind of cruelty by the survival of a few very old ones from among the number which civilization has already made obsolete, appears to me not over consistent with the doctrines of elimination of abominations and gradual cleansing of life which scientific believers have accepted in exchange for the old æsthetical paradise promised by Christianity. Yet another and equally favourite argument consists in confronting us with all the various advantages which we have reaped at the expense of pain and injustice; summoning us to renounce this or that advantage inherited from the past, because we cannot be quite sure whether the hands, of man or of fate, which got us that advantage were quite clean; representing to us that we have been moulded by a cruel and unjust nature with many a cruel and unjust instrument; the logical result of all of which is intended to be that if our forefathers made their fortune by cheating customers or robbing travellers, we ought ourselves to condone, if not to practise, the same kind of trade. This is not an argument, it is a theatrical effect, intended to stagger the conscience. 'Are you sure,' says the devil to the honest woman, 'that your mother was not unchaste and that you yourself are not the fruit of adultery?' And this also, this upsetting of the moral judgment by appeal to the imagination, this degrading of the present and the future by pointing to the ignoble past, seems to me more akin to the branding and chaining into eternal prostitution of the woman who has once sinned, than to the principle that man is for ever on the road to a greater moral good, and must with every step leave the original slums further behind and cast from him their befouled rags. This (as it appears to me) flagrant moral contradiction due to the one choice of evil, is summed up, almost in a kind of allegory, by the fact that the flower of moral rhetoricians, the very prince of dainty *connoisseurs* in charity and justice, M. Ernest Renan, writing—with the same hand that had written of Christ 'for all those who suffered'—the superb description of the august priest of truth, Claude Bernard, surrounded by the fumes of the blood of the living beasts whom he had poisoned with curare into a state 'of the most atrocious sufferings' (to use his own words) 'that the imagination of man can conceive.'[1]

"I know it well: it is in his *Eloge* of Bernard, spoken when he replaced him in the French Academy," answered Michael; "but unless you have studied the subject as I have, you can have no conception of the strange condescensions to ignoble moral argument into which the desire of defending vivisection has forced men fully conscious of right and wrong, nay, even experts in moral beauty. I need scarcely say that, the principle once established that the advancement of science and the diminution of human aches is the highest moral test, it must have become a positive duty to sacrifice to this end any scruples not only as to infliction of pain, but also as to the mutilation and disfigurement of truth; of which any one who will note the innumerable evasive answers, the actual flagrant contradictions in statement, and the general denial of the evils of vivisection registered in the Blue-book of the Royal Commission, may persuade himself; and, if he desire further persuasion, obtain it by comparing the vague accounts of the trumpery pains of vivisection, the mere prickings and

[1] *Revue des deux mondes*, Sept. 1864, p. 173. It should be observed that Bernard expressly says in his "Leçons de Physiologie Opératorie," p. 168, that "curare is now employed in a vast number of experiments as a means of restraining the animals. There are but few observations the narrative of which does not begin by notifying that they were made on a curarized dog."

ticklings, given in the reviews by various eminent physiologists and physicians to the suspicious public at large, with what may be found in any advanced physiological handbook or physiological periodical in the way of innumerable admirably clear recipes for day-long torturings. But the degradation of a wrong moral choice carries with it not only horrid prostitutions of conscience but melancholy stultifications of intellect; makes not only honourable men argue according to dishonourable standards, but makes intelligent men talk rubbish. When, for instance, Professor Humphry has said that nothing has shaken his faith in the moral sensitiveness of Englishmen so much as the movement which has subjected vivisection to moral scrutiny; when Professor Owen has declared that a day's pigeon-shooting in one place inflicts more agony than a year's physiological experimentation all over the world; when Dr. Wilks has stated that it is clear that in the anti-vivisection agitation the real motive was fear of atheism, while the plea of cruelty was a mere subterfuge; when such astounding nonsense has been talked by men who are trained to logical thought; there remains possible only one further degree of audacious absurdity of argument, reserved oddly enough for one of the most eminent scientific thinkers of the day, Professor Virchow, who warned the public that if vivisection should ever be prohibited, the logical sequel to refusal to permit the infliction of agony on living beasts would evidently be a prohibition to dissect stone-dead corpses. But there has been worse stultification than this; stultification stranger and much more lamentable, because on the part, not of an infuriated physiologist or plausible doctor, but of a man apparently defending vivisection from a mere abstract desire for the diminution of human pain, a man proved in other fields a most powerful and original thinker, and obviously almost nervously careful in weighing the rights and wrongs of either side. Mr. Edmund Gurney suggests, with saint-like simplicity, that the evils of vivisection may easily be abolished by referring to a board of eminent physiologists and physicians the question whether this, that, or the other experiment may be authorized in consideration of the distinct medical or surgical results which it promises. And he does this in the face not only of the obvious fact that vivisection is an infinitely varied system of experimentation by which abstract truth is sought, as by every other scientific process, on the principle of digging and seeing what may turn up; a system, moreover, of experiment repeated hundredfold for suggestion, verification, re-verification, correcting, refuting, and demonstrating, exactly analogous to the hundredfold experimentation of chemistry or physics; and of the equally obvious fact that by restricting their own experiments English physiologists and physicians would simply be virtuously condemning themselves to hopeless inferiority to the untrammelled experimenters of the Continent, a degree of self-sacrifice, little less than suicide ; but in the face of the distinct assertions of the highest physiological authorities, summed up by Dr. Wilks, that it is utterly absurd for a Government official to ask experimenters 'before he permits them to commence their work, what good object they can foresee in pursuing their researches,' and that 'the only answer which a really scientific man could give would be—knowledge.'"

The train had stopped, and Baldwin and Michael had walked through the unearthly electric flare, with its strange blue shadows and its apparent alterations of distances, of the station.

"It seems to me, in my present mood," said Michael, as they got out of the din and glare, "that modern civilization has a sort of mark of the beast—a something hideous and Moloch-like, even where it is most obviously subservient to our comfort and welfare. The angel of progress makes a sound with his wings, and has a sulphurousness in his breath which is oddly suggestive of hell. Vivisection somehow seems to fit very neatly into it."

Baldwin laughed.

"I told you that you were growing a retrograde," he said, as they walked along the silent, shadowy streets on to the embankment. You forget that this is a moment of transition. You forget that if we have new evils, we have also new sensitiveness to them. In former days there was no such hideosity as a large London railway station, but I question whether there was either any capacity for feeling its hideousness as we do. So also as to vivisection. Our great-grandfathers were comparatively free from this modern vice; but I greatly question whether, had it existed then to the same extent as nowadays, there would have been among our ancestors one-tenth of the moral doubt and dispute and crusading zeal which it has provoked in our times."

Michael did not answer for a minute, but looked vaguely at the lights dotting the darkness on the opposite shore, at the wide yellow reflections from the the gaslights, shivered and heaving on the river; at the spectral towers of Westminster, dim in the dim sky, where the watery moon went in and out among the suffused, buff-tinted clouds.

"Do you think," he said, "that any man or woman whose heart is really in the progress of modern ideas will ever allow that physiology should be fettered, that the discovery of facts and laws should be retarded, that one science should be separated by a moral barrier from the full data which it covets? Why, to these people such a decision would seem positively sinful, impious, frightful."

"It would not be so frightful if we looked well at the matter, nor by any means so unique. Physiology would not really be placed in a position so wholly different from that of the other sciences as one is at first apt to think. For in reality there are few, if any, sciences, which are permitted to obtain directly all the materials they require: barriers exist for them, sometimes almost enclose them—barriers across which only the strong muscle of analogical argument can raise itself to peer, the strong wing of imaginative reason can fly—barriers, which we are apt to forget, of place and time, hopeless barriers of chaos and vacuity and obliteration which separate the historian, the geologist, the astronomer, the physicist, the sociologist, from the facts which he covets. Moreover, this very science of physiology, in its higher levels of human biology, of mental physiology, has between it and its facts a wall as yet solid and unbroken, the wall of public opinion, of long habit, perhaps almost prejudice, which will not let the investigator experiment on the living nerves and brain, the living imagination and passions of a human victim. These walls exist for all science; their presence is borne with patience, and mankind does not fret at the long and roundabout ways by which knowledge must wearily proceed. A bit more wall or a bit less, a little more patience and a little more fortitude, a little more ingenuity in hewing out the difficult paths of thought where we cannot follow the broad highway of experiment: this is what would be meant to men of science by the prohibition of vivisection. A little more manly endurance of physical and mental pain; a little more wise recognition that with the pain mankind has equitably drawn a possible and probable lot of pleasure ; a little more truthful perception that the pains which we suffer are largely due to the folly and vice of ourselves and our fathers; a little more grateful perception that the joys of mind, and eye and ear and heart, are multifold with which man can compensate himself for the sufferings of the body— a certain amount of gained moral vigour: this is what the prohibition of vivisection would mean to mankind at large."

"You are not a real believer in evolutional morality, Baldwin," said Michael.

"Pardon me, I think that way of seeing the question is due precisely to my believing in evolutional morality more completely than other folk. Let us see. Here we have on either side a loss and a gain. Which shall we choose ? To me it seems that to the man who not merely superficially knows and repeats, but whose thoughts and feelings are saturated with our new creed of the perpetual development of the nobler by perpetual elimination of the baser motives of our nature, it will be clear, sooner or later, that the improvement of bodily condition, the advancement of our knowledge, must be a retrogressive step if bought at the expense of the infliction of manifold and daily increasing tortures on creatures who will participate in no way thereby ; on creatures who have not our innumerable consoling pleasures of thought, sentiment, hope, and æsthetic perception ; who, if they suffer, lose all and everything they possess, nay rather, are basely cheated and robbed like some poor serf of their miserable birthright of painless existence by us, their lords, rich with a hundred inherited riches, rich with a hundred riches within our grasp. And similarly, it seems to me, that to every man imbued with the noble religion of choice and improvement, it should appear that the patient foregoing of knowledge thus to be bought, the manly endurance of suffering at such a price to be diminished, must be a great step in the great journey of human bettering; must be, both in the large act of preference of justice to injustice, and in the minor attendant acts of cherished forbearance from the coveted, of fortitude in pain, of thoughtful weighing of good and evil, of candid listening to our conscience, one of those choices of the higher rather than the lower which have made us what we are, which shall make us what we should be."

ON NOVELS.

ON NOVELS.

"AFTER all," said Mrs. Blake, the eminent novelist, "with the exception of very few touches, there is nothing human in 'Wuthering Heights;' those people with their sullenness and coldness and frenzy are none of them real men and women, such as Charlotte Brontë would have given us had she written the book instead of her sister. You can't deny that, Monsieur Marcel."

They had clambered through the steep, bleak Yorkshire village, which trickles, a water-course of rough black masonry, down the green hillside; past the inn where Branwell Brontë drank and raved; through the churchyard, a grim, grassless garden of blackened tombstones; under the windows of the Brontës' parsonage; and still higher, up the slippery slope of coarse, sere grass, on to the undulating flatness of Haworth Moor.

André Marcel, the subtle young French critic and novelist, who had come to Yorkshire in order to study the Brontës, listened to Mrs. Blake with disappointed pensiveness. Knowing more of English things than most Frenchmen, and with a natural preference for the exotic of all kinds, it was part of his mission to make known to the world that England really was what, in the days of Goethe, Italy had falsely been supposed to be: a sort of exceptional and esoteric country, whence æsthetic and critical natures might get weird and exquisite moral impressions as they got orchids and porcelain and lacquer from Japan. Such being the case, this clever woman with her clever novels, both so narrow and so normal, so full at once of scepticism and of respect for precedent, gave him as much of a sense of annoyance and hostility almost as his placid, pessimistic, purely artistic and speculative nature could experience.

They walked on for some minutes in silence, Marcel and Mrs. Blake behind, Baldwin and his cousin Dorothy in front, trampling the rough carpet of lilac and black heather matted with long withered grass and speckled with the bright scarlet of sere bilberry leaves; the valleys gradually closing up all around; the green pasture slopes, ribbed with black stone fences, gradually meeting one another, uniting, disappearing, absorbed in the undulating sea of moorland, spreading solitary, face to face with the low, purplish-grey sky. As Mrs Blake spoke, Dorothy turned round eagerly.

"They are not real men and women, the people in 'Wuthering Heights,'" she said; "but they are real all the same. Don't you feel that they are real, Monsieur Marcel, when you look about you now? Don't you feel that they are these moors, and the sunshine, the clouds, the winds, the storms upon them?"

"All the moors and all the storms upon them put together haven't the importance for a human being that has one well-understood real character of Charlotte Brontë's or George Eliot's," answered Mrs. Blake, coldly.

"I quite understand your point of view," said Marcel; "but, for all my admiration for Charlotte Brontë and George Eliot, I can't agree that either of them, or any writer of their school, can give us anything of the value of 'Wuthering Heights.' After all, what do we gain by their immense powers of psychological analysis and reconstruction? Merely a partial insight into a certain number of characters—characters which, whatever the genius of the novelist, can be only approximations to reality, because they are the result of the study of something of which we can never completely understand the nature—because it is outside ourselves."

Mrs. Blake, who could understand of Marcel's theories only the fact they were extremely distasteful to herself, began to laugh.

"If we are never to understand anything except ourselves, I think we had better leave off novel-writing at once, Monsieur Marcel," she said.

"I don't think that would suit Marcel at all," put in Baldwin, "and he does not by any means condemn the ordinary novel for being what he considers a mere approximation to reality. All he says is, that he prefers books where there is no attempt at completely solving what he considers the inscrutable—namely, the character of every one not oneself. He perceives, more than most people, perhaps even too much, the complexity of human nature; and what to you or me is a complete moral portrait is to him a mere partial representation. I personally think that it is all the better for us if we are unable to see every little moral nerve and muscle in our neighbours: there are in all of us remains of machinery which belongs to something baser, and is little or not at all put in movement. If we could see all the incipient thoughts and incipient feelings of even the best people, we should probably form a much less really just estimate of them than we do at present. It is not morally correct, any more than it is artistically correct, to see the microscopic and the hidden."

"I don't know about that," said Marcel. "But I know that, by the fatality of heredity on one hand, a human being contains within himself a number of different tendencies, all moulded, it is true, into one character, but existing none the less each in its special nature, ready to respond to its special stimulus from without; on the other hand, by the fatality of environment every human being is modified in many different ways: he is rammed into a place until he fits it, and absorbs fragments of all the other personalities with whom he is crushed together. So that there must be, in all of us, even in the most homogeneous, tendencies which, from not having met their appropriate stimulus, may be lying unsuspected at the very bottom of our nature, far below the level of consciousness; but which, on the approach of the specific stimulus, or merely on the occasion of any violent shaking of the whole nature, will suddenly come to the surface. Now it seems to me that such complications of main and minor characteristics, such complications inherited or induced, of half-perceived or dormant qualities, can be disentangled, made intelligible, when the writer is speaking of himself, may be shown even unconsciously to himself; but they cannot be got at in a third person. Therefore I give infinitely less value to one of your writers with universal intuition and sympathy, writing of approximate realities neither himself nor yourself, than to one who like Emily Brontë simply shows us men, women, nature, passion, life, all seen through the medium of her own personality. It is this sense of coming really and absolutely in contact with a real soul which gives such a poignancy to a certain very small class of books—books, to my mind the most precious we have—such as the Memoirs of St. Augustine, the 'Vita Nuova,' the 'Confessions' of Jean-Jacques Rousseau; and 'Wuthering Heights, although an infinitely more imaginative book, seems to me worthy to be ranked with these."

Dorothy Orme had been walking silently in front, her hat slung on her arm, her light curly hair flying in the wind, filling her arms with pale lilac heather, and seeming to the Frenchman a kind of outcome of the moor, an illustration of "Wuthering Heights;" something akin to Emily Brontë's heroine, nay, rather to Emily Brontë herself, as she existed for his imagination. She turned round as he spoke, and said, with a curious mixture of surprise, pain, and reproach:

"I am glad you put 'Wuthering Heights' with the 'Vita Nuova;' but how can you mention in the same breath those disgusting, degraded 'Confessions' of Rousseau? I once tried to read them, and they made me feel sick."

Marcel looked at her with grave admiration. "Mademoiselle," he said, "the 'Confessions' are not a book for you; a diseased soul like Jean-Jacques ought never to be obtruded upon your notice: you ought to read only things like 'Wuthering Heights' and the 'Vita Nuova,' just as you ought to walk on these moors, but not among the squalor and confusion of a big town; you fit into the one, and not into the other. But I put the 'Confessions' by the side of these other books because they belong, in their deeply troubling way, as the 'Vita Nuova' is in its perfect serenity, to that very small class of scarcely self-conscious revelations of personality which may teach us what the novel should aim at."

Dorothy did not answer. This young man, with his keen appreciation, his delicate enthusiasm alike for purity and impurity, puzzled her and made her unhappy. She felt sure he was good himself, yet his notions were so very strange.

"At that rate," put in Mrs. Blake, "there is an end of the novel as a work of art, if we are to make it into a study of the mere psychology of a single individual. As it is, the perpetual preoccupation of psychology has pretty well got rid of all real interest of plot and incident, and is rapidly getting rid of all humour; a comic character like those of Dickens, and even those of Thackeray, will soon be out of the question. Did you read an extraordinarily suggestive article by Mr. Hillebrand, which appeared in *The Contemporary* last year, contrasting the modern novel with the old one? It was very one-sided, of course; but in many things wonderfully correct. I felt that he must condemn my novels along with the others, but I was pleased; it was as if Fielding's ghost had told us his opinion of modern novelists."

Dorothy Orme was not addicted to literary discussions; but the recollection of this article seemed suddenly to transform her.

"I read it," she cried, eagerly; "I hated it. He was very angry with George Eliot because she had made the story of Dorothea and Casaubon tragic, instead of making it farcical, as I suppose Fielding or some such creature would have done ; he would have liked some disgusting, ridiculous comedy of an old pedant, a sort of Don Bartolo, and a girl whom he bored and who made fun of him. Did he never ask himself whether the reality of a situation such as that of Dorothea and Casaubon would be more comic or tragic, whether we should be seeing things more as they really are, whether we should be entering more into the feelings of the people themselves, whether we should be placing ourselves more in the position to help, to diminish unhappiness, by laughing at Dorothea and Casaubon, or by crying at their story ? I am sure we are far too apt to laugh at things already. I dare say that the sense of the ridiculous is a very useful thing ; I dare say it helps to make the world more supportable ; but not when the sense of the ridiculous makes us see things as they are not, or as they are merely superficially ; when it makes us feel pleased and passive where we ought to be pained and active. People have a way of talking about the tendency which the wish for nobility and beauty has to make us see things in the wrong light ; but there is much more danger, surely, of that sort of falsification from our desire for the comic. There's Don Quixote—we have laughed at him quite long enough. I wish some one would write a book now about the reverse of Don Quixote, about a good and kind and helpful man who is made unjust, unkind, and useless by his habit of seeking for the ridiculous, by his habit of seeing windmills where there are real giants, and coarse peasants where there are really princesses. The history of that man, absurd though it may seem as a whole, would yet be, in its part, the history of some little bit of the life of all of us; a bit which might be amusing enough to novelists of the old school, but is sad enough, I think, in all conscience, when we look back upon it in ourselves."

Marcel looked up. To him the weirdest and most exotic flowers of this moral and intellectual Japan called England, were its young women, wonderful it seemed to him in delicacy, in brilliancy of colour, in *bizarre* outline, in imaginatively stimulating and yet reviving perfume; and ever since he had met her a few days ago, this cousin of his old friend Baldwin, this Dorothy Orme, painter, sculptor, philanthropist, and mystic, with the sea-blue eyes, and the light hair that seemed always caught up by the breeze, this creature, at once so mature and so immature, so full of enthusiasm, so unconscious of passion, so boldly conversant with evil in the abstract, so pathetically ignorant of evil in the concrete, had appeared to him as almost the strangest of all these strange English girls who fascinated him as a poet and a critic.

Baldwin had affectionately taken his cousin's arm and passed it through his own.

"You are quite right, Dorothy," he said; "you have put into words what I myself felt while reading that paper; but then, you know, unfortunately, as one grows older—and I am a good bit older than you—one is apt to let oneself drift into looking at people only from the comic side; it is so much easier, and saves one such a deal of useless pain and rage. But you are quite right all the same. A substitution of psychological sympathetic interest for the comic interest of former days has certainly taken place in the novel, and is taking place more and more every day. But I don't think, with Mrs. Blake and Hillebrand, that this is at all a matter for lamentation. Few things strike me more in old fiction, especially if we go back a century, than the curious callousness which many of its incidents reveal; a callousness not merely to many impressions of disgust and shame, which to the modern mind would counterbalance the pleasure of mere droll contrast, as is so constantly the case in Rabelais (where we can't laugh because we have to hold our nose), but also to impressions of actual pain at the pain, moral or physical, endured by the person at whom we are laughing; of indignation at the baseness or cruelty of those through whose agency that comic person is made comic. After all, a great deal of what people are pleased to call the healthy sense of fun of former days is merely the sense of fun of the boy who pours a glass of water down his companion's back, of the young brutes who worry an honest woman in the street, of the ragamuffins who tie a saucepan to a cat's tail and hunt it along. Sometimes it is even more deliberately wanton and cruel; it is the spiritual equivalent of the cock-fighting and bull-baiting, of the amusement at what Michelet reckons among the three great jokes of the Middle Ages: 'La grimace du pendu.' It is possible that we may at some future period be in danger of becoming too serious, too sympathizing, of losing our animal spirits; but I don't see any such danger in the present. And I do see that it is a gain, not only in our souls, but in the actual influence on the amount of good and bad in the world, that certain things which amused our ancestors, the grimace of the dupe, of the betrayed husband, of the kicked servant, should no longer amuse, but merely make us sorry or indignant. Let us laugh by all means, but not when others are crying."

"I perfectly agree with you," said Marcel. "What people call the comic is a lower form of art; legitimate, but only in so far as it does not interfere with the higher. Complete beauty in sculpture, in painting, and in music has never been compatible with the laughable, and I think it will prove to be the same in fiction. To begin with, all great art carries with it a poignancy which is incompatible with the desire to laugh."

"The French have strangely changed," exclaimed Mrs. Blake. "It is difficult to imagine that you belong to the country which produced Rabelais and Molière and Voltaire, Monsieur Marcel."

Marcel sighed. "I know it is," he said; "it is sad, perhaps, as it is always sad to see that one is no longer a child, but a man. Our childhood, at least as artists, is over; we have lost our laughter, our pleasure in romping. But we can understand and feel; we are men."

Mrs. Blake looked shrewdly at the young man. "It seems to me that they were men also, those of the past," she answered. "They laughed; but they also suffered, and hoped, and hated; and the laugh seemed to fit in with the rest. Your modern French literature seems to me no longer French: it all somehow comes out of Rousseau. Balzac, Flaubert, Zola, Baudelaire, all that comes out of those 'Confessions' which you choose to place by the side of the 'Vita Nuova.' And as Rousseau, who certainly was not a true Frenchman, has never seemed to be a genuine man either, but a sickly, morbid piece of half-developed precocity; so I cannot admit that the present phase of French literature represents manhood as opposed to the French literature of the past. Had there remained in France more of the old power of laughter, we should not have had your Zolas and Baudelaires, or rather the genius of your Zolas and Baudelaires would have been healthy and useful. Don't wish to lose that laugh of yours, Monsieur Marcel; our moral health here, in England, where evil is brutish, depends upon seriousness; yours, in France, where evil immediately becomes intellectual depends upon laughter. I am an old woman, so you must not be offended with me."

"There is a deal of truth in what you say," said Baldwin. "The time will come, I am sure, when Frenchmen will look back upon the literature of the last twenty-five years, not as a product of maturity, but rather as a symptom of a particular sort of humourless morbidness which is one of the unbeautiful phases of growth."

Marcel shook his head. "You are merely falling foul of a new form of art because it does not answer to the critical standards which you have deduced from an old one. The art which deals with human emotions real and really appreciated is a growth of our century, and mainly a growth of my country; and you are criticizing it from the standpoint of a quite different art, which made use of only an approximation to psychological reality, for the sake of a tragic or comic effect; it is as if you criticized a landscape by Corot, where beauty is extracted out of the quality of the light, of the soil, and the dampness or dryness of the air, without a thought of the human figure, because it is not like the little bits of conventional landscape which Titian used to complete the scheme of his groups of Saints or Nymphs. Shakespeare and Cervantes are legitimate; but we moderns are legitimate also: they sought for artistic effects new in their day; we seek for artistic effects new in ours."

Baldwin was twisting a long brown rush between his fingers meditatively, looking straight before him upon the endless, grey and purple, thundercloud-coloured undulations of heather.

"I think," he said, "that you imagine you are seeking new artistic effects; but I think, also, that you are mistaken, simply because I feel daily more persuaded that artistic aims are only partially compatible with psychological aims, and that the more the novel becomes psychological the less also will it become artistic. The aim of art, of painting, sculpture, music, and architecture, is, if we put aside the mere display of technical skill, which, as a rule, appeals only to the technically initiated—the aim of art is the production of something which shall give us the particular kind of pleasure associated with the word *beautiful*, pleasure given to our æsthetic faculties, which have a mode of action and necessities as special and as impossible to translate into the mode of action and necessities of our logical and animal faculties as it is impossible to translate the impressions of sight into the impressions of hearing. All art addresses itself, however unconsciously and however much hampered by extraneous necessities, to a desire belonging to these æsthetic faculties, to a desire for the beautiful. What I may call the freely inventive arts, music and architecture, do this most obviously. We are apt to think that painting does so less, because

painting is at present seeking for beauty in a region
—the region of effects of mere atmosphere, light
and colour independent of linear form—where it
was not sought in the past, and where we are therefore not prepared to acknowledge it at present, like
a certain eminent painter of the old school, who
complained to me that Corot had no sense of
beauty, because Corot painted grey drizzly skies
instead of the blue ones in which beauty used exclusively to reside in former days. But painting,
even in the branch which happens to address a non-
artistic desire, even in portraiture, is intensely pre-
occupied with arrangements, the sole aim of which
is that specific quality which we call beauty. If a
painter select this or that arrangement of light
wherein to place what in itself may be ugly; if he
say 'such a dress, such an attitude, is better;' if he
rack his brains to make his sitter the centre of a
scheme of colour; he does this, however, unconsciously, under the impulse of the artistic desire for
beauty. We outsiders are apt to overlook, when we
see a painter painting some very simple scene or
person, neither of which comes up to our idea of
beauty, the special sort of beauty which he pursues
when, for instance, he changes the tint of the sky
in order to give a greater value to the tint of the
rocks or so forth. We do not perceive the thought
and labour expended, for instance, in arranging the
hands of several figures, or the fingers of the hands

of a single one; still less do we reflect that if the painter were aiming at mere psychological character or truthfulness to nature, he would have placed those hands or those fingers no matter how. Hence, I say, all real art addresses itself mainly, however unconsciously, to a desire for beauty. Now, to postulate such a predominant desire for the beautiful in a literary work dealing exclusively with human emotion and action seems to me utterly absurd. First, because mere beauty, the thing which gives us the specific æsthetic impression, exists, I believe, in its absolute reality only in the domain of the senses and of the sensuous impressions recalled and reconstructed by the intellect; and because I believe that it is merely by analogy, and because we perceive that such a pleasure is neither unreasoning and animal nor intellectual and utilitarian, that we apply to pleasing moral impressions the adjective beautiful. The beautiful, therefore, according to my view, can exist in literature only inasmuch as literature reproduces and reconstructs certain sensuous impressions which we name beautiful; or as it deals with such moral effects as give us an unmixed, direct unutilitarian pleasure analogous to that produced by these sensuous impressions of beauty. Now, human character, emotion, and action not merely present us with a host of impressions which, applying an æsthetical word to moral phenomena, are more or less ugly; but, by the very fatality of things, nearly always require for the production of what we call moral beauty a certain proportion of moral ugliness to make it visible. It is not so in art. A dark background, necessary to throw a figure into full light, is as much part of the beautiful whole as the figure in the light; whereas moral beauty—namely, virtue—can scarcely be conceived as existing, except in a passive and almost invisible condition, unless it be brought out by struggle with vice; so that we can't get rid of ugliness in this department. On the other hand, while the desire for beauty can never be paramount in a work dealing with human character and emotion, at least in anything like the sense in which it is paramount in a work dealing with lines, colours, or sounds; there are connected with this work, dealing with human character and emotion, desires special to itself, independent of, and usually hostile to, the desire of beauty—such desires as those for psychological truth and for dramatic excitement. You may say that these are themselves, inasmuch as they are desires without any proximate practical object, artistic; and that, in this sense, every work that caters for them is subject to artistic necessities. So far you may call them artistic, if you like; but then we must call artistic also every other non-practical desire of our nature: the desire which is gratified by a piece of scientific information, divested of all practical value, will also be artistic, and the man who presents an abstract logical argument in the best order, so that the unimportant be always subordinate to the important, will have to be called an artist. The satisfaction we have in following the workings of a character, when these workings do not awaken sympathy or aversion, is as purely scientific as the satisfaction in following a mathematical demonstration or a physiological experiment; and when these workings of character do awaken sympathy or aversion, this sympathy or aversion is a moral emotion, to which we can apply the æsthetical terms 'beautiful' and 'ugly' only by a metaphor, only in the same way that we apply adjectives of temperature to character, or adjectives belonging to music to qualities of painting. The beautiful, as such, has a far smaller share in the poem, novel, or the drama than in painting, sculpture, or music; and, what is more, the ugly has an immeasurably larger one, both in the actual sense of physical ugliness and in the metaphorical sense of moral deformity. I wonder how much of the desire which makes a painter seek for a peculiar scheme of colour, or a peculiar arrangement of hands, enters into the production of such characters as Regan and Goneril and Cousine Bette and Emma Bovary; into the production of the Pension Vauquer dining-room and the Dissenting chapel in Browning's 'Christmas Eve and Easter Day'? To compare a man who works with such materials, who, every now and then at least, carefully elaborates descriptions of hideous places and odious people, with an artist like Corot, seeking for absolute loveliness in those less showy effects which previous painters have neglected, is simply an absurdity. The arts which deal with man and his passions, and especially the novel, which does so far more exclusively and completely than poetry or the drama, are, compared with painting, or sculpture, or architecture, or music, only half-arts. They can scarcely attain unmixed, absolute beauty; and they are perpetually obliged to deal with unmixed, absolute ugliness."

There was a moment's silence.

"I can't make out our friend Baldwin," said Mrs. Blake; "he is too strangely compounded of a scientific thinker, a moralist, and an æsthete; and each of the three component parts is always starting up when you expect one of the others. Yesterday he was descanting on the sublime superiority of literature over art; now he suddenly tells us that, compared with art, literature is an ugly hybrid."

Dorothy Orme had been listening attentively, and her face wore an expression of vague pain and perplexity.

"I can't understand," she said. "What you say seems dreadfully true; it is what I have often vaguely felt, and what has made me wretched. Human nature does not seem to give one that complete, perfect satisfaction which we get from physical beauty; it is always mixed up, or in conflict with, something that gives pain. And yet one feels, one knows, that it is something much higher and nobler than mere combinations of lines, or sounds, or colours. Oh, why should art that deals with these things be the only real, the only thoroughly perfect art? Why should art that deals with human beings be a mistake? Don't you feel that there is something very wrong and very humiliating in such an admission?—in the admission that an artist is less well employed in showing us real men and women than in showing us a certain amount of heather and cloud and rock like that?"

And Dorothy pointed to the moor which spread, with immediately beneath them a sudden dip, a deep pool of rough, spray-like, blackish-purple heather round half-buried fragments of black rock, for what might be yards or miles or scores of miles; not a house, not a tree, not a track, nothing but the tufts of black and lilac heather and wind-bent rushes being there by which to measure the chain of moors: a sort of second sky, folds and folds and rolls and rolls of grey and purple and black-splashed cloud, swelling out and going in, beneath the folds and folds and rolls and rolls of the real sky, black-splashed, purple and grey, into which the moorland melted, with scarcely a line of division, on the low horizon.

"I make no such admission, my dear Dorothy," answered Baldwin. "Nay, I think that the artist who shows us real men and women in their emotion and action is a far more important person than the artist who shows us trees and skies, and clouds and rocks; although the one may always give us beauty, and the other may often give us ugliness. I was saying just now that the art dealing with human character and emotion is only half an art, that it cannot fulfil the complete æsthetic purpose of the other arts, and cannot be judged entirely by their standard; but while fiction—let us say at once, the novel—falls short of absolute achievement on one side, it is able to achieve much more, something quite unknown to the rest of the arts, on the other; and while it evades some of the laws of the merely æsthetical, it becomes liable to another set of necessities, the necessities of ethics. The novel has less value in art, but more importance in life. Let me explain my idea. We have seen that there enter into the novel a proportion of interests which are not artistic, interests which are emotional and scientific; desire for the excitement of sympathy and aversion, and desire for the comprehension of psychological problems. Now one of the main differences between these emotional and scientific interests and the merely æsthetic ones is, I think, that the experience accumulated, the sensitiveness increased, by æsthetic stimulation serves merely (except we go hunting for most remote consequences) to fit us for the reception of more æsthetic experiences, for the putting out of more æsthetic sensitiveness; familiarity with beauty training us only for further familiarity with beauty. Whereas, on the contrary, our emotional and scientific experiences obtained from art, however distant all practical object may have been while obtaining them, mingle with other emotional and scientific experiences obtained, with no desire of pleasure, in the course of events; and thus become part of our *viaticum* for life. Emotional and scientific art, or rather emotional and scientific play (for I don't see why the word art should always be used when we do a thing merely to gratify our higher faculties without practical purposes), trains us to feel and comprehend—that is to say, to live. It trains us well or ill; and, the thing done as mere play becoming thus connected with practical matters, it is evident that it must submit to the exigencies of practical matters. From this passive acquiescence in the interests of our lives to an active influence therein is but one step; for the mere play desires receive a strange additional strength from the half-conscious sense that the play has practical results: it is the difference, in point of excitement, between gambling with markers and gambling with money. There is a kind of literature, both in verse and in prose, in which the human figure is but a mere accessory—a doll on which to arrange beautiful brocades and ornaments. But wherever the human figure becomes the central interest, there literature begins to diverge from art; other interests, foreign to those of art, conflicting with the desire for beauty, arise; and these interests, psychological and sympathetic, in mankind, create new powers and necessities. Hence, I say, that although the novel, for instance, is not as artistically valuable as painting, or sculpture, or music, it is practically more important and more noble."

"It is extraordinary," mused Marcel, "how æsthetical questions invariably end in ethical ones when treated by English people; and yet in practice you have given the world as great an artistic literature as any other nation, perhaps even greater."

"I think," answered Mrs. Blake, who was always sceptical even when she assented, and who represented that portion of reasoning mankind which carries a belief in spontaneous action to the length of disbelief in all action at all—"I think that, like most speculative thinkers, our friend Baldwin always exaggerates the practical result of everything."

They had turned, after a last look at the grey and purple and blackish undulations of the moors, and were slowly walking back over the matted sere grass and the stiff short heather in the direction of Haworth; the apparently continuous table-land beginning to divide once more, the tops of the green pasture-slopes to reappear, the valleys separating hill from hill to become apparent; and a greyness, different from the greyness of the sky, to tell, on one side, of the neighbourhood down below of grimy, smoky manufacturing towns and villages, from which, in one's fancy, these wild, uncultivated, uninhabited hill-top solitudes seemed separated by hundreds of miles.

"I don't think I exaggerate the practical effects in this case," answered Baldwin. "When we think of the difference in what I must call secular, as distinguished from religious, inner life, between ourselves and our ancestors of two or three centuries, nay, of only one century, ago, the question must come to us: Whence this difference? Social differences, due to political and economical ones, will explain a great deal; but they will not explain all. Much is a question of mere development. Nothing external has altered, only time has passed. Now what has developed in us such a number and variety of moral notes which did not exist in the gamut of our fathers? What has enabled us to follow consonances and dissonances for which their moral ear was still too coarse? Development? Doubtless; just as development has enabled us to execute, nay, to hear, music which would have escaped the comprehension of the men of former days. But what is development? A mere word, a mere shibboleth, unless we attach to it the conception of a succession of acts which have constituted or produced the change. Now, what, in a case such as this, is that succession of acts? We have little by little become conscious of new harmonies and dissonances, have felt new feelings. But whence came those new harmonics and dissonances, those new feelings? Out of their predecessors: the power of to-day's perception arising out of the fact of yesterday's. But what are such perceptions; and would mere real life suffice to give them? I doubt it. In real life there would be mere dumb, inarticulate, unconscious feeling, at least for the immense majority of humanity, if certain specially gifted individuals did not pick out, isolate, those feelings of real life, show them to us in an ideal condition where they have a merely intellectual value, where we could assimilate them into our conscious ideas. This is done by the moralist, by the preacher, by the poet, by the dramatist; people who have taught mankind to see the broad channels along which its feelings move, who have dug those channels. But in all those things, those finer details of feeling which separate us from the people of the time of Elizabeth, nay, from the people of the time of Fielding, who have been those that have discovered, made familiar, placed within the reach of the immense majority, subtleties of feeling barely known to the minority some hundred years before? The novelists, I think. They have, by playing upon our emotions, immensely increased the sensitiveness, the richness, of this living keyboard; even as a singing-master, by playing on his pupil's throat, increases the number of the musical intervals which he can intone."

"I ask you," went on Baldwin, after a minute, "do you think that our great-grandfathers and great-grandmothers would have been able to understand such situations as those of Dorothea and Casaubon, of the husband and wife in Howells' 'Modern Instance,' as that of the young widow in a novel which I think we must all have read a couple of years ago—Lucas Malet's 'Mrs. Lorimer'? Such situations may have existed, but their very heroes and heroines must have been unconscious of them. I ask you again, Mrs. Blake—for you know the book—could you conceive a modern girl of eighteen, pure and charming and loving, as Fielding represents his Sophia Western, learning the connection between her lover and a creature like Molly Seagrim, without becoming quite morally ill at the discovery? But in the eighteenth century a nice girl had not the feelings, the ideal of repugnances, of a nice girl of our day. In the face of such things it is absurd to pretend, as some people do, that the feelings of mankind and womankind are always the same. Well, to return to my argument. Believing, as I do, in the power of directing human feeling into certain channels rather than into certain others; believing, especially, in the power of reiteration of emotion in constituting our emotional selves, in digging by a constant drop, drop, such moral channels as have already been traced; I must necessarily also believe that the modern human being has been largely fashioned, in all his more delicate peculiarities, by those who have written about him; and most of all, therefore, by the novelist. I believe that were the majority of us, educated and sensitive men and women, able to analyze what we consider our almost inborn, nay, automatic views of life, character, and feeling; able to scientifically assign its origin to each and trace its modifications — I believe that, were this possible, we should find that a good third of what we take to be instinctive knowledge, or knowledge vaguely acquired from personal experience, is really obtained from the novels which we or our friends have read."

The discussion, somehow, was dropped at this point; and it was not till some hours later, as they were returning home from their visit to Haworth and the moors, that Baldwin reverted to the subject. They were driving along one of the green hillsides, ribbed with fences of black stone, and dotted here and there with one of those low black stone houses, with long narrow mullioned windows for the hand-loom, which bring home to one the days, scarcely beyond those of our fathers and yet seemingly so distant, when the dales of Yorkshire, now crowded with manufacturing towns, belonged to a scattered population of peasants who spun and wove the wool of the sheep of their moors. In the valley below lay the huge black city, spreading up and down the neighbouring hills, as if all the world were soon to be covered with streets and factories and warehouses. The day's work was over, and the last smoke lazily rising into the sky, or rather into the cloud of smoke which already enwrapped the city, and overhung it as far as one could see. The sun was setting, invisible in this strange artificial twilight; but as it sank, unseen, its light permeated the smoke, dividing it into huge masses of dull coppery and leaden cloud, and turning its lividness into a vague ethereal goldeness, against which the hundreds of factory chimneys, their base lost in the smoky twilight, stood out dim and spectral like the masts of innumerable gigantic ships.

"Look at that," said Marcel: "ought not such a sight to convert any one to modern art, to show beyond controversy that, no matter how ugly a thing may be, a great artist can always find a moment in its existence when it becomes as beautiful as the most intrinsically perfect and noble object?"

"This sudden transfiguration of our hideous city," remarked Baldwin, "makes me think again about our conversation on novels. As it is with towns, so also is it, I think, with human beings: there are comparatively few so utterly base, so utterly deserted by all better influences, that they have not, however rarely, moments when they are worthy of being shown us, moments when their soot and smoke is glorified by the light within or without them. We must all have remarked such moments in others and in ourselves: nobler moments, during which the individual is loosened from the selfish and petty interests and habits of every day, and rises to a state of consciousness, of emotion, of perception and sympathy with higher things; only to be caught once again by the baser interests, to flop down again to where life is languid, and the horizon narrow." . . .

Marcel shook his head sadly. "Don't speak of them," he said; "they are the bitterness of life. Without them, without these nobler revelations of ourselves and others which last only a minute, we could be happy and even dignified, like the beasts around us."

Baldwin laughed. "Nay," he answered, "that was not at all my thought. What I was going to say was, on the contrary, ought we not rather to be grateful rather than disgusted at such things? Heaven forbid that I should pretend that in such moments we see the real individual despoiled of the merely accidental; the real individual is whatever he may be in the bulk of his nature: weak if that bulk be weak, strong if it be strong, mixed if it be mixed. These nobler moments are not moments of revelation of the reality; they are moments of transfiguration of the possibility; and for this very reason they are much more useful and worthy. They are in truth the sports, in Darwinian language, of our nature: out of these nobler accidents comes progress. Thousands of such must be wasted for one to come to good, as thousands of germs must rise on the wind for one to fall on the right soil. But it is the experience of such moments as these, brief as they may have been, which enables us to conceive nobler characters than our own in the abstract, to sympathize and co-operate with them in the concrete. Dorothy was talking this morning about some letters which had been written to her by a rather morally mediocre woman, in circumstances which greatly shook this woman's nature. Dorothy seemed to think it rather disgusting, as you do, Marcel, that a person should be able to feel nobly only to descend again into a life of rather mean feeling. That this particular woman in question, whose letters my cousin was showing me, has by this time descended most thoroughly from the height of those sentiments, I am perfectly prepared to admit; but that those sentiments should have been there is none the less a good thing for her, for the world, and for Dorothy and me. It is good for us to have witnessed this momentary transfiguration; both practically and because every memory of such a thing is or ought to be valuable, as a pleasure, in the same sense as a remembered melody, or picture, or couplet.

"It is one of the noble uses of literature, especially of the novel," continued Baldwin, looking down on the city, whose forest of slender chimneys was gradually fading into greyness, as the last yellow suffusion died away out of the smoke and mist of the sky, "and one of the things which puts this sort of half-art above the perfect arts which can attain perfect and unmixed beauty;—this, that it artificially increases these rare moments when our meaner part is in abeyance, our better in activity ; that it connects, with its network of imaginary emotions, those few and far between noble real ones ; that it records, as a painter might have recorded the sunset which has just glorified this ugly mass of brick and smut and smoke, those nobler moments which would otherwise fade away forgotten, into the uniformity of our trivial existence."

II.

"I am sorry that Miss Dorothy should have been reading 'Une Vie,'" said Marcel, as he sat next morning after breakfast in the country house near the big black Yorkshire city; "the book is perhaps the finest novel that any of our younger Frenchmen have produced, and I wish I, instead of Maupassant, were its author. But I shrink from the thought of the impression which it must have made upon this young girl, so frank and fearless, but at the same time so pure and sensitive. I am very sorry it should have fallen into her hands."

"I have no doubt that my cousin felt very sick after reading it," said Baldwin, coldly ; "but I think that if there is any one who might read such a book without worse result than mere temporary disgust, it is exactly Dorothy. What I feel sorry about is, not that an English girl should read the book, but that a Frenchman, or rather the majority of the French people, could write it."

Marcel looked surprised. "The book is a painful one," he said; "there is something very horrible, more than merely tragic, in the discovery, by a pure and ideal-minded woman, brought up in happy ignorance of the brutish realities of life. But I cannot understand how you, Baldwin, who are above the Pharisaism of your nation, and who lay so much—so far too great (I think)—weight upon the ethical importance of the novel, can say that 'Une Vie' is a book that should not have been written. We have, I admit, a class of novel which panders to the worst instincts of the public; and we have also, and I think legitimately, a class of novel which, leaving all practical and moral questions aside, treats life as merely so much artistic material. But 'Une Vie' belongs to neither of these classes. There is, in this novel, a distinct moral purpose: the author feels a duty——"

"I deny it," cried Mrs. Blake, hotly; "the sense of duty in handling indecent things can never lead to their being handled like this; the surgeon washes his hands; and this Guy de Maupassant, nay, rather this French nation, goes through no similar ablution. The man thinks he is obeying his conscience; in reality he is merely obeying his appetite for nastiness and his desire to outdo some other man who has raised the curtain where people have hitherto drawn it."

"Pardon me," answered Marcel, "you seem to me guilty of inconsistency; Baldwin to his theories of the ethical importance of novels: you, Mrs. Blake, to the notions which all English people have about the enlightenment of unmarried women on subjects from which we French most rigorously exclude them. Looking at the question from your own standpoint, you ought to see that such a sickening and degrading revelation as that to which Maupassant's heroine is subjected, is due to that very ignorance of all the realities of married life in which our girls are brought up, and which you consider so immoral. This being the case, what right have you to object to a book which removes the sort of ignorance that turns a woman into a victim, and often into a morally degraded victim?"

"My dear Monsieur Marcel," said Mrs. Blake, "I quite see your argument. I do consider the system of education of your French girls as abominably immoral, since they are brought up in an ignorance which would never be tolerated in entering upon the most trifling contract, and which is downright sinful in entering upon the most terribly binding contract of all. But I say that a woman should get rid of such ignorance gradually, insensibly; in such a manner that she should possess the knowledge without, if I may say so, its ever possessing her, coming upon her in a rush, filling her imagination and emotion, dragging her down by its weight; she ought certainly not to learn it from a book like this, where the sudden, complete, loathsome revelation would be more degrading than the actual degradation in the reality, because addressed merely to the mind. Hence such a book is more than useless, it is absolutely harmful : a blow, a draught of filthy poison, to the ignorant woman who requires enlightenment ; and as to the woman who is not ignorant, who understands such things from experience or from the vicarious experience gleaned throughout years from others and from books, she cannot profit by being presented, in a concentrated, imaginative, emotional form, these facts which she has already learned without any such disgusting concentration of effect. Believe me, respectable, Pharisaic mankind knows what it is about when it taboos such subjects from novels ; it may not intellectually understand, but it instinctively guesses, the enervating effect of doubling by the imagination things which exist but too plentifully in reality."

"I perfectly agree with Mrs. Blake," said Baldwin. "We English are inclined to listen to no such pleas as might be presented for 'Une Vie,' and to kick the man who writes a book like this downstairs without more ado ; but I regret that, while the instinct which should impel such summary treatment would be perfectly correct, it should with most of my countrypeople be a mere vague, confused instinct, so that they would be quite unable to answer (except by another kick) the arguments which moral men who write immoral books might urge in defence."

"But why should you wish to kick a man because

he does not conceal the truth?" argued Marcel. "Why should that be a sin in an artist which is a virtue in a man of science? Why should you fall foul of a book on account of the baseness of the world which it truthfully reflects? Is not life largely compounded of filthiness and injustice? is it not hopelessly confused and aimless? Does life present us with a lesson, a moral tendency, a moral mood? And if life does not, why should fiction?"

"Because," answered Baldwin, "fiction *is* fiction. Because fiction can manipulate things as they are not manipulated by reality; because fiction addresses faculties which expect, require, a final summing up, a moral, a lesson, a something which will be treasured up, however unconsciously, as a generalization. Life does not appeal to us in the same way, at the same moment, in the same moods, as does literature; less so even than science appeals to us in the same way as art (and yet we should be shocked to hear from a poet what would not shock us from a doctor). We are conscious of life in the very act of living—that is to say, conscious of it in the somewhat confused way in which we are conscious of things going on outside us while other things are going on inside us; conscious by fits and starts, with mind and feelings, not tense, but slack; with attention constantly diverted elsewhere; conscious, as it were, on a full stomach. The things which are washed on to our consciousness, floating on the stream, by the one wave, are washed off again by another wave. It is quite otherwise with literature. We receive its impressions on what, in the intellectual order, corresponds to an empty stomach. We are thinking and feeling about nothing else; we are tense, prepared for receiving and retaining impressions; the faculties concerned therein, and which are continually going off to sleep in reality, are broad awake, on the alert. We are, however unconsciously, prepared to learn a lesson, to be put into a mood, and that lesson learnt will become, remember, a portion of the principles by which we steer our life, that induced mood will become a mood more easily induced among those in which we shall really have to act. Hence we have no right to present to the intellect, which by its nature expects essences, types, lessons, generalizations —we have no right to present to the intellect expecting things which it graves into itself, a casual bit of unarranged, unstudied reality, which is not any of these things; which is only reality, and which ought to have reality's destructibility and fleetingness; a thing which the intellect, the imagination, the imaginative emotions, accept, as they must accept all things belonging to their domain, as the essential, the selected, the thing to be preserved and revived. Hence, also, the immorality, to me, of presenting a piece of mere beastly reality as so much fiction, without demonstrating the proposition which it goes to prove or suggesting the reprobation which it ought to provoke. Still greater, therefore, is the immorality of giving this special value, this durability, this property of haunting the imagination, of determining the judgment, this essentially intellectual (whether imaginative or emotional) weight to things which, in reality, take place below the sphere of the intellect and the intellectual emotions, as, for instance, a man like Rabelais gives an intellectual value, which means obscenity, to acts which in the reality do not tarnish the mind, simply because they don't come in contact with it. In fact, my views may be summed up in one sentence, which is this: Commit to the intellect, which is that which registers, re-arranges, and develops, only such things as we may profit by having registered, re-arranged, and developed."

Dorothy had entered the room, and presently she and Marcel were strolling out on the lawn, leaving Mrs. Blake and Baldwin to continue their discussion.

"What is the use of talking about such things with a Frenchman?" exclaimed Mrs. Blake. "I could scarcely refrain from laughing when I saw you gravely arguing about morality and immorality in novels with that young man, who would give one of his fingers to have written 'Une Vie'; and who, after talking pessimistic idealism with Dorothy, and going on by the hour about the exotic frankness, and purity, and mixture of knowledge and innocence of English girls, probably shuts himself up in his room to write a novel the effect of which upon just such a girl he positively shrinks from thinking of, as the morbid, puling creature said about 'Une Vie.' Do you remember the preface to the 'Nouvelle Héloïse'? Rousseau declaring that if any modest girl read the book he had just written, she would be lost? That is how all the French are: they can neither understand that their books are sickening, nor that a decently constituted human being can recover after five minutes from the feeling of sickness which they inspire. It is impossible to argue with them on the subject."

"It *is* very difficult to argue with them on the subject," answered Baldwin, "but not so much for the reasons you allege. The difficulty which I experience in attacking the French novel to a Frenchman is, that I cannot honestly attack it in the name of the English novel; the paralyzing difficulty of being between two hostile parties which are both in the wrong. The French novel, by its particular system of selection and treatment of subject, by choosing the nasty sides of things and investing them with an artificial intellectual and emotional value, falsifies our views of life and enervates our character; the English novel, on the other hand, falsifies our views of life and enervates our character in a different way, by deliberately refusing to admit that things can have certain nasty sides, and by making us draw conclusions and pass judgments upon the supposition that no such nasty factors really enter into the arrangement of things. A girl, for instance, who has read only

English novels has not merely got a most ridiculously partial idea of life, an idea which can be only of the most partial practical utility, but she has, moreover, from the fact of the disproportion between the immense amount of talk on some subjects and the absolute silence on others, acquired an actually false idea of life, which may become actually practically mischievous. I have taken the example of a girl, because men get to know but too easily the ugly sides of things and of themselves; and it has always struck me that there is something absolutely piteous, and which should make an honest man feel quite guilty, in the fact of girls being fed exclusively upon a kind of literature which conduces to their taking the most important steps, nay, what is almost worse, which conduces to their forming the most important ideals and judgments and rules of conduct, in ignorance of the realities of life, or rather in a deluded condition about them."

Mrs. Blake looked at Baldwin with an air of whimsical compassion. "My dear friend," she said, "I am an old woman and an old novelist. When I was young I thought as you do, for, permit me to say, all that array of scientific argument seems to tend to prolonging people's youth most marvellously in some respects. You say that it is unjust that women should be permitted to form ideals and rules of conduct, that they should be allowed to make decisions, while labouring under partial and erroneous views of life. Is that not exactly what Marcel answered when you called 'Une Vie' a filthy book? What does that book do, if it does not enlighten the ignorance of which you complain?"

Baldwin shook his head. "You misunderstand me. I said to you just now that the English novel is pernicious because it permits people, or rather let us say women (for the ethics of novels are, after all, framed entirely for the benefit or detriment of women), to live on in the midst of a partial, and therefore falsified, notion of life. That has nothing to do with my strictures on 'Une Vie' or upon any other French novel whatsoever. I objected, in answer to Marcel, that a book like Maupassant's gave a false impression of life, because it presented as a literary work—that is to say, as something which we instinctively accept as a generalization, as a lesson—what is in truth a mere accidental, exceptional heaping up of revolting facts, as little like a generalization of life as a hump-backed dwarf is like a figure in a book of artistic anatomy; and I objected to it still more because, like nine out of ten French novels, it dragged the imagination over physical details with which the imagination has no legitimate connection, which can only enervate, soil, and corrupt it; because, as I said, it gave an intellectual value to facts with which the intellect cannot deal with the very smallest profit in the world. I said just now that, in attacking the French novel, I felt the disadvantage of not being able to do so in the name of the English novel; at present the case is exactly reversed: I feel the difficulty of attacking the restrictions of the English novel, because the excesses of the French novel are staring me in the face. I assure you that one pays a price for the satisfaction of remaining independent between two rival systems of novel-writing, as one does for remaining independent between two rival political or religious parties: the price of being continually isolated and continually in antagonism; dragged, or rather pushed away, from side to side, sickened, insulted in one's own mind, told by oneself that one is narrow-minded and immoral by turns. I know that, if I wrote a novel, it would be laughed at as stuff for schoolgirls by my French and Italian friends, and howled down as unfit for family reading by my own country-people."

"Very likely," answered Mrs. Blake, "and it would serve you right for not having the courage to decide boldly between the timidity of the English and the shamelessness of the French."

"I do decide. I decide boldly that both are in the wrong. I cannot admit that a man should give his adherence to either party if he think each represents an excess. At that rate, it would be impossible ever to form a third party in whom justice should reside, and things would always go on swinging from one absurdity or one evil to the other. I see that you consider me already as a partisan of the French novel. Permit me to say that I would rather that the English novel were reduced to the condition of Sunday reading for girls of twelve than that such a novel as Maupassant's 'Une Vie' or Gautier's 'Mademoiselle de Maupin' should be written in this country. I tell you frankly that I can scarcely think of a dozen modern French novels in which I should not like to cut out whole passages, sometimes whole chapters, from Balzac to Daudet. Let me explain myself, and recapitulate what I consider the sins of the modern French novel. One of these, fortunately rare, but gaining ground every day, can be dismissed at once: I mean the allusion to particular kinds of evil which are so exceptional and abnormal that any practical advantage derivable from knowledge of them must inevitably be utterly outweighed by the disadvantage of introducing into the mind vague and diseased suspicions of unprovable but also undisprovable evil. The other principal sins of modern French novelists are, to my mind, first: the presentation of remarkable evil without any comment on the part of the author, or without any presentation of remarkable good to counterbalance, by its moral and æsthetical stimulus, the enervating effect of familiarity with evil. The sight of evil is not merely necessary, if evil is to diminish; it is wholesome, if it awakens indignation : it is good for us to maintain our power of taking exception, of protesting, of hating ; it is good for us, in moral matters, to have the instinct of battle. But this becomes impossible if evil is represented as the sole occupant of this earth: in that case we no longer have any one to fight for, and we run the risk of forgetting how to fight for ourselves. So much for the demoralizing effect of the pessimistic misrepresentation, or at all events the representation of an unfairly selected specimen of life. It distinctly diminishes our energies for good. The other, and I decidedly think even worse, great sin of French novelists is their habit of describing the physical sides of love, or of what people call love, whether it be socially legitimate or socially illegitimate. Such descriptions are absolutely unnecessary for the psychological completeness of their work, since, as I said to Marcel, they drag the mind and the intellectual emotions into regions below their cognizance, and cram them with impressions which they can never digest, which remain as a mere foul nuisance; besides, by stimulating instincts which require not stimulation, but repression, they entirely betray the mission of all intellectual work, which is to develop the higher sides of our nature at the expense of the lower. There is not a single description of this kind which might not most advantageously be struck out, and I could have gone on my knees to Flaubert to supplicate him to suppress whole passages and pages of 'Madame Bovary,' which I consider a most moral and useful book. I don't think you yourself would be more rigorous in dealing with the French novel."

Mrs. Blake looked puzzled. "I confess I can't well conceive 'Madame Bovary' with those parts left out," she said; "nor do I clearly understand, since you are so uncompromising with the French novel, why in the world you cannot rest satisfied with the English one. You seem to me to be merely removing its limits in order to fence the French novel round with them. What do you want?"

"I want absolute liberty of selection and treatment of subjects to the exclusion of all abnormal suggestion, of all prurient description, and of all pessimistic misrepresentation. I want the English novelist to have the right of treating the social and moral sides of all relations in life, as distinguished from treating their physical sides. I want him to deal with all the situations in which a normal human soul, as distinguished from a human body, can find itself. I want, in short, that the man or woman who purports to show us life in a manner far more minute and far more realistic than the poet, should receive the same degree of liberty of action as the poet."

"As Swinburne in the first series of 'Poems and Ballads'?" asked Mrs. Blake, with a sneer.

Baldwin looked quite angry. "If people are irrational, is that my fault?" he exclaimed. "You know perfectly well that if I condemn Maupassant, and Daudet, and Zola, I condemn Swinburne, in the poems you allude to, a hundred times worse, because he has no possible moral intention to plead, because his abominations are purely artistic. The liberty which I ask for the English novelist is the liberty which is given to a poet like Browning, or Browning's wife—the liberty in the choice of subject which we would none of us deny to Shakespeare. Does the English public disapprove of 'The Ring and the Book,' of 'Aurora Leigh,' of the plot of 'Othello' or of 'Measure for Measure'? Well, ask yourself what the English public would say of a novelist who should treat 'Othello' or 'Measure for Measure,' who should venture upon writing 'Aurora Leigh' or 'The Ring and the Book,' in prose. Let us look a moment at this last. You will not, I suppose, deny that it is one of the most magnificent and noble works of our day; to my mind, with the exception perhaps of the 'Misérables,' by far the most magnificent and the most noble. Now the plot of 'The Ring and the Book' is one which no English novelist would dare to handle; Mudie would simply refuse to circulate a novel the immense bulk of which consisted in the question, discussed and re-discussed by half-a-dozen persons: Has there been adultery between Pompilia and Caponsacchi? Has Guido Franceschini tried to push his wife into dishonour, or has he been dishonoured by his wife? Ask yourself what would have been the fate of this book had it been written by an unknown man in prose. Every newspaper critic would have shrieked that the situation was intolerable, and that the mind of the reader had been dragged through an amount of evil suggestion which no height of sanctity in Pompilia or Caponsacchi could possibly compensate. I foresee your answer: you are going to rejoin that poetry addresses a select, a higher, more moral, more mature public than does the novel; that the poet, therefore, may say a great deal where the novelist must hold his tongue. Is it not so? Well, to this I can only answer (forgive me, for you are a novelist yourself) that I would rather never put pen to paper than be a novelist upon such terms. What, is a man or woman who feels and understands and represents as strongly and keenly and clearly as any poet, to be thrust into an inferior category merely because he or she happens to write in prose instead of writing in verse? Is the novel, the one great literary form produced by our age, as the drama and the epic were produced by other ages, to appeal to a public of which we are to take for granted that it is so infinitely less mature, so infinitely less intelligent, and less clean-minded than the public of the poet? A public of half-grown boys or girls, too silly to understand the bearings of things; a public of depraved men and women, in whom every suggestion of evil will awake, not invigorating indignation, but a mere disgusting and dangerous response? Tell me: is the novelist to confess that he addresses a public too foolish and too base to be addressed plainly?"

Mrs. Blake did not answer for a minute. In her

youth, while she had still believed in the nobility of mankind, she had written a novel which had been violently attacked as immoral; and ever since, in proportion as her opinion of men and women had become worse and worse, she had carefully avoided what she called "sailing too near the wind;" a woman, the morality, as people called it, of whose books was due to deep moral scepticism, in the same way that the decorum, the safety, of certain great cities is due to the State's acquiescence in the existence of shameful classes.

"That's all very fine," she answered, "in theory; but look at the practical result of letting novelists treat certain subjects in a pure-minded way; you have it in France. In order to prevent people getting to the thin ice, we must forbid their going on to the pond; we must fence it round and write up 'No trespassing allowed.' Believe me, were the English novelist permitted to write a 'Ring and the Book' or an 'Aurora Leigh' in prose, he would have written 'Une Vie' or 'Nana' before the year was out."

Baldwin shook his head. "You are entirely mistaken," he said; "these novels are, could not be, the result of greater liberty being given to the English novel, for they are not the result of the liberty given to the French novelist. They are the result simply of the demoralization of France, and of all nations influenced by France, in certain matters: a demoralization due partly, perhaps, to a habit engrained in the race; partly, most certainly, to the abominable system of foreign female education and of foreign marriage; due, in short, to the fact of French civilization (and under the head of French I include Italian, Spanish, and Russian) being to a much greater extent a masculine civilization, made by men for men, and therefore without the element of chastity which women have elaborated throughout the centuries, and which only women can diffuse. The French may not be more licentious than the English; but they are less ashamed of licentiousness, or, rather, not ashamed of it at all; and when I say the French I mean the Latin peoples and the Russians and Poles as well. If you had lived abroad as much as I have, you would know that the incidents which revolt us most in French novels are the incidents which are taken as matter of course in French-speaking countries, that the allusions and discussions which seem to us most intolerable are made freely wherever, out of the presence of unmarried women, French or Italian is spoken. No thoroughbred English person—at least, no thoroughbred Englishwoman — can have a conception of the perfect simplicity, the innocence of heart I might almost say, with which French and Italian and Russian women absolutely virtuous in their conduct and even theoretically opposed to vice, bandy about suggestions, suspicions, accusations, which would make an Englishman's hair stand on end. There is, in what I may call the French world, a positive habit of putting nasty constructions upon things, which is as striking in its way as our English habit of always pretending that such a thing as vice cannot exist among our respectable neighbours, a perfect Philistinism — or even Pharisaism—of evil, as conventional as our Philistinism of good. The immorality of the French novel is simply the immorality of French society."

"And you think," asked Mrs. Blake, sceptically, "that English society is not sufficiently immoral to produce, if allowed to do so, a French novel? My poor Baldwin!"

"I think so, most certainly. And I think that if English society were sufficiently immoral to produce a French novel, the sooner it did so the better ; for in that case our English novel would be almost the worst sign of our weakness and depravity—a white leprosy of hypocrisy and cowardice. If England were sufficiently immoral to produce a French novel, and restrained from so doing merely by conventional reasons, why the whole of our nation would simply be no better than a convent-bred young French girl of whom I heard lately, who was not permitted to go to a ball for fear of meeting young men, and who slipped out every night her mother was at a party, and took a solitary walk on the boulevards."

"Speaking of girls, there is your cousin walking along the road with Marcel," interrupted Mrs. Blake. "I think, considering the sort of young ladies to whom, according to his novels, he is accustomed, it would be as well that we should accompany these representatives of a moral and an immmoral civilization on their walk."

Baldwin laughed. "You are more French than Marcel himself!" he exclaimed.

Baldwin and Mrs. Blake had soon overtaken the two young people on the road which, leading to a patch of moor that had got enclosed among the pasture land, wound along the round hills, covered with grass and corn and park land, above the big manufacturing city, which lay, wrapped in grey fog, with its hundreds of chimneys smoking away, invisible in the valley. The morning was fine. One appeared to be walking in the sunshine, feeling it on one's back and accompanied by one's shadow; but this sunlit patch extended only a few paces around one, and moved on as one moved, leaving all the rest of the earth veiled in a dense and not at all luminous mist of blackish grey—of the grey in which there is no blue at all, but which seems like a mere dilution of black; the grey of coal-smoke, heavy all round, but perceptibly thickening and gaining blackness in one spot, where the hidden chimneys of the black city slowly poured their blackish-grey smoke-wreaths into the blackish-grey sky.

"Oh, how can you write about such women," Dorothy was saying to Marcel, "and write about them so quietly—look at them and paint them as if they were merely a curious effect of light, merely a strange sky like this one?"

"What else are they?" answered Marcel. "I mean, what else can they be to an artist or a psychologist? We cannot destroy such women because there are other women, like you, Miss Dorothy, who are all that they are not, any more than we can forbid this smoke, this fog, to exist because there are mornings full of light, and breeze, and freshness. We cannot prevent their existing, and cannot hide from ourselves that as this fog, this smoke, has beauties strange and eerie, which make it valuable to a painter; so also such women, weak, perverse, heartless, destructive, have a value, a strange unhealthy charm for the imagination."

There was a brief silence; then Baldwin and Mrs. Blake heard Dorothy's voice, earnest and agitated, answering the languid voice of Marcel, as they walked on enveloped in the mist.

"No, no," she said; "you think that, because you have never felt what those women are, because it has never come home to you."

Marcel sighed. "I fear it has come home to me but too much, Miss Dorothy," he answered.

"That is not what I mean. You may have known women like that—I dare say you have—and still not have known all that their wickedness means. If you had you could not talk like that about skies and light and mist. I have known such a woman, known the full meaning of such a woman. I can't very well explain ; my ideas are rather confused, you know ; but I understand that I understood that woman's real meaning. I had a friend once ; she was beautiful, and young, and noble, and she was dying ; and her husband, instead of caring for her, cared for a woman such as you describe in your novel ; the two betrayed and outraged her, and made her last years bitterness and ignominy. She is dead now, I am thankful. Last year I went to the play in Paris. They were giving one of those horrible, vulgar vaudevilles, full of half-dressed people, and horrid, hideous songs and jokes ; it was all about a burlesque actress, a sort of apotheosis of her. There were lots of people in the theatre ; and some one pointed out to me, in one of the boxes, the woman who had made my friend so unhappy. She was what people call a lady, quite young, beautifully dressed, with a beautiful, delicate face, and she was laughing and blushing a great deal behind her fan, and looking very happy. It was the first time that I had ever seen her, and I never expected to see her there. I could not take my eyes off her. I can't tell you how I felt : as if a precipice had suddenly opened before me. I shall never forget it. She seemed somehow to be the concentration of what was going on on the stage ; the play seemed to be about her, the songs about her. She seemed to be framed, as it were, beautiful and delicate though she was, in all that indecency and vulgarity, those hideous gestures, that frightful music, those disgusting jokes. And the play seemed to become terrible, tragic, as if some one were being killed somewhere. I don't know how to explain it. But ever since that evening I have understood what a bad woman is."

Dorothy's voice died away, hot and hoarse.

"Did you hear?" Baldwin whispered to Mrs. Blake. "Well; what my cousin has just been saying is a thing which an English novelist would not be allowed to say; he would not be allowed to show us the bad woman in her box; and he would not be allowed, therefore, to show us what was passing in that girl's heart, all the rebellion of outraged love and respect, all that great and holy indignation. And yet, to have seen the contents of Dorothy's heart at that moment, braces our soul, does us more moral good than the sight of all the bad women in Christendom could do us harm; for it means that we have stood for a moment in the presence of the Lord, of the true God, whose name is Love and Indignation."

They got up with Marcel and Dorothy, and walked for a little while silently in the moving luminous gap in the body of the blackish grey mist. All colour seemed removed from out of things: green pastures, on the hills, thick tangles of bluish-green trees in the river-courses between them, patches of ripening grain; all were reduced to the same blackish-grey smoke of the sky, against which stood out, sharply defined and in preternatural blackness, the telegraph posts and wires covered with birds, the circling rooks, the few wind-warped beeches with black trunks and blackened leaves, the long low black walls, or rather lines of heaped-up black stones in the fields. The foreground started into vivid relief and colour: the grass, divided by the lines of black stones, was of Alpine greenness, the heather and ling intensely purple, the oats and barley strangely yellow; but even into this colour (and this was the strangest part of that strange effect) there seemed to enter a quantity of black, as of a thick sprinkling of cinders; the bit of moorland was dabbed with black patches of gorse and withered heather among the pale lilac and the deep purple of the flowers, and shot with the blackness of heather roots and long sere grass; the ripening oats were picked out with a sort of black granulation in the light; the very grass, in its intense greenness, seemed sparkling with the black glint of coal dust, making it but the more vivid and shining in its freshness; the houses were of black stone, the dust of the road, pulverized stone and dried peat, was blackish as if coal had been crushed into it; and all round, as if to emphasize the blackness, as if to show the underlying quality of earth and sky, of grass, and grain, and heather, the inky black was scattered about in the walls which streaked the blackish green of the fields; in the stones which patched the pale violet, the strong purple, land with blackness of stems and sere grass, of the moorland.

"Are you still talking of novels?" asked Baldwin of Dorothy and Marcel.

"I wish no more novels might ever be written," answered Dorothy. "I wish no novels ever had been written. Life is too hideous and melancholy to be painted."

"That is to say, life as painted in 'Une Vie,' my dear child," said Mrs. Blake, feeling her own art attacked.

At that moment, as if to make things complete, there came riding through the lane a little girl on a white horse, emerging out of the mist, entering, taking body in the luminous space in which they seemed to be walking. In that light concentrated between the grey mist, the fair flesh, the blond hair, in long curls, of the child, took, with their grey shadows, their greyish blond high lights, a diaphanous, almost an unearthly, loveliness.

"She looks like a sister of Velasquez's Infanta Margaret," said Marcel, looking back as the little figure on the pony vanished once more in the mist.

"Yes," answered Dorothy, "she is lovely. And that is what is so horrible in life, and in all art which deals with life, instead of dealing merely with visible things; this, that while there is scarcely a thing which, at some moment, is not worth painting, not a light in which something does not look beautiful and impressive, in life, on the other hand, we may go on for hours and miles seeing only uninteresting and ugly moral sights. Such a morning as this, with the fog and the smoke, is like death, at first sight; and yet, did you notice how lovely and charming that child looked in the black smoke and mist? But when once we come to moral questions, to life, all is confusion and ugliness: the good people seem so unreasonable and intolerant, their attempts to do good seem so often foolish and mischievous; the people, on the other hand, who understand, and are just and tolerant, seem so half-hearted and useless. There is no satisfaction to be got anywhere. The 'how things are' seems for ever, hopelessly, opposed to the 'how things should be.' If we paint reality, we paint imperfection; if we paint perfection, we paint unreality. I wish, therefore, that people would write only about trees and skies and effects of light. I wish they would give up writing about human beings. I wish they would never write any more novels."

Mrs. Blake laughed. "That is not very encouraging for Monsieur Marcel and me," she said.

"What you say is perfectly true, Dorothy," said Baldwin, "but I think it is a reason that novels should be written, and not the contrary. It is most true that, as you say, the 'how things are' is for ever militating against the 'how things ought to be.' The best people, those with most desire for good, and most self-sacrificing power of attaining it, seem usually also to be those who are most ignorant, most credulous, most blind. The knowledge of what men and women really are, the knowledge of the inevitable sequence of cause and effect which has made them so, of the complication of actions and reactions which necessarily render all changes slow and partial—this comprehension of how things are makes us, we cannot doubt it, gradually cynical and indifferent and passive, deprives us of initiative for good. And yet, without such knowledge, what is the use of the most ardent aspirations? Dealing with the unknown, improvement is rarely attained; and in the attempt to improve, heaven only knows how much additional evil is not created. Surely three-quarters of all the foolish regulations which hamper life, divert it into unnatural channels, and create vice and misery, have been framed by people wishing to do good, and believing they could do it. It is sad to see this double waste—the waste of knowledge which becomes conducive merely to cynical indifference; and the waste of generous impulse which results merely in abortive or mischievous attempts. And from the mediæval saints, who, ignoring the baser necessities of human nature, aimed at impossible ideals of conduct and produced new evils, bodily and mental, in trying to cure old ones; from these to the good people who try, from some interpretation of Scripture, to prevent a man marrying a woman with whom he has no blood connection, and who may be the fittest guardian of his and her dead sister's children, a good half of human history consists in such abortive and mischievous results of generous feeling. On the other hand, as I have said, those who see and understand are too apt to acquiesce. When we perceive how naturally all manner of base things have come about, how difficult it is to get rid of them, how universal they are, and how inextricably interwoven in normal life, we get sad and useless for effort. Besides, we see, what they others do not, the good things which are mixed up with the bad, and we are paralyzed; we sympathize with the good in faulty mankind, and condone its faults; above all, we are angered in our sense of logic and justice, by the unreasonableness, the injustice of the people of noble aims: they ask so much that is impossible, they spurn so much that is good; they are so stupid and uncharitable often. And yet, without them, how little improvement in life, and how little nobility in it! Does not the whole of the world's life consist in the balancing of these two tendencies? and is not that balancing, at present, a conflict, a terrible waste and misery? If only, instead of conflicting, they could be united, they would be as fruitful of good as, in their conflict, they are fruitful of evil. To make the shrewd and tolerant a little less shrewd and tolerant; to make the generous and austere a little more sceptical and easy-going—this seems to me pretty well the chief problem of life; and also the chief use of the novel. But, for that attempt to be possible, the novel itself must represent a compromise between the knowledge of how things are, and the desire for how things ought to be ; the novel must represent what there is of good in the scientific spirit of France, and what there is of good in the moral spirit of England."

"I don't know if it is you or the weather, but I feel less dismal about life, Baldwin," said Dorothy.

"It is the weather," answered Mrs. Blake.

The mist had gradually thinned, the luminous space about them had widened, the greyish-black vapour, gradually turning white, was rising into clouds, leaving the tree-tops distinct and green against a rift of moist, bright sky.

THE VALUE OF THE IDEAL.

THE VALUE OF THE IDEAL.

The old painter smiled in his beard: that gently ironical smile which meant that age had brought with it scepticism, but scepticism of the reality only of mean and foolish things.

"My dear boy," he said, laying his delicate veined white hand on Carlo's shoulder, "when you are as old as I, you will have given over being a realist."

The obvious retort was that, not being so old as Sir Anthony, he could not be an idealist; for, to Carlo's mind, saturated with cosmopolitan modernnesses, idealism appeared in connection with the mahogany and rep furniture, the crinolines of thirty years ago. But, irritated though he was at having his ideas measured by an obsolete standard; and also at being, as he considered, twitted with his youth, he could not even feel the temptation of cheap sarcasm towards Sir Anthony; the young realist unconsciously bowed before something ideal in this old man's personality. And the bitter thing was that Sir Anthony's smile, although the smile of the champion of a false æsthetical theory, had nevertheless a power of scattering his triumphant realistic arguments.

"But why," cried the young man, the curious arch-modern outcome of mixed nationalities—"why should any one want idealism nowadays? Surely there has been enough of it in the past! Surely people have shown us sufficiently often how things don't look; it is time that they show us a little how they do look! Idealism nowadays," he went on, delighted at recovering possession of his favourite arguments—"idealism is a waste of time and energy. Why should a man paint us his conception of an olive tree, a stick with five little branches, each with five little leaves and five little berries upon it; and his conception of marigolds, little yellow paper stars arranged like the pattern of a Persian rug, when he could paint us the reality of olives and marigolds—such a reality as that?"

Baldwin, who had been watching the beautiful ironical face framed in white hair and beard; and the eager, dark young face, full of energetic curiosity, like that of some frescoed Italian of the Renaissance, turned his head in the direction whither Carlo was pointing. They were sitting on the wall of Sir Anthony's Tuscan villa, the foxglove in the chinks forming rich crimson and yellow dabs on the inky-black stone beneath them; the pomegranate blossoms standing out, in luminous scarlet, against the distant, constantly receding, and yet all-pervading blue luminousness of the sky over their heads. Below stretched the farm-lands, a shimmer of half-ripe corn, of pale green vines hanging in garlands from maple to maple, of bluish-green reed tufts, enfolded in the smoke-like blue haze of the hill-side. And opposite, catching the sun, was a raised plantation of olive-trees, their smooth, twisted trunks shining like silver, their silvery leafage, more feather-like for pale new sprouts and spray of white blossom, detaching itself delicately and clearly from the bright air in which it seemed to swim, as the light, pale weeds swim in the transparent water of a stream. And at the gnarled roots of the olives, clustered, golden, against the grey, the thick growth of orange marigolds.

"It is downright wastefulness to go in for idealism in the face of such reality as this," repeated Carlo; "to give us, with the brush, a mere symbol, a mere suggestion, a thing which any writer could do as well with the pen, when we might be given the real appearance of the thing, which only the painter can give."

The old painter of strange, gorgeous, symbolic creatures drummed lightly on the warm black stone of the wall, where, every now and then, darted a bright-green lizard amongst the fallen pomegranate petals.

"You speak of wastefulness," he said, slowly; "have you ever asked yourself whether realistic art is not wasteful?"

"In giving us the picture of what we have already got?" answered Carlo quickly, ready to crush this conventional argument. "Yes, I know idealists say that; but it is not wasteful, because there is no wastefulness in teaching us to see in the picture of a thing the characteristic qualities which we may have missed seeing in the original; or in giving us once more, greatly enhanced, the pleasure which we had already received from perceiving them in the original. No, I think this is no argument against simply showing us reality, because no wastefulness is really proved."

"My plea against realism has nothing to do with that," answered Sir Anthony. "You were saying just now that idealism means wastefulness, because idealism (according to you, at least) implies that painting, instead of giving us what can be given only by itself, attempts to give us such things as are better given to us by literature—was not that your argument? Well, I want to show you that realism, on its side, can result, and indeed has resulted, in just the same sort of wastefulness. Your realistic painters, the French and Italian particularly, go upon the principle that art has the power, by means of faithful representation, of giving us pleasure out of the slightest things; is it not so?"

"Yes; and the principle is, I think, a true one,"

replied Carlo, proudly. "Modern art has proved to us that a thing too trifling to be mentioned, a little dust and sky, for instance, will make a picture, and a picture which may be delightful; and that, once outside the domain of absolute æsthetic satisfaction in the beautiful, there is nothing so trumpery, vulgar, nay, ugly, that it cannot serve at least to display the technical skill, the individuality of eye and mind and hand, of the painter. Do you remember Manet's picture of the 'Bar of the Folies Bergères?' Nothing more trumpery, or even more vulgar, could be imagined than the coloured liqueur-bottles and glasses on the counter, the wet cab-roofs in the distance; and yet there was interest, and even beauty, in those coloured bottles and glasses, in those wet, blue, shining cab-roofs."

Sir Anthony nodded.

"Exactly," he remarked. "Well, modern writers of the sort calling themselves realists have recognized this power in modern painting, nay, in some instances they seem to have guessed the intention of art, and to have forestalled it. Hence, especially on the Continent, where realism reigns supreme, a deluge of minute descriptions which the mind strains to realize, and which, realizing, it most often loathes. Hence, what is even worse, the mania for the minute enumeration of the colours and shapes of things as seen at a given moment; all action in time carefully left out, because action in time cannot be shown in a picture. Every visible object in a room or a street catalogued, as if instant death would follow on the smallest omission. Everything there, appallingly there, except—except, what do you think? Except those things which are the essential, unique property of literature: action, feeling, sequence of ideas, association of impression—the things, in short, which a painter cannot give, and a writer can."

"Modern descriptive passages," said Baldwin, "always remind me of the fury of an old music-master of mine with the stupidity of those fellows who make piano-arrangements of operas; he used to point out to me how they carefully copied into their versions every little note of the full orchestral score, forgetting that the note which, given by an insignificant instrument in the midst of a whole orchestra, merges into the general effect without being individually perceived, will, if given on the piano, and therefore in perfect equality with the other notes, acquire a value, a distracting, fatiguing, impertinent value, which was never intended by the composer."

"That's just it," answered Sir Anthony; "these young realistic writers think it necessary to transcribe all those things which the artist transcribes, forgetting that he copies them on to his canvas, that is to say, on to a second reality, which affects the mind with much the same graduation as the original reality; whereas the writer copies them directly on to the consciousness of the reader, where they have a very different value. They are thrust upon him, like the unnecessary notes of the piano-arrangement, instead of going thereby to form part of a vague general impression. They are treated as if they were the equals of those more important items which the mind has instinctively selected and re-arranged in its reproduction of the real scene. The result is complete falseness of perceptional and emotional values; the impression produced is crowded, out of perspective, utterly crude and glaring. And this is not all. There is the much worse result of falsifying our impressions by leaving out, or, at all events, clogging and checking, those effects which only words can produce, and which are as inevitable and indispensable to our intellectual perception of things as are the shadows, gradations of tints, and the hundred and one similar details, to our visual perception of them. To leave out, in a description, the action we understand, the emotion we guess at, the feelings we ourselves share, is as false in point of fact as to leave out in painting the ground upon which people move, the light in which they are seen; indeed, it is even falser, since what is shown to our eyes, however badly, we do actually see; but what is shown badly to our mind we do not see at all. I have ventured to make these remarks," added the old painter, subsiding from the excitement of unwonted discussion to his usual gentle and delicately ironical manner, "because you accused idealism of being wasteful, of doing the thing which need not be done, and omitting the thing which requires doing. It seems to me, so far as I can judge, that modern realistic description is itself an instance of this mode of proceeding."

Carlo rose from the wall.

"You must give me time to muster my thoughts, Master," he said. "I feel as if you had bowled me over; and yet—and yet—" he added, laughing, "I feel as if I were a realist still."

The old painter strolled along the grassy path, powdered over with hemlock, between the low sweeping garlands of green vines, accompanying his two friends out of the villa grounds.

"You will not always remain a realist, take my word for it," he said, with that curious smile in the curls of his beard, as he stood under the ivied penthouse gate, looking after Baldwin and Carlo strolling out into the corn-fields, which shimmered and throbbed, all a hum and a buz with insects, in the yellow afternoon sun.

The two young men walked along for a moment in silence, which the half English, half Italian, and wholly cosmopolitan lad was the first to break.

"I don't know what to think about it," he said to Baldwin. "I know that my portfolio is crammed with manuscript descriptions of which I was very proud ten minutes ago, and which exactly answer to the Master's account of everything that a description should not be: pages and pages of inventory of tints and shapes, and effects of light without a scrap of human interest about them. And yet, at the same time, I feel that there's sophistry somewhere; and that although my descriptions, and every one else's nowadays, may be all wrong, Sir Anthony's pictures are not all right."

"Sir Anthony's pictures are all wrong for the selfsame reason that your descriptions are all wrong, my dear Carlo;" answered Baldwin; "and, what is more, his attack upon your school of literature is well founded, for the same reason that your attack on his school of painting is well founded also. Both of you are theoretically for each art doing the particular sort of work which it does better than the other arts; and both of you are practically for your own art attempting the work which it does less well. He tries to produce literary effects in painting, and you try to produce pictorial effects in literature."

"You think, then," said Carlo, "that the Master was merely carrying the warfare into the enemy's camp, when he argued that realistic art is just as wasteful as idealistic; that he was merely retorting about a minor point? You don't think that what he said really affects the question of the superiority of idealism or realism?"

"I think," replied Baldwin, "that Sir Anthony is

a remarkably clever man, who knows how to get the better in an argument; but I think that, like most artists, he can reason only in self-defence. After all, he merely attacked you upon the very same point upon which you had attacked him: you had demonstrated that idealism, or what you consider idealism, is occasionally wasteful; he demonstrated that one could say just as much about realism."

"That's true," said Carlo, cheerfully: "what he said proved nothing against the theory of realism. It's very silly of me to have let myself be shut up. I suppose these old idealists are full of little dodges of attack and defence like this."

Baldwin laughed.

"You feel as if you were up to all these little dodges, now, don't you?" he asked; "as if you could demolish poor Sir Anthony and the ideal for good and all?"

"Why do you say that? I am not so conceited, indeed. But I think you could do the demolishing, and I should like to look on. Will you tackle him this evening? Oh, do, Baldwin, do please demolish the ideal in my presence."

Carlo's eagerness to become his disciple, his curious mental attitude, at once modest and militant, like that of one of Plato's youths, greatly tickled Baldwin.

"But what will you say to me if I answer that I can't demolish idealism, Carlo; and if I confess to you why I can't demolish it?"

"Why can't you, Baldwin? Why? You are not afraid of the Master, surely?"

"I'm not afraid of the Master; I am afraid of you. You will never listen to me again if I tell you why I can't attempt to demolish idealism."

Carlo seized Baldwin's hand.

"Oh, Baldwin," he cried, "please, please tell me!—don't be disagreeable!—please tell me!"

Baldwin laughed as he looked at this eager, humorous young philosopher, trying to wring the drops of wisdom out of him.

"Well, but how shall I put it? Prepare yourself for something very startling and dreadful. I can't demolish the ideal, my dear Charlie, because—because—because, in short, I believe in it myself! I am an idealist, there's for you."

Carlo stopped for a moment, not knowing whether to be amused or perplexed. The young enthusiast for modernness had sought out Baldwin because he had always heard of Baldwin as a man of advanced modernness of views; and he had always a lurking fear, being endowed with a good sense of humour, that his self-chosen guide and philosopher might be taking a pleasure in seeing how much the disciple could be made to swallow on the score of modernness.

"You are making fun of me, Baldwin," he said, his dark Renaissance face perplexed with an incipient laugh, as he mechanically dissected a lace-like star of hemlock-flower.

"I am not making fun of you," said Baldwin, "I am merely saying the truth. I believe, for my part, in idealism quite as much as Sir Anthony."

"No, I can't believe that you are serious." exclaimed Carlo; "don't be so cruel as to tease me. How can you believe in idealism—you who are always saying that we must face the reality of things? How can you, who are always refusing to submit to arbitrary standards, admit of art which does things by a compromise, making them a little less real here, a little more real there? Nonsense! I remember how you answered the Master the other day, when he said that ideal portrait-art was the representation of the individual as he never is at any given moment, but as you get him by striking an average."

"I certainly don't believe in Sir Anthony's idealism," answered Baldwin, stopping to light his cigarette; "but can't you conceive any idealism besides his? To me idealism has value only inasmuch as it develops the resources of art and enables art to do more for us. Now, idealism, such as Sir Anthony understands it, does just the reverse: it gives a scientific formula instead of an artistic manifestation; it transfers the necessities of our mode of thought to the mode of existence of real things. An abstraction of a man such as he would like to paint is no better than a diagram in a book of anatomy."

"I know; that is what you said to him. And

what I can't understand is that, having said that, you should now stick up for just that same sort of deliberate alteration of things in conformity to some abstract notion."

Baldwin shook his head.

"Not at all," he answered. "Make up your mind to this, that when I speak of idealism I mean something quite different from what Sir Anthony means. To me, idealism does not imply deliberate alteration in conformity to an abstract notion; it does not even necessarily imply alteration of any sort whatever. It means merely the attempt, conscious or unconscious, to obtain for the soul a special sort of satisfaction, or something approaching to such a special sort of satisfaction, which may, according to the case, be obtained by mere selection, or by mere accident, or, again, may be obtained by what you call the alteration of things. For me the ideal means simply the sufficiently beautiful, the something that satisfies, the great desideratum; and the desire for this perfect satisfaction, the quest of this supreme desideratum, is what I call idealism."

They were strolling along through the fields, which the sun filled with a vague golden green haze before hiding behind the high Apennine peaks all round. The leaves of the vine-supporting poplars quivered like flakes of greenish gold in the sunshine; the poppies flamed like drops of scarlet fire by the road-side, and here and there a clump of rye, no longer green, but not yet yellow, stood out in the bright light, each separate long silvery blade and lustrous bristly ear seeming to twist and erect itself like wire which rebounds.

"But why call it idealism?" asked Carlo. "What has the desire for beauty to do with the idealism of men like Sir Anthony, that you should confuse them together? If you want something perfectly satisfying, something supremely desirable, why seek for it outside reality? Doesn't an evening like this one, in such a spot, nay, in a hundred such spots, give you all you can wish: does it not satisfy you? Or rather—how shall I express it?—does it not give you something more almost than satisfaction, a sort of half nostalgic feeling, due not to deficiency in the object, but to deficiency in our own power of enjoying, to the strain on our feelings of taking in so much delight, the sort of feeling which makes all beautiful music pathetic? Don't you feel that the reality of this moment gives you that?"

As he spoke, and the low light enveloped his brown face in a sort of aureole, the lad really looked as if he felt that strain of incapacity to take in so much pleasure.

"Certainly I feel that," answered Baldwin, as they walked along; "but did I not tell you just now that this satisfaction, which I call ideal, can come to us by mere accident, that we can receive it, and do receive it constantly, ready made at the hands of nature? Why, it always seems to me that the artist of landscape, the man who has the keenest desire for the superlative satisfaction of external things, may require to do but little save study, and nothing more than select. Hills and valleys, and light and sky and plants, are just as beautiful as we can conceive them; a painter need only bring home their beauty to us, or pick out the rarest instances of that beauty. There is so much physical beauty in the world that one might think that, except as regards the human form, we might almost dispense with art; or, rather, that art is scarcely more than the result of the joy which we have had, its multiplication by its very richness, the means of fixing these joys for ourselves, or of pointing them out to others."

"I suppose that is what Ruskin meant by saying that art is the expression of our pleasure in God's works," mused Carlo.

He had sat down on a bank of ferns, under solitary chestnut tree, which shed its white tassels on the moss.

The sun was just sinking over a high mountain; a little more and it would be completely hidden behind it. Its rays, thrown up in great dust-like beams, among the grey clouds above, expanded over the mountain side, veiled it, nay, rather drowned it, in a broad, luminous, grey pallor, a wash of lustreless smoke-like silver, in which all shapes of trees were lost, and only the deep embosomings of the hills appeared as unsubstantial blue depths on that silvery unsubstantial faintness. Against the spectral luminous grey of this smoky hill-side stood out the luminous tops of the tremulous poplars by the river, a tuft of uncertain shimmer; and, spread on their scintillating clear silveriness, the tall bearded stems of a ripening rye-field, visible almost separately or interweaving like cobweb in the sunshine. And in front, in the immediate foreground, the tall silver poplars (which sing the same note in the southern quire of colour as the lady birches do in the north) intertwined, in large simple lines, their dazzling white trunks, their dazzling silver branches, against the luminous grey smoke of the mountain side, against the shimmer of the silver sky.

"Art," said Baldwin, "is, as Ruskin says, the expression of man's pleasure in the works of God. But art is also, and quite as much, the expression of man's dissatisfaction with them."

"I don't follow your meaning, Baldwin."

"I mean," answered Baldwin, "that art is simply the practical result of a hunger of our soul, which the real things of this world may or may not happen to satisfy."

"At that rate," remarked Carlo, "art would give us merely the same sort of satisfaction as nature."

"As nature sometimes gives us, mind you, but as nature frequently also refuses."

"Then art is, according to you, in a position somewhat analogous to cooking: it helps out nature. We paint a picture or compose a symphony because the sights and sounds of nature are not sufficient to satisfy our spiritual hunger, exactly on the same principle that we cook a piece of meat because there are not enough apples or oranges to live off—is that it?"

Baldwin laughed. "And also because we are so constituted that a diet of nothing but raw fruit would make us ill, my dear Carlo."

Carlo leaned back on the bank, and looked up for a moment at the green fans of narrow, sun-permeated leaves and the tassels of white blossom which the Spanish chestnut tree printed, like some huge Japanese ornaments, on to the pale blue sky.

"Then allow me to say that you are contradicting yourself," he remarked, after a minute. "You now say that we can no more be satisfied with the mere beauty of nature than we can be satisfied with mere raw fruit. You compare art with the process of cooking in so far as it changes the quality of our mental food. And yet you seemed to imply that the use of art is merely the same as the use of beautiful nature. If that is the case, why should not nature suffice?"

"I certainly think that the function of art is the same as the function of beautiful nature. They both feed our soul in exactly the same way. As to your culinary image, I can explain in a minute what strikes you as a contradiction in my views."

"No, don't!" exclaimed Carlo—"not yet, please, because I think I can see my own way. I think I have got hold of a train of thought; I am not sure of it yet, but I want to catch hold of it. I think I see where you are wrong; I think I can hit the mark. May I try, Baldwin?"

Baldwin laughed. There was something very pleasant in this young creature's delight in intellectual movement quite independent of all personal vanity or personal bias—the delight of a young horse galloping round a paddock.

"Don't nip my idea in the bud, please, please, Baldwin!" he went on, "but let me explain. I think that, just as there is a difference between cooked food and raw food, so there is a difference between the pleasure we derive from nature and the pleasure we derive from art. Haven't you left one item out of your calculation? Haven't you forgotten that art is the expression of the mind of the artist?"

"I have not forgotten it any more than I have forgotten the other great truth that cooked food is the expression of the mind of the cook, my dear boy."

"There you are making fun of me again, Baldwin! I think it is very cruel, when I am trying hard to understand. Do you mean to deny that every work of art owes the greater number of its constituent qualities, of what makes us recognize it, to the peculiar qualities of the artist who has produced it?"

"To the peculiar artistic qualities, certainly; but can you deny that the constituent qualities of a dish are not due to the culinary qualities of the cook? I bring in your favourite culinary simile once more, because I want to lay particular stress upon the fact that the peculiarities of a work of art are due to the peculiarities of the machinery which produces it, which machinery is the artistic organization of the artist. If the artist is a colourist, colour will be the predominant quality; if a draughtsman, drawing; if a melodist, melody, and so forth. In this I don't at all see how a work of art differs from a natural object: that also owes its peculiarities to the causes which produce it. If those hills are rounded in the particular way which, as you express it, makes us recognize them, I suppose it is because they were produced by a geological process which results in rounding; if this soil is red, I suppose it is because there is a certain amount of iron in it; if those mists take that particular silvery tone, I suppose it is because the light strikes upon them in the way which makes mists silvery. All one can say is that things answer to their producing cause; whether that producing cause be what we call a natural force or a mental force seems to me to make no difference in the value which the result may have, in the artistic enjoyment which they afford us."

Carlo was silent for an instant.

"That is just where I think you are a little bit

sophistical. You talk of a work of art as the produce of artistic machinery, as you would talk of natural effects, like the shapes of these hills, the colour of these mists, and so forth, being the produce of natural machinery. You suppress one fact, which is that the artistic machine to which we owe a picture, a statue, a symphony, or a poem, happens to be a man, a thing with consciousness, sympathies, a character, opinions, and life, a whole individuality finding its expression in his work."

"I suppress nothing of the sort, because nothing of the sort exists to be suppressed. Don't look at me as if you thought I was joking, Charlie; but let me explain. I said that a work of art is produced by an artistic mechanism, which is the artist. Into this artistic mechanism, this artist, there enters only so much of the peculiarities of the man of whom this artist is a part as can possibly influence the work of art. You may cook a piece of meat on a fire made of oak branches or of oak carvings by Grinling Gibbons; the roast beef may be better or worse for the wood being dry or damp, hard or soft, but the fact of the wood being carved into an ornamental garland won't make the smallest culinary difference And similarly with art. The fact of your Michael-Angelo being a man of haughty and melancholy and violent character may account in some measure for the haughty and melancholy and violent faces which he draws or models; but the domestic relations and political views of the man have nothing to do with his artistic work."

"But the domestic relations and political views of Dante have a great deal to do with the 'Vita Nuova' and the 'Divine Comedy.'"

"Did I not say just now that the peculiarities of the man enter into the artist in proportion as they can affect the art? The very stuff of which the 'Vita Nuova' and the 'Divine Comedy' are made happens to consist of what you call domestic relations and political opinions; of course, therefore, the particular nature of those of Dante comes into play and is expressed. But this does not alter the fact that in a great many cases the man does not, and cannot, enter into the artist; and that it is therefore no more necessary that we should see the traces of an artist's human emotions in his works than that we should find a proportion of iron in every sort of soil. The iron is sometimes there and sometimes not there, but its presence or its absence does not affect the question whether the soil is or is not worth looking at and painting. And it is exactly the same with art: the fact of finding in it the expression of the artist's nature has a scientific, but not an artistic, value. This theory of art as an expression of an artist's personality is due, I think, to our constantly viewing art through the medium of critical literature, which is, indeed, specifically, the expression of the author's mind. All that art can show us, unless indeed it take the artist's feelings as its absolute subject matter, is that each particular artist sees things somewhat differently from his fellows, has preferences, and reproduces in a different way the object of these preferences. I prefer fair people, you prefer dark ones; I paint on rough canvas with a big brush and a liking for cool colours, you paint on smooth canvas with a fine brush and a liking for warm colours: these are really the principal things which a picture can tell us about the man who has painted it. And therefore I say that we have no right to consider that beauty in art affects us, artistically, at all differently from beauty in nature."

Carlo mused for a moment.

"I don't think you are right," he said; "there still remains, for all that you have been saying, a something in art which does not exist in nature. Do you remember Goethe says somewhere that art is that which gives form? Now, if it gives form, it must evidently give form to something—there must be a contents, a thought contained within this form."

"Art certainly gives form. And do you know to what it gives form?—to its constituent elements, line, colour, light and shade, or sound. The mistake is to suppose, by a false analogy, that this form necessarily encloses something; a mistake due to a metaphor which has quite passed into the language of æsthetics, where we are always talking of contents, of that blessed German invention, *Inhalt*. Now it so happens that the non-artistic matter of art is in no respect a contents. That is a false metaphorical expression originating probably in the time when art was looked upon as symbolic, its forms being a mere shorthand writing ; and when consequently art, like the symbols of ordinary writing, like a letter or a book, got spoken of as having a contents. The form does not contain anything—remember that. It may have attached to it the more or less arbitrary thing called a subject, or it may—I mean the form—be constituted of elements fraught with emotional or imaginative suggestion ; but in neither of these two cases does the form contain the subject in the same way as the body was supposed to contain the soul. The elements of the non-imitative arts are fraught with emotional and imaginative suggestion. In the case of music it is the direct nervous power of tone and movement, and the blurred and confused associations of feeling with it ; a suggestion due to the fact that tone, rhythm, and so forth, are recognized dimly and unconsciously as having been modes or concomitants of expression. In the case of the imitative arts it is the power of evoking past and distant images and trains of thought owing to the fact of the things used by the artist having been seen before in reality, and suggesting therefore the significance which they had therein. But this emotional and imaginative suggestiveness engrained in the elements used by the artist exist equally outside the art, and they may either be deliberately used or deliberately neutralized or merely overlooked by the artist ; and whether he deliberately employ or merely neglect these suggestive elements, is a question outside the jurisdiction of his special art, although within that kingdom of emotion and imagination which surrounds it. Some of the art which is most absolutely art is wholly without intellectual contents; you must have remarked this yourself."

"It is true as to pattern art, and colour art, generally," answered Carlo, hesitating. "I suppose there is really no intellectual contents, no *Inhalt*, in a Persian carpet, a Moorish lustre plate, or in the things which come nearest to that—the pattern mosaics of San Vitale and Galla Placidia at Ravenna. And I suppose there are certain Venetian pictures which are pretty well in the same case. Do you remember the little picture of the death of Sophonisba, by Paul Veronese, of which I am so fond? The pale girl in the shot iris and opal dress being stabbed by a red-capped negro, the indifferent young man in scarlet, the indifferent old man in shot purple and yellow—all these are as simply and entirely so many notes of colour as are the pale sky and the opalescent clouds. The absolute negation of interest on the part of actors and artist in what is going on makes it perfectly impossible to feel the slightest interest or emotion connected with this picture. I suppose you would say, Baldwin, that such a picture as this appeals to us in the same way as a sunset or an evening sky?"

"Not only this picture, but every picture, in so far as it is a picture. Some of the noblest works of linear art (for you have been speaking of colour), not merely arabesques of carving or stalactite of architectural decoration, but actual human figures, appeal to us, and can appeal to us, only as form: the draped fragments from the Parthenon, the Belvedere Mercury, the naked men of Signorelli, the draped virgins of Andrea—all these appeal to us as exclusively by their form as does a pattern in lace. It is useless to object that they represent something, namely, men and women; we perceive that only as part of the fact of their being form, and form only. In none of these things, if we enjoy them, do we seek for an *Inhalt*."

"Don't you think you are turning artistic enjoyment into something rather soulless, Baldwin?"

"My dear Carlo, I am merely arguing that we enjoy art in the same way that we enjoy nature; and I have never heard it called soulless to enjoy nature. Ask yourself where is the difference? Don't the marvellous peacock harmonies, the branching, spreading, and interlacing sea blue, and sea green, and russet gold of those Ravenna mosaics, appeal to the same faculties as the even more marvellous colour harmonies of the peacock's tail and breast; don't the sun-permeated flesh and shot draperies of Veronese's pictures affect us exactly as would the sun-permeated flesh, the shot draperies of some living woman; and don't the throat and neck and head of the youths in Signorelli's frescoes arrest our attention as would the similar throat and neck and head of a beautiful real youth? We do not seek for an explanation of the how and why, for an expression of the artist's nature, in natural things; nor for an intellectual contents of their beauty; and, as a matter of fact, we do not look for any of these things at the moment that we are really enjoying art. And therefore I say that art merely adds to the stock of beauty which nature has given us: it completes and multiplies it when deficient."

"You may be right, so far," remarked Carlo, half assentingly. "But I don't see how what you have been saying just now bears upon the question of realism and idealism."

They were strolling once more along the grassy path, between the compact masses of tall dark green hemp, and the heavy garlands of vines hanging from tree to tree. The sun was now hidden behind the high mountain peaks; the valley was filled with a greyish-green mist, a dewy freshness, as of all this young green, and with the vibration of the long, quavering note of the cicalas in the trees and the crickets in the grass.

"What I have been saying, namely, that the beautiful things of art give us the same sort of emotion as the beautiful things of nature, supplement them so to speak; what I have been trying to prove to you, my dear Charlie, bears upon the other question because I told you before, that our soul is for ever craving after something sufficiently beautiful, something satisfying, which something I call the ideal."

" But why should you call that satisfaction ideal ? " insisted the lad, to whom the word was particularly obnoxious.

" In contradistinction to the real; because the enjoyment of this particular quality, and the desire for it, are independent of the fact of its existing in reality, or of its being artificially made up. Because, more particularly, the standard by which we measure this desideratum is not outside ourselves, but inside ; not in real things, but in our feelings."

" Upon my word, Baldwin, one would think that you believed in innate ideas!" exclaimed Carlo.

" I don't believe the least in innate ideas," answered Baldwin, amused at the young man's look of horror ; " but I don't believe either that our minds and feelings are merely whitewashed walls, on which the external world projects its magic-lantern figures. Every real impression that we receive decomposes and leaves behind it a greater or lesser amount of fragments of itself : broken-down impressions, sometimes a mere minute dust, which live on within us. And the aggregate, constantly shifting, of all this living dust of broken impressions, lives and has its necessities of life, its sympathies and desires. In speaking of the æsthetic or imaginative sides of our life," went on Baldwin, "we are apt to think of them as composed of distinct impressions, voluntary and well-defined, the seeing of a picture or piece of architecture, the reading of a poem, the hearing of a song or symphony. Nothing could be further from the fact. Our æsthetic life goes on within us, or if not constantly in fact, constantly at all events potentially; and in this the new sights or sounds play no more part—nay, I think, play less—than do new facts in our intellectual life. As this latter is an almost permanent process—a process of constant weighing and comparing and classifying of our ideas—so likewise is our æsthetic life an almost permanent process, infinitely vaguer and more delicate, and, to a great extent, unconscious, a kaleidoscopic shifting and rearranging of all pleasant impressions of colour, sound, form, or emotion. The fact is, that we live much more in the past of our æsthetic impressions than in their present: our æsthetic life consists really in the fluctuations, the movements, of these, if I may call them so, living molecules of æsthetic feeling; it consists of the action and reaction produced within us by any new impression that we receive. It is for this reason that the value of art must not be measured, as I said, by conformity to a reality which is outside us, but by conformity to these feelings within us. Remember, what you realists forget, that there is not merely the real constitution of external nature to be taken into account;

there is, what is much more important, the real nature of our soul."

For a moment Carlo did not answer.

"Then, according to you," he said, as they walked along a narrow lane between the ridges of corn and hemp, where goats and sheep nibbled at the fern and honeysuckle; "according to you, art is there, so to speak, for the express purpose of gratifying the fantastic requirements of this fantastic living mass of heterogeneous broken-down impressions within us— art is not there to register our knowledge of reality?"

" Only incidentally, so far as reality is, after all, the storehouse whence the majority of our impressions come. Art registers our knowledge of reality when reality happens to coalesce with that which constitutes, as I have said, our æsthetic life; when, in short, reality is what we term beautiful."

"But art is continually doing the very opposite, registering reality pure and simple, merely because it is reality, Baldwin."

"Art does it, and does it especially at present; but to do so is, whenever it happens, a new, a false start, due to the mixing up of scientific interests, or to the usurpations of technical knowledge or skill, the usurpations of the *power of doing*. But you will find that while left to itself, while in possession of unexhausted means, and while absolutely spontaneous, all art tends, as Pater has said, to the condition of music. I don't know what Pater exactly meant by that remark."

"I think he was probably merely repeating Hegel's old theories about music being the romantic art, and all other arts tending towards the romantic condition," interrupted Carlo.

"I dare say he did. But the saying to me expresses a far more important truth: all art tends to the condition of music, that is to say, to the condition of producing freely, with reference not to a pre-existing reality, but to the desires of our soul."

"At that rate," answered Carlo, incredulously, "a perfect piece of artificiality, a monstrosity, like the opera, is the typical form of art."

Baldwin was not at all put out by this remark.

"Exactly so," he said; "and so, from the Greek tragedy to the great ceremonial altar-pieces of the Venetians, where madonnas and saints and real people sit and stand among clouds and lamps and garlands, none taking heed of his companions, all the greatest and most spontaneous art has been. And this is exactly what I want to prove to you, and what I shall prove to you in five minutes, I hope—I mean that realistic art is an after-thought, an artificial growth; and idealistic, unreal art, a direct, spontaneous one. I hope we may be in time for the demonstration of this fact."

And Baldwin nodded in the direction of the village towards which they were walking, its semicircle of black walls, overtopped by houses and a ruined castle and belfry, and open loggias, nestling among the poplars and vines of the hill-side, against the ultramarine of distant mountains, like the background of some picture by Cima or Bellini.

"Where are we going?" asked Carlo.

"You shall see," answered Baldwin. "To something which will, I hope, illustrate my theory."

The lane was now steep and roughly paved, between banks where the lilac mint and starry hemlock grew beneath trellisses of delicate green vines, and high box edges, through the gaps in which you caught a distant glimpse of hills, a sheen of mulberry and wheat and vines, burnished golden green by the sun, which had not yet disappeared in that wider part of the valley. Women with great stacks of freshly-mown grass and clematis and vinetrails on their heads, clattered past them up the paved lane in their light wooden clogs; little brown boys and girls, barefoot, bare-armed, and bare-legged, drove sheep and lazy grey cows down from the village to browse along the road-side. From the little crown of fortified houses, bristling with towers, came the jangle of bells. The time for work was over; on to the fields, the lanes, the farmyards which they passed, peacefulness seemed to descend, permeating, like rain, with the golden mist of the sunset.

"Such idealism, such artificiality," went on Baldwin, "will, you may object, shock us? We think so, but the event proves the contrary. However much we may appreciate the reality of Zola, we care none the less for the unreality of Shakespeare. And why? Simply because the faculties appealed to by realism are not the same that are appealed to by idealism: the one have reference to what exists—are scientific, analytic; the others are creative, are longings of our nature. To these longings of our nature things are right, quite independently of any prototype they may or may not possess in reality; they are right, in the sense that a pattern, a wilfully altered, composed arrangement of lines and colours, is right to the æsthetic sense. That people in great passion should use the language of Lear or Hamlet is absolutely incorrect to our perception of what is; but it is all right to our desires, which, after all, are the best judges of what they want. Nor are such desires unreasonable. They attempt to combine, by means of one art, effects existing scattered in our soul. Thus in the balcony scene of 'Romeo and Juliet,' where the words of the lovers give us not merely the impression of their own sentiment, but also of that sentiment which is awakened in us by the knowledge that they are in a garden, and in the presence of dawn, the poetry merges the thing actually presented to our mind with the impressions which that object finds dormant already in it, and wakes up with its presence. In this way the garden scene, objectively false in the sense that no two people would have spoken in that way, becomes subjectively most correct, embodying all the confused artistic elements in ourselves. Similarly," went on Baldwin, as they clambered up under the high walls of the fortified village with foxglove and wild fig growing on their blackness, "similarly with all that which I should call the decorative and musical effects introduced into the Shakespearian drama; they are perfectly true to our state of mind. Have you never remarked how the thought of heroism, love, misfortune, brings with it a perfect train of sights and sounds? Except in our scientific moods, we feel about Napoleon (when his face suddenly turns up on a coin, or, for instance, as when you saw his medal on that old tattered beggar the other day) with a vague splendour as of Mantegna's triumphs, a vague clangour as of Cherubini's music about him. And we easily think of any dear and noble dead person on a wave of music, and with a flutter of flowers and a fragrance of incense. Is there not a sort of framework of I know not what exquisite things—light, music, pattern, nay, rather a visible and audible aureole, round the figure of Dante's Beatrice—nay, almost round any quasi-Beatrice of our own? Our desire for beauty, our sense of it, is not analytic, like that for truth, but synthetic, collecting round one image the gold-dust of a thousand bruised impressions."

They had got to the gate, surmounted by the

Virgin's image, of the little place. Everything seemed very deserted, looking up its steep black street between the high black houses; and at the well outside, under the big chestnut-tree, there remained only two women, one wringing out linen over the big stone tank, the other waiting for her brass pitcher to be filled out of the rudely-carved lion's head. And from a neighbouring group of farm-buildings, hidden among walnut trees and box hedges, came a scraping of fiddles, a quavering of flutes, and gusts of a strange guttural chant.

"We are still in time. I am so glad. I feared it might be all over," exclaimed Baldwin, and he beckoned Carlo to follow him between the black walls of the farm-buildings, to the place whence the sounds came, now broken with loud clapping and shouts, namely, a threshing-floor closed in by boarding and sheets.

"What is all this?" asked Carlo.

"It is the demonstration of my æsthetic theory," answered Baldwin.

II.

The peasant play drew to a close. The last sunbeam grazed the black farm-buildings, with the fishing-nets and silkworm-mats fastened to their walls, making the women's faces behind the sweet basil and red cloves at the windows glow, red spots surrounded by a halo of sun-transfigured hair, against the square of darkness; merging the spectators crammed on the threshing-floor beneath into a light-drowned confusion of auburn and blond of heads, and scarlet and yellow and purple and black of kerchiefs and hats and dresses; creeping, a golden braid, in between the ill-jointed deal boards, the ill-sewn sheets, which closed in the rustic theatre.

The peasant play drew to a close. The tyrant had been defeated; the monster, with very obvious blue trowsers protruding from his furry hide, had been killed; the two hapless princesses rescued. The surviving virtuous persons were heaping benedictions, in the long phrase of archaic chant, upon the conqueror, while the fiddles and flutes and accordion closed in each verse with two or three bars of symphony. When all evil had been set right, and the throne of Ormuz vainly offered to the good knight-errant, when, so to speak, the world of that rustic drama was filled with peace and glory, the principal actors united into a group on the front of the stage, the hero in the middle, and raised up their voices, men and boys, into solemn choral song in praise of virtue. The low yellow light eddied round their heads, transfiguring the make-shift robes and caftans of old rags and patches, the armour of tinsel and tin-foil, into magnificent spots of crimson, and green, and ultramarine, and shimmerings of steel and of gold, while the good Prince, overtopping the rest in his scarlet tunic, beat time slowly with a solemn movement of his beautiful strong bare arms, his blond young head thrown back in beatitude like some painted St. Sebastian; the poplars and young vines behind the boarding quivered golden in the setting sun, and above the stage rose the circle of fortified village, bristling among the green with belfry and towers, and higher up, further yet behind, the ultramarine mountains with delicate clear outline against the white evening sky, flecked here and there with rosy cloud-feathers.

Baldwin and Carlo walked slowly homewards through the fields, while the rapid Italian twilight fell around them over the plantations of ripening corn and vines and serried fresh-scented hemp.

"I understand what you wanted me to see," said Carlo, after a moment; "it was very impressive and beautiful. But art such as that is not possible for us. Those people may pursue, and may attain, that which to them is the ideal, because they are peasants, because to them a story out of Ariosto, or Tasso, or the Lives of the Saints, a few red and blue dresses, a little tinsel, a little scraping of fiddles, constitutes the ideal. But with us it is different. Our purely æsthetic faculties are no longer so clamorous, and our other faculties cry out for reality. We have no great works, at least no great spontaneous works (for I don't count your pre-Raphaelite eclectic decorativeness of Morris and Swinburne) that belong to such a conception of art."

"In the first place," answered Baldwin, "I cannot admit of the justice of treating the art of Swinburne and Morris as mere eclectic, culture stuff; it is as spontaneous, given our civilization into which the past enters so largely, as the art of Chaucer or Spenser was spontaneous at the period when the present ruled much more despotically. But letting alone Swinburne and Morris, and putting aside Tennyson, whom you might also accuse of not being sufficiently spontaneous, there remains in our day one of the greatest monuments of ideal art, great in magnitude and completeness of beauty in the same sense as some temple front or fresco decoration on an immense scale: your own favourite poem, which, by the way, I made you read: 'the Ring and the Book.'"

Carlo almost jumped for astonishment.

"Good gracious, Baldwin!" he exclaimed, "you must be stark staring mad! Why, if ever there was an instance of realism, it is 'the Ring and the Book'! Why, you will be putting down Zola's novels as ideal art next!"

"Zola's novels are not without their bits of idealism every now and then," answered Baldwin. "The girl who suffocates herself with the flowers in 'L'abbé Mouret,' the madness of the husband and wife in the 'Couquête de Plassans'—do you think realism is responsible for that? But to return to 'the Ring and the Book'—do you remember the remarks of your friend, the little Neapolitan novelist, about the chapter called after Caponsacchi? That speech of Caponsacchi's, he said, is the most impossible rhetoric; no man could by any kind of chance hold forth in that way—the whole thing was absolutely unnatural. And, from the realistic point of view, so it is."

"Not at all," cried Carlo. "Caponsacchi is perfectly natural, and every word he utters is perfectly natural, when once we understand the man and the circumstances in which he is placed. . . . That talk with our realist friend made me think over the 'Ring and the Book' very much, and I tried to note down my impressions upon Caponsacchi. I think I may have those notes in the book in my pocket: would you mind—would you just let me read them to you, Baldwin?"

"Certainly, my dear boy, if there is light enough for you to read by."

The enthusiastic young man had pulled a voluminous note-book out of his pocket—a thing in which, with the ardour of a young writer, he noted down every little impression he received.

"May I really read it?" he repeated, with his thumb between the pages. "It won't bore you, Baldwin? I should so much like you to hear that note, because it bears upon the subject, and also because I think it's the best thing I have done, so far."

Baldwin nodded, and they slackened their pace a little.

"To understand its naturalness—I am speaking of Caponsacchi's speech to the judges, you know," began Carlo—"to understand its naturalness, we must understand not merely Caponsacchi in general, but Caponsacchi at that moment. To say that he is a good, pure, and chivalrous man is to understand only part of the matter. The moment when Caponsacchi is called to rescue Pompilia coincides with the climax in the awaking of a singularly earnest, noble, and, above all, singularly reverential and poetical character in a man who has hitherto been (as some natures undoubtedly remain during years) morally dormant and, in a way, only half fledged. The end of his original state of half-life is heralded by a daily increasing discomfort therein; the soul, so to speak, quickening within the body. We have, in a much baser character, a somewhat similar phenomenon in Alfieri; we have it very notably in St. Augustine. When, therefore, this soul is finally awakened, or rather born, it finds among all its surroundings nothing that answers to its cravings, since Caponsacchi has seen religion too close to become an Augustine; and these cravings, ideal in their very essence, become the more so for remaining unsatisfied, for it is the nature of the desire for the always higher never to find satisfaction. At this moment Pompilia crosses his path; his urgent desire for something to which to devote his stored-up moral energies flings, fastens itself upon her, attracted by what to such a nature is a great attraction, the thought of injustice, and stimulated by the inherent tendency of such a late-born soul—which, however much its possessor may have lived before its existence, has not lived long enough to be blunted by reality—the tendency, I mean, to make more beautiful and appealing whatever is so already.

"Pompilia, to this man, is not merely the reality, the merely pure and lovely and injured woman; she is the first thing that may become that which his soul longs for, the ideal; and hence she becomes it. He knows her no better than Dante knows Beatrice; he really sees not her, but the state of mind she produces in himself. A priest seeking for a new god, Caponsacchi's soul bows down to Pompilia; not to the woman, but to the whole splendid moral vision which he has evolved out of this woman. Such is his state when he rescues her. Magnify this, then, by the fact that, despite all his efforts, the victim has succumbed, that the saint has become a martyr, and you have the man's condition when he addresses the judges. Nay more, and more potent: consider that between him and this woman has come death, that the already ideal has become, alas! the unattainable; consider that his poetic and idealizing nature is convulsed, thrown into hundred-fold activity, by the sudden fact of the martyrdom, by the sudden disappearance of the thing for which he has lived from out of the reach of the living ; consider all this, and you will understand that there never was in all poetry a moment more entirely lyric. All care of reality had long ago ceased, aspiration after the unknown perfection had long since begun ; and now, under the stress not merely of love and reverence, but of grief, and in the presence of death, the tempestuous desire for moral perfection, the tempestuous longing for the lost beloved, unchain all other vague desires for beauty, and his soul is swept by them. His speech is henceforth poetry—one might almost say, music. All that is noblest and most lovely rises to the surface : the rare, the exceptional only exists, and leaves below it, far away, the ideas and words of ordinary life. Over the body, transfigured, of Pompilia, he casts the flowers which have bloomed up within his mind; and, as he sinks upon his knees before the martyred saint, he does not speak, he sings."

Carlo's voice trembled as he read the last lines of the note ; and there was a brief interval of silence after he had replaced the note-book in his pocket.

"All that you say about Caponsacchi is very just, my dear Charlie, and I congratulate you on your note. But what I can't at all understand is that, having written that note, you should still imagine that you are a realist."

"I am a realist, but I don't at all deny that there is within us, and even within me, a tormenting desire for the beautiful, the perfect—if you choose, the unreal. But I consider this as one of our misfortunes. The desire merely deludes us, for our ideal can never be attained; we rush after it, neglecting whatever of interest we might find to our right and left, and all that we get is disappointment and bitterness. Prose, prose, everything around us is prose!" he suddenly burst out, angrily beating the grass and flowers from side to side with his stick as he went along; "don't you think, Baldwin, that I have found that out yet, even at my age? and don't you see that it is just because I know that the ideal torments us that I think a man should boldly cast in his lot with mere reality? You laughed at me because I got so excited over that old man, with the hairy chest and the medal of the Napoleonic wars, who turned up at the villa. Well, that was idealism on my part, what you laughed at. There was a gush, a spurt at least, of poetry, of something fine—a moment's imaginative emotion. If only one could have fixed that moment! But the very next the mind, working on the subject, meets trivial details. This old man—after all, what is he? What has been his life in its detail? Nay, what were those very campaigns, which seem so poetical, in their details? Prose, the ugly, the unsatisfactory; that on which the mind does not care to dwell. Is all, then, a mere moment, a combination, as it were, at a certain angle, of our own fancy and the things outside us? the smallest alteration in the thing outside, or in our own attitude, destroying all? Is poetry, the beautiful, the noble, in life, only as the breadth of a grain of sand? I am getting to think so, Baldwin."

Baldwin looked long at Carlo.

"Young idealist," he said, "who are merely shifting your hopes to the real—that is what you are. Of the things which we desire most, we can taste but little, that is true ; and true especially as regards such desires as these. And yet they do come, and they are poignant and memorable, those moments when in the real you find interwoven a thread of that which our imagination spins, the dream-stuff which makes the heroes and heroines of poetry. Is it not so, Carlo? There is nothing like it in the pleasure which we receive from nature : the only thing coming near to it is music. I have been watching you and your psychological studies of late, my dear boy ; and I know how you felt when there came home to you the knowledge that in that splendid woman of the world whose gait and manners and toilettes you wanted to copy into a realistic novel, there existed a sort of primitive, homogeneous, heroic soul ; that there existed, under the same roof with you, and in a seemingly prosaic creature, an all-absorbing passion of sexless love and devotion. Nay, don't feel ashamed of the pleasure which you felt. It was like having seen a grand sunrise or storm, like having heard some great symphony. I understand what you felt, my realist: you felt that you had clutched the ever-retreating garments of the ideal, heard the tremendous rustle of its wings, breathed its breath as it rushed by——"

Baldwin had put his arm affectionately round Carlo's shoulder, and smiled as he noticed the shyness, and almost shame, with which the lad admitted that he could possibly be enthusiastic about anything more human than an idea or a form.

It was rapidly growing dark. Here and there an isolated hill-side pine or cypress printed its feathery clearness upon the milky luminousness of the sky; but the valley was filled with mist and vagueness, while the sawing of the cicala in the trees flagged, and the hum of the beetles and crickets, the long quavering note of the frogs in the reeds, made a sort of twilight of sound. Between the garlands of vines and the high-growing corn and hemp, now mere blackish masses, there flickered the distant lights of a procession which was winding through the fields, the white shimmer of the wax, the white wreaths of the incense, the white cowls of the peasants bearing banners and crucifix, mingling, ghost-like, with the greyness of the fields. There was something solemn and pathetic, and at the same time pagan, bringing with it vague reminiscences of Virgil and Tibullus, in this ending of a holiday.

"Yes—I did feel like that," admitted Carlo, "but even in the midst of that feeling, I said to myself, 'Shall I see things in this light this time next year —nay, even this time to-morrow?' And that is why," he went on, "I say let us have none of this idealism in art. If the ideal torments us, cheats us, if we cannot see the reality in life, let us see it boldly in art."

Baldwin smiled.

"You crave for the ideal in life, and you are to seek after the real in art! You strange creature! Does it not strike you that it might be more logical to employ art to realize that ideal which escapes you in life?"

Night had closed in about them. The hills were mere huge round masses of unsubstantial darkness; the trees stood out as solid black masses, with but a few leaves trembling clear on the topmost twigs, against the moonless deep blue sky. But between the shadowy trees the fireflies seemed to weave a mystic network, as they rose and fell, crossed and recrossed, palpitating sparks of green fire floating swiftly across the path, and all around the mountain slope heaved and scintillated with a thousand quivering specks of light, a wave of darkness with innumerable ever-changing, ever-moving, rippling, glittering, phosphorescent tips.

"I don't see that it is necessary," Carlo answered. "Art has other things to do than to strain after our ideals. You said that a man who paints landscape need do little besides copy what he sees, nothing more than select. Why, then, should a man who paints human character and emotion be called upon to enlarge, and alter, and idealize?"

"Because moral beauty is in quite a different case from physical beauty. It exists not in space, but in time; it exists not in the simple thing nature, but in the complex thing man. It exists in momentary flashes; rarely permanent and never perfect. There is, in our search after moral beauty, an element of dissatisfaction, nay, despair; at best of unrest and suspicion, very different from the complete and quiet satisfaction derivable from physical beauty. The state of mind which produces an heroic action has but a brief duration; before and after it lies very often what is trivial, sometimes what is base. Nay, worse, the heroic action, the noble sentiment, do not occupy the whole personality at once: heaven only knows what mean desires may not be crawling over some other part of the soul. Thus it continually happens that we see in physical nature an object, a scene, quite as perfect as we can conceive it; he or she is fortunate, or very blind, who can find a character of man or woman which, even during the time we might spend looking at a sky or a group of trees, could be so perfect throughout that they could bear being looked at as long or as closely as a painter looks at his model. Hence it is, that in our search for the moral equivalent of physical beauty, we are all of us so much less realists; we have to make up so much. In order to enjoy a full and satisfying joy like that given us through our eyes so often, we are forced to take the creatures who are to give it us out of reality into the domain of art. Art, not of the professional artist in human feeling, called poet or novelist, but art of our affections and enthusiasms. Most of us, at least of the better, are as great artists in this line as any Phidias or Titian; we know exactly what to blur and what to accentuate, how to correct here, to leave out there, how to place the creature from whom we expect moral delight, or rather its image, in the very most favourable light; we make ourselves this corrected, perfected image, and call it the reality. We must all know, all of us who long for such impressions, how we manipulate our conceptions of people and events, how we almost consciously hide all that detracts from our pleasure and magnify all that gives it; we know the pain, dull or sharp, of having to undo our arrangements of light and colour, of having to own that the portrait which we have adored is idealized as no bodily portrait ever was. In this matter we are all artists on our own behalf, for we all seek beauty that transcends reality; and hence, I think, the necessity that, so far from being enclosed within reality, art should boldly step into this region of the ideal."

"Even at the risk of departing from reality?" asked Carlo.

"Certainly—or I should rather say, in order to depart from reality. To escape, at least, from its interference, to get to a place where we need no longer be afraid of the pleasure which we expect being continually spoilt by a lot of trifling matters."

"But don't you see, Baldwin, that in order to prevent the spoiling of these pleasures—the pleasures dependent upon the realization, or partial realization of the ideal—you would deprive us of the pleasure which we derive from the perception of the reality. I give you up Caponsacchi, because you say that Caponsacchi is himself, so to speak, idealism incarnate. But look at the other hero of the 'Ring and the Book,' Guido Franceschini. What would become of him if Browning had set up his poetical workshop in that famous region of the ideal? And yet you must admit that we feel a poignant pleasure in reading his speeches, a sort of thrill all over us when we exclaim, 'How true!'"

Baldwin nodded. "I was just going to mention Guido Franceschini myself, as an exemplification of part of my theory about the necessity for the ideal. It is perfectly true that when we think of Guido Franceschini we exclaim to ourselves, 'How true!' and believe we have thereby explained everything. As it happens, Guido is in reality very far from true, infinitely less true than many a character in a novel before which we do not gape and cry, 'How true!' Nay, Guido is, in great measure, false. Have you ever come across a little book by a man called Ademollo, 'Le Giustizie di Roma'?"

"Never," answered Carlo.

"It is a collection of summings up of the chief criminal cases of Rome from the end of the seventeenth century, a sort of death register kept by the confraternity which attended the condemned in prison and on the scaffold. And among these summings up is that of the murder of Pompilia and her reputed parents by Guido Franceschini. Well, there you get the real Guido, and you see that this man whom Browning has shown us as great, a creature of the stature of Faust or Othello, was what such a cardinal's parasite, outwitted cheat, and sneaking murderer, could not help being—a very small person indeed."

"The Franceschini of history may have been only that, Baldwin; but Browning had a right to create a new Franceschini of his own; and the Franceschini of Browning's creation is true to nature, although he may be false to history."

"Not at all. A man of the intellect and passion of Browning's Guido, a man who could feel and think and speak as he does, would certainly not have spent his life tormenting a wretched little wife, nor ended it ignominiously for a bungled murder: he would have been a Sforza, a Napoleon, at the least a Cæsar Borgia. Why, therefore, do we instinctively exclaim, 'How true?' In point of fact not because that particular exclamation expresses our feeling, but because we have a feeling to express, and we make use of the exclamation which comes most readily. Now, owing to some original misconception of things, owing to one of those many æsthetical bungles with which the world is rife, mankind has got to associate feelings of admiration for the creations of the poet (and in a measure those of the painter) with the recognition of the fact that these creations have a familiar prototype in reality; than which few errors could be more erroneous. We recognize, indeed, forms and characters which we have seen before, we stretch out, as it were, our mental feelers towards them, suck them in; but every faculty of our nature recognizes, as the needle may be said to recognize the loadstone, the special object of its desires—it sucks them in; and the fact of the recognition by certain æsthetic appetites of the things which are their food has in reality no more to do with the recognition of resemblance between a natural object and its artistic imitation, than the recognition by a hungry man of the smell of roast meat has to do with the recognition of a tune we have heard before: both are lively stretchings forth of our faculties, and that is all. We exclaim, therefore, 'How true!' partly from an engrained theory that only *true things* (whatever exact meaning we may choose to connect with those terms) give us pleasure—'Rien n'est beau que le vrai, le vrai seul est aimable,' as Boileau taught mankind, which, by the way, the whole experience of the pattern arts, music, architecture, and so forth, goes to belie. And we exclaim, 'How true!' partly from a dim perception of the analogy existing between the recognition by our mind of something which it had seen before, and the recognition by our desires of the desired object. Forgive this long piece of metaphysic, you will see in a moment how it bears upon Guido Franceschini, and how Guido Franceschini bears upon the question of realism and idealism. Well, as to Guido. In this case recognition is not the recognition by our mind of the reality of a villain, since, if only we think over the matter, we see that the likeness is far from perfect; it is the recognition by our æsthetic desires of one of their special desiderata: the grand. The colossal proportions of Guido's intellect and passions, absolutely false to history, are delightful to our cravings for moral (or immoral) ideals in the same way, and as unintelligibly, as the particular curve of a hill or the particular modulation of a song is delightful to our cravings for form or melody. Do I make myself understood, Carlo?"

"Perfectly, Baldwin; but——"

"Have patience a moment, my dear Charlie. This, I say, is the explanation of a thing being *true to our wants*, as distinguished from being true to our powers of recognition; and, as our powers of recognition have ample scope in daily life, while our æsthetic wants are kept on short commons, the emotion attendant on the recognition of the object of such wants, is infinitely more powerful than the emotion attendant on our recognition of mere resemblance, and therefore the artist who can awaken such emotion takes so much higher rank."

Carlo was silent for a moment.

"But there is an emotion, and hence a foundation for art, in all perception of reality," he said; "an emotion in all recognition, quite apart from beauty, moral or physical."

"Yes; but it is an emotion whose pleasureableness or painfulness must be decided by other circumstances, being in itself negative in nature. The representation of a thing which we have seen before awakens our attention, but that is all, unless some circumstance of beauty or importance, of pain or pleasure, be attached to the thing in question. There may be a little more excitement, apart from the excitement of technical criticism (which, of course, is another matter) in the picture of a kettle than in the kettle itself; but the excitement is neither pleasant nor unpleasant. But when the object represented is one which has already produced in us an emotion either pleasant or unpleasant, the going over the track, the re-opening of the cicatrice left in our soul by this emotion, is often more strongly perceived than the original making of the track or cicatrice. There is an increase of effect in the very act of recognition; the description of a beautiful scene delights us because we were delighted with the original; but if we return to the original, we shall be more delighted with it, in consequence of our delight with the description, and in consequence also of that storage and dissemination of connected impressions of which I have spoken before."

"You are always taking for granted a sort of internal manipulation of our impressions, Baldwin—always taking for granted something beyond the mere impression from without, and the mere perceiving mind, it seems to me."

"I am taking for granted, as I already told you, that our mind is neither empty nor inactive; that it has an already assimilated contents, and instincts of fresh assimilation; that it is, in short, a living thing with living necessities. And herein, by the way, lies the chief fundamental difference between a realist of your school and an idealist of mine; herein, that while the realist thinks only of the impression from without, the idealist thinks also of the mind for whose benefit the impression from without is to be elicited. Art, my dear boy, exists, not because the things outside us clamour to have their portraits taken; but because the things, the desires, within us clamour for a particular kind of satisfaction. After all, we paint pictures and write poems to please ourselves, not to please the stones and trees and skies, the dead heroes and heroines who are none the wiser for our proceeding."

"To return to Guido Franceschini, or rather to the

discussion which made us mention him," said Baldwin, after a moment. " I said, at the beginning of our conversation, that the artist who deals merely with trees and skies and light and shade need scarcely do more than copy, and nothing more than select ; and you, my dear Carlo, said, if I remember correctly, that as regards human character and emotion, the beautiful, the noble, what we call poetry, is only as the breadth of a grain of sand. Do you remember ? "

" I remember, and I remember also my conclusion that it would be wiser to learn to do without this beauty and nobility and poetry of which we are permitted to taste only that we may long for it and starve," answered Carlo, fiercely.

" We cannot do without it, and we must not starve. And art is there to prevent our starving ; and to prevent our forgetting the nobler food of our soul, and learning to live a baser life on baser spiritual food. I told you that, as regards life and feeling, and the men and women in whose life our feelings live, we are all artists on our own behalf, seeking to obtain, making up, a beauty that transcends reality ; craving for a kind of pleasure which is the most acute and exquisite that our soul can enjoy. For this sort of pleasure, which, when given us by reality, is so far less perfect, is rarer than any other, but, when obtained, more poignant : no physical beauty can make our souls brim over with delight as this moral loveliness when we see it—see it in our mind, not imperfect and fleeting as in reality, but with the steady and complete perfection into which our soul has wrought it. We have such works of art, idealized portraits, all of us, in our souls; but they are portraits which fade and alter, and against which our reason and our love of truth are for ever revolting. Hence the good done to us (far greater than the good done by any selecting artist of material things) by the artist who gives us certain imaginary creatures. Such beings are, alas! so ideal, that in contemplating, for instance, Pompilia or Caponsacchi, or Jean Valjean, we experience something more than the mere humdrum pleasure in the beauty of painting and sculpture, arts so near reality. We feel the pleasure in artificial harmony and perfection, the same sort of pleasure, nay, almost the very same pleasure, which is given us by the art of beauty without a prototype on earth: I mean music."

They had entered Sir Anthony's villa, and were waiting for the old painter on the terrace which adjoined his improvised studio. For a few minutes they leaned against the parapet in silence, looking out into the summer night, vibrating with the quavering notes of insects; vibrating, one might almost say, with the poignant scent of vague flowers and distant hayfields. The moon, very nearly full, was not very high in the heavens, and small and luminous with a pale sheen. While the sky opposite was a sea-green blue which seemed to shed a light of its own, so bright that not a star could be seen; the sky, on the contrary, surrounding the moon was a pale, opalescent luminousness, as of the bluish iridescence of mother-of-pearl, through which the larger stars trembled as if they were infinitely distant. Against it lay the line of hills, misty, bodiless, blue, turned by the moon into something of its own substance; and underneath, the trees of the villa gardens. Not a ray caught their leaves, not a shimmer about them; not a cypress stood out solid against the sky; but everything lay wonderfully distinct and diaphanous: the white blossom of some trees clear and shaken out, as it were, in the pale blue night; the other trees, cypresses, elms, cedars, poplars, surrounded by an atmosphere of blue luminousness, in which their branches, nay, almost their leaves, seemed to float spread out, every leaf and twig far apart and distinct, like the weeds spread out upon the surface of a stream, the light separating their parts, spreading them out like lace; the adjacent trees separate in this flood of opalescent blue; even the cypresses become semi-transparent, like the veined and ribbed rose petals dried in a book.

"Ah! we want it, we want it, that something which you call the ideal," said Carlo, leaning on the terrace and looking into the night; "we want it, Baldwin; and it is useless pretending that we do not. We want, on such a night as this, the belief in a Cordelia, a Clarissa, a Caponsacchi, a Jean Valjean; as we want, sometimes, a voice to sing clearly out the part, to bring it home to us, when we are playing some exquisite music on a beautiful instrument. We want it; but is it right that we should have it? The satisfying, the perfect, eludes us for ever in this world of reality; it can exist only, as you say, in our imagination. But have we a right to pursue the unattainable, we who have so many realities to clutch and to hold; have we a right to live in company with the imaginary, we who must struggle for ever with the remorselessly real?"

Baldwin nodded silently as he listened to the lad.

"We struggle for ever with the real," he said, "and we must struggle with it for ever. But ask yourself, Carlo, in whose name does this battle go on; or rather, what is it within ourselves that urges us to struggle, that struggles for us? The ideal; the desire, if you choose to call it so, of the unattainable, through which alone all higher things are ever attained."

"People nowadays," he continued, after a pause, "have a way of talking as if the one useful thing, the one necessary, were to know the world such as it is. True enough: but only in order that we should know how to make the world, each of us so far as his power goes, a little more like what it should be. With us, who are no longer plants or beasts, a new kind of selection comes into play; and that selection means the setting up in our mind of the model to which we may as yet be unable to conform the things outside us. Let us know the reality, and know the unreal;

above all, know the border-line of both. Let us crave for complete satisfaction of our souls that we may not grow enervate in satisfaction which is but partial; let us seek the unattainable in order that we may not stick fast and rot in the attainable."

"Then life, according to you, is to be a constant straining after the unreachable, a race, a battle?"

"Life is that already; all else is death."

"But that is dreadful, Baldwin; dreary and dreadful. Don't you see that you are telling us to care for nothing which really exists? to be dissatisfied with everything that is not the creation of our own nature, with everything, in fact, which is a reality and a certainty?"

"As you grow older," answered Baldwin, "you will learn that what your imagination and your heart have made for you, and what resides within your own soul, is the one and only thing of which you can be certain, the one and only thing which can never alter and can never betray you. You will learn that the great reality which is yours, unalterably and eternally, is the ideal.'

Sir Anthony had come out on to the moonlit terrace, and listened to the discussion.

"Well, young realist," he asked, "has Baldwin converted you to believe in the ideal?"

"Not yet!" answered Carlo, "not yet. The ideal is too distant, too vague. And the real seems to me so full of endless and uncounted beauty and satisfaction. Look there!" and he pointed to the valley, lying clear and blue in the moonlight, the soft, short note of Shelley's Aziola gently dividing, as water is divided by a boat's keel, the sort of silence made up of the vague hum of insects. A firefly rose slowly, shining green against the dark bushes, then golden against the blue sky, till it was lost, a brighter star merged gradually in the dimness of the real stars in the heavens.

Sir Anthony smiled; that curious, gentle, ironical smile of scepticism towards everything foolish and base.

"For the moment," he said, "be a realist, my dear boy. At twenty-one you can still afford to seek in reality for everything that you desire; you can still seek in reality for the ideal."

OF DOUBTS AND PESSIMISM.

OF DOUBTS AND PESSIMISM.

"What a pity gondoliers can't sing Tasso any longer!" said Marcel, in his whimsical way, letting his finger tips caress the green water as they rowed slowly across the lagoon in the low afternoon light. "I should have liked to hear the canto where the fairy steers the knights across the summer sea, towards the enchanted island, within sight of the great dead cities of the Past—'cadano le città, cadano i regni; e d'essere mortale par che l'uom sdegni'—do you remember? It must have been so like this, don't you think? Do repeat it to us, Miss Olivia; or, better still, make us the song of the fairy, about weighing anchor for the land of unreality, and drifting, drifting, into the sunset, down into peace and nothingness."

"One doesn't feel sentimental and sing songs like that when one is a professional poet, Monsieur Marcel—one writes verses only when there is a volume to finish and a publisher in the background;" answered Olivia, with that pleasure in treating poetry as a mechanical trade, which was one of the waywardnesses of her wayward poet's nature. " Besides, I don't think our friend Baldwin would at all approve of such songs as that, would he, Charlie?"

Carlo looked up to his half-sister from where he sat, meditating, with boyish rapture, upon possible adjectives as the boat skirted the long hedges of pale yellow matting and pale grey tamarisk, overtopped here and there by the russet leaves of a peach tree, the vermilion fruit of a pomegranate; while above, in the sky of lilac blue, the sea-gulls eddied like snow-flakes.

"No, indeed!" he exclaimed; "Baldwin might capsize the gondola from utilitarian motives, if we were to sing anything of the kind. Baldwin likes us to be rational beings and to discuss philosophy, and he thinks nothingness the most immoral thing that was ever invented; don't you, Baldwin?"

Baldwin laughed from where he stood rowing at the prow of the gondola, and, turning round, showered the drops from his oar on to Carlo's head.

"Little boys mustn't make impertinent remarks to old folk who know exactly when they were taken out of Eton jackets," he said, as Carlo screamed in the midst of his tirade. "I beg, moreover, to add," he continued, working away at his oar, "that if any of the present company decidedly prefer arguing on metaphysics to looking about, it is not my unworthy self, but my old friend Olivia and our distinguished guest, Monsieur Marcel. Why, they were discussing free-will and necessity like German mystics of the fourteenth century all the time we were at Chioggia, as if there were no houses, or sky, or water, or yellow sails, or pretty girls to look at. My own discussions are strictly limited to cases where a definite solution or a practical result seems possible."

"That is because you are a utilitarian, Baldwin," answered Olivia; "you don't really care for metaphysics."

"I hate them," interrupted Baldwin, as his oar cut a deep turquoise gash in the green water.

"I know you hate them. That's your mistake in life. You persist in thinking that logic has a practical value, that we can get at what you call definite solutions and useful results by its means; Monsieur Marcel and I don't feel at all so sure about that; but we have the candour to admit that while we don't expect to be much the wiser, or much the more comfortable for our logical straw-splitting, we find that logical straw-splitting, in itself, one of the most delightful employments in life."

"After all," she continued, her metaphysical spirit, which was as the prosaic side of her singular lyric gift, once aroused—"after all, thought is only one of our modes of existence, logic is but one factor in life; so where is the use of applying the laws of thought to our other modes of existence, emotional or æsthetical, or whatever they may be? Where is the use of seeking a logical explanation for our feelings, for our preferences of good to bad and beautiful to ugly, when logic has absolutely nothing to do with these preferences? All these things are separate, parallel; and we may walk on till doomsday before we find their meeting place."

Carlo had taken his head in his hand. The young man, devoured with a boyish passion to understand all modern problems, to be a modern man, looked up with perplexed and conflicting admiration at the superiority of his elder sister, of her former playfellow and domestic philosopher, Baldwin, and at this subtle and brilliant Marcel, whose every written word seemed fraught with a kind of clairvoyant suggestion.

"Half of our life at least," pursued Olivia, "is a matter of the emotions; and tell me whether our emotions are logical? You might as well say that digestion is due to our reasoning faculties."

Baldwin handed over his oar to Carlo, and sat down near Olivia and the young French critic.

"I perfectly agree," he answered; "but you forget that to subordinate non-logical impressions and activities to logical motives is one thing, and to seek out by logical analysis the reasons of these non-logical impressions and activities is another. Thought does not make us prefer beauty to ugliness, nor good to evil; but thought, by explaining the structure of the emotional or æsthetic apparatus, may explain the reasons of their peculiar mode of action; thought, to take up your metaphor, is certainly no factor in digestion; yet it may enable us to understand what digestion is, and why it is so."

The poetess shook her head. She was one of those rare creatures, blond and tall, in whom thinness, instead of angularity, means only a strange half artificial exquisiteness of outline and movement, a bodily perfection more transcendent for its very immateriality, and which affects one like a kind of intellectual superiority. That things for her should move for ever in the region of mere abstract thought and fancy seemed only right and natural: her own beauty was an abstraction, unconnected with material wants or purposes.

"But thought can never approach emotion, or any of the realities of our inner life," she persisted; "if it does, it becomes absolutely inconsistent. Look at Stuart Mill; there was a man, if ever there were, who might be considered as the incarnation of logic and utilitarianism. Well, Stuart Mill, while believing firmly that there survived of his dead wife nothing that might derive pleasure or profit from any posthumous expression of love and respect, yet did all that he could in the way of such expressions of love and respect. Yet this man was the most logical and practical that ever lived. Surely this is enough to show the uselessness of logic."

"By no means," answered Baldwin. "Logic, while explaining to Mill that there could remain of his wife nothing to appreciate such demonstrations on his part, explained or might have explained to him also that it was impossible for the complicated train of emotional action and reaction set up in his mind by his wife while she was living, to be cut short, snuffed out like her physical existence. Logic explained that the image of her must persist much longer than the reality; nay, that the very act of dying, which put an end to her objective existence, must inevitably, by the sudden heightening of desire and appreciation and vivid imaginative perception implied in grief, have immensely reinforced this emotional activity which resulted in a sense of her presence to the survivor."

"That is true," interrupted Marcel, to whom all personal psychology had a peculiar charm; "indeed, I question whether there is a moment of subjective existence, of existence in the consciousness of others, superior to that immediately following on death, that is to say, on the cessation of all objective existence."

"Hence," continued Baldwin, "while logic, applied narrowly, shows us that Mrs. Stuart Mill could not profit by her husband's expressions of grief and affection; logic also, when applied more largely, to the cause and not to the result, shows us that it must have seemed to her husband's feelings as if these expressions would give her satisfaction. In the same way, while logic explains that this or that religious belief is absolutely mistaken, it explains also why that same religious belief has been or is inevitable in given circumstances."

"That," put in Carlo, "is the difference between the attitude of Renan and modern students of religions, and the attitude of the old school, who thought that because dogmas were absurd and pernicious, the men who taught them—the Bonzes, Fakirs, and Old Men of the Mountain, as Voltaire calls them in his stories—must have been either knaves or fools."

"Exactly," said Baldwin. "And it is one of the practical, strictly utilitarian advantages of logic that it teaches us why we must sometimes be illogical."

They rowed on for some while in silence, absorbed once more in the strange beauty of the islands and sandbanks which their gondola skirted on its northward way towards Venice. Broken only by orchards was a long line of little villages, their rows of houses reflected in the sea—houses whose red scoriated bricks, and worn white and rose-coloured plaster, illumined with intensity by the reflected light from the water, had, against the lilac blue, hot, opaque sky printed with slender pink belfries and white-funnel, shaped chimneys, a strange powdery brilliancy of colour, full of thick white and rose as of pastel: unreal, exquisite in tone, like some canvas by Veronese, or fresco by Tiepolo. Indeed, only the sea seemed real, consistent, made of something less illusory than delicate tinted chalks on reddish prepared paper; the sea, with white and orange sails flecking it like butterflies, which was of a thick marble smoothness, grey with blue and lilac veinings, and opalescences, in the low light, as of glass spun with gold dust.

"But as logic, even according to you, Baldwin," remarked Marcel, "is perpetually teaching us that we cannot be logical, so also, in the course of discussing any kind of practical matter, we are constantly learning that all such discussion is vain. The longer one lives the more plainly one sees, unless one be a fool or a fanatic, that the world is made up of one-sided views on all matters, obstinate, not to be reasoned with, because constitutional; that wherever one expects to be able to reason out a truth for oneself and others, the place is already filled by bulky preconceived ideas, or guarded by invincible preconceiving tendencies. Where is certainty? Where is reason? Nowhere, perhaps, save in the very fact of that conflict between excessive views. Here again, therefore, logic can demonstrate only logic's practical impotence."

"I quite agree with you," answered Baldwin, "that the intellectual and moral life of the world is largely carried on by means of exaggeration, prejudice, and injustice. Every day impresses me more and more with the seeming necessity of excess in all things in order that excess may be checked. I am sometimes quite oppressed by the sense that one idiotcy, one selfishness, nay, one dangerous enthusiasm or dangerous self-sacrifice, is required to balance and correct some other."

"But then," exclaimed Carlo, suddenly resting on his oar, "is no one to see the light? Are we all to be excessive, unjust, monstrous, having our injurious excessive opinions and actions counteracted by those of others; and counteracting, rendering nugatory, theirs? Is the world to be carried on thanks to our irrationalism and pigheadedness and self-righteousness and selfishness?"

"I don't know," replied Baldwin: "it certainly seems as if justice and lucidity were scarcely compatible with feeling and action; as if seeing all things would prevent doing anything. But after all, is it necessary that the person who understands and judges should be the one who at that moment feels and acts? Is it not sufficient that, as Butler said better than Herbert Spencer could say it, we should all

> 'Compound for sins we have a mind to
> By damning those we're not inclined to'?"

Is it not sufficient that each of us should, turn about, correct by his power of seeing the power of feeling of another, and be corrected in his turn; or will not a habit of seeing lucidly and judging justly when we are not in the moment of feeling and acting, prepare, as it were, a safer channel in which our feeling and action may flow? Must conflict inevitably imply wastefulness and destruction? Sometimes it seems to me that it must; that of wastefulness and destruction consists all life. But it is this wastefulness and destruction which makes life as sterile as death. Surely the day will come when the conflict of mere constitutions, of mere inherent tendencies and interests, may be enough; the conflict of partial truth with partial truth, not of error with error. I believe meanwhile in the possibility of compromise instead of conflict; I pray for the equitable distribution of belief and scepticism, of pushing on and hanging back; and I pray, therefore, for the reign of lucidity, which is the reign also of justice."

Marcel shook his head.

"You are an optimist, Baldwin," he said, sadly.

"Not at all. I am merely not a pessimist, Marcel."

"You speak, Baldwin," put in Olivia, "as if the result of what you call lucidity would be certainty. But what do we see in the moments—very rare moments—when the scales of personality seem to fall from our eyes, when there comes to us a revelation of the real reality of the world and our position in it? I see that every creature is a centre, a meeting-point of different and incongruous ideas; that each creature understands and tolerates and loves so many creatures and ideas and tendencies which hate one another; that each creature is a sort of point of justice, a point of equilibrium, a centre, as I said; and that each creature is at the same time a diverging ray in some other system; is, as regards some other person's feelings and ideas, a misunderstanding, an injustice, a blindness; that each of us is at once a reconciler and an irreconcilable, a dealer out of justice and a judged thing. And thus on, circle cutting circle, centre touching circumference, rays uniting and diverging in all directions, all moving, whirling, acting, reacting; an universe of egos, of wills and judgments and feelings, to which the stars in the heavens, with their interlacing systems, are as a diagram in the first book of Euclid. Have you ever grasped that; and if you have, do you not know the paralyzing awe of that moment of comprehension?"

Baldwin nodded.

"I have realized it, I do realize it every now and then. But such a knowledge has virtually no effect on our feelings and actions, any more than the knowledge that this seemingly steady earth is spinning about at a furious rate; or that our body, which seems so completely ourself, is for ever changing and being made anew. Such things go against our consciousness. We see, at most, and not every one sees even so much, that there are other centres and other circles which cut our own. To do this is as much as we can permanently realize without falling into a kind of metaphysical trance; and it is therefore enough, and more than enough."

"But this metaphysical trance carries us into the presence of Truth," answered Olivia, "even as the mystic trance brought the saints of old into the presence of God."

"And, as the saints of old, indulging in this mystic trance, ceased to feel or act, so should we also cease to feel and act, cease to be of any use in this world, were we to indulge in such metaphysical contemplations; growing dizzy and cataleptic from trying to fix our mental eyes upon more than we can see. Such truth as you speak of is not truth with reference to our nature: we are individual, limited, and cannot grasp the infinite and absolute."

"We can and we should," cried Olivia. "Not the larger and most remote infinite and absolute— for, as measured by our faculties, there is infinite beyond infinite, absolute beyond absolute, a series of ever receding horizons. There is in all of us something that makes us akin to the universal and absolute, there is in our souls somewhat of the infinite; though limited on all sides by the barriers of personality, though prevented, by the narrow vessel which contains it, from mingling freely in the ocean of infinite life and thought and feeling. Our every aspiration, our every ideal, proves it: we, at least the nobler of us, are striving for ever to get beyond the actual, the narrow, to press forward towards something in which we may rest in satisfaction and peace; love, art, the desire to know, all prove this."

"I fear," put in Baldwin, with a smile, "that I am, then, not of the nobler sort. I notice, indeed in others, and I feel in myself, those aspirations and ideals which you describe, those strivings for more complete satisfaction. I know that when we pursue beauty or truth, that when we idealize, as we always do, any beloved object, we are manifesting dissatisfaction with the reality of things and of ourselves. But I know also that these desires and strivings are merely the expansion of our individuality, not the breaking its bounds; they are the efforts to obtain a response to our most personal cravings, not the efforts to be rid of our personality. If we desire to see the manifestation of greater goodness or beauty than habitually comes before us, it is merely as we desire to eat a greater amount of food, to get a greater amount of sleep, or take a greater amount of exercise than at present: our individual powers are clamouring for satisfaction. The infinite and the absolute have nothing to do with this."

"You do not understand," persisted Olivia, "or rather you refuse to understand, Baldwin. There is the positive desire to get rid of our individuality; to get rid of the personality which prevents our seeing the whole truth and feeling the complete truth——"

"To be, in short, less naughty and less stupid than we are," put in Baldwin; "to improve——"

"No, not to improve. To cease to be ourselves, to cease to live our lives; to live in a larger life not our own, to see and feel vision and feelings vaster than ours."

"Hero-worship, then. You wish to abdicate your emotions and ideas into the hands of some one else."

"I do not wish to abdicate in favour of anyone, although that also is a great temptation: to feel a larger life than one's own. I wish merely, in this case, to get rid of my own personality, moral and mental and physical."

"That would be a dreadful loss to every one," murmured Marcel, his eyes fixed upon that strange diaphanous blond beauty, less a woman, as he had once remarked, than a series of exquisite movements.

"My own personality which is for ever hampering and checking me, preventing me from moving; getting between myself and the things I desire to see and embrace. And also," added Olivia, a sort of childish waywardness and impertinence coming over her, "I wish to get rid of the tiresome, contradictory, doctrinaire, utilitarian personality of other folk."

Baldwin smiled and bowed.

The sun was beginning to set in a sky of perfect purity; and as the gondola glided over the lagoon towards the westernmost point of Venice, the shallow water was turned into a pavement veined and streaked like jasper, almost solid in its marble stillness, and tesselated with gold, down whose middle ran a narrow golden pathway, leading towards a strip of shining, steel-like water, above which, and above the vague grey line of terra firma, the sun was descending, a vast disc of gold.

"I wish," went on Olivia, screening her eyes with her hand, and looking far into the sunset, as if indeed, as Marcel had suggested, its golden causeway might lead into the mysterious country where the soul strips off all individual baseness and falls asleep in the wings of the ideal—"I wish, I long, to shuffle off my own self and all the pettinesses of identity. I should like to stand in the presence of absolute truth and absolute good, to feel myself absorbed into the real reality."

Baldwin smiled.

"You are a poet. Do you not also wish to walk to the rainbow's foot and dig for the gold that is buried there? As the rainbow has no foot, and you might walk on till doomsday without finding the place to dig in, so also this transcendent good and transcendent truth would for ever elude you. It is an abstraction, and does not exist."

"But abstractions are the only real realities," cried Olivia; "they are the only things which do not change."

"They do not change simply because they do not really exist. They are merely the expression of our mode of seeing things intellectually. All these fine things which we make into ideals exist only in our mind; and it is for that reason that they can be our ideals. Mankind—the humanity which our Comtiste friends would bid us worship, where may it be found? Has any one seen it yet? Is it a crowd? No; it is an abstraction. The real existence is the individual man, and of him endless numbers, the individual man with his necessities and powers and vices and virtues. And so also of good and truth : real good and real truth is the good which each man does and aspires to do, the truth that he sees and strives to see. In order to increase this good and this truth, we must increase it in the individual. To destroy the personality in hopes of getting at a higher good or a higher truth is to cut off one's head to cure the toothache. Prune away the base peculiarities, improve the individual by comparing him with as many other individuals as you like ; make an abstraction, if you please, of all that you love best in all individuals ; but do not expect that this abstraction can ever become a reality except in each separate creature ; do not strive to grasp what remains only as a mental conception, an emotional desire. We are the sole realities, we individuals ; and our law is the improvement of the individual : to loosen the individual's limits and become united with transcendent good or transcendent truth, is to be dissolved into nothingness."

Olivia was silent for a minute. She respected Baldwin, and perceived his greater lucidity of thought, the stronger grasp he possessed over ideas ; and she could not deny that what he said seemed true. But a habit of certain modes of imagination and feeling which she mistook for ideas, the essentially poetical bias of her nature that, loving metaphysics, she mistook for a peculiar speculative aptitude, prevented her from being satisfied with his conclusions. The transcendent, the mysterious, fascinated her imagination ; and she believed in its existence as, in her childhood, she would have believed that, could they only row out sufficiently long, they would have reached, not the sandbank, and stagnant waters, and stunted willows of the mainland, but the real country of the setting sun.

"But, Baldwin," she persisted, "have you never felt choked by your own personality—choked as a man buried alive would feel choked by the bricks and mortar and earth? Have you never felt that you were being prevented, not by any one else, but by your own self, from being just, from uniting, as you should, in sympathy and affection with some person outside you?"

"I know what you mean;" answered Baldwin, "but that does not prove that we should or could unite ourself with any abstract truth or good. It means merely, I think, that we are some of us, perhaps most (perhaps all), made, so to speak, of several pieces; of an inner and innermost *myself* and of a number of outer ones. It means, what we have, alas! nearly all of us, occasion to experience, that our real soul which can appreciate, love, help, is sometimes fenced in, as the just king is in his palace, by a crowd of habits of thought and manner, of accidentally or deliberately made up spurious *myselfs* hedging the reality in, preventing it from seeing other realities, or at least from uniting with them. I think, were we to look round in our past, we should most of us see some cause we ought to have joined, some friend we ought to have loved, which have passed across our life and been nothing in it."

Marcel had been sitting, "meditating a description," as Carlo maliciously defined it to himself, looking before him over the water as the gondola advanced across the sea floor paved with golden scales, in the direction of the little black island of Saint George of the Sea-Weed, with its lonely madonna shrine on the watery path standing out against the amber of the sky, out of which the sun was slowly descending into a narrow pool of silver-sparkling water; turning his eyes sometimes from the scarce endurable sunset effulgence to the opposite side of the sky, where it and the water were of vague, coldest moonlight blue, with the little crescent moon rising and the black fishing boats moored motionless.

Although his pessimism and a vague poeticalness frequently led him to sigh after an extinction of the individual, a blissful nirvana that should deliver him of a soul which he felt to be unhealthy and ill at ease, Marcel, as a prominent member of the school of psychological criticism, or, as some consider it, of soul pathology studied in artificially induced cases, could not hear Olivia's abuse of the individual without feeling that she would deprive him of what made the world and himself supremely interesting in his eyes. And the principles of his school of literary criticism— a school which has much if not complete reason on its side—were also aroused by this constant seeking after an abstract and absolute standard of truth and right which seemed to him a positive nuisance.

"I think," he said, "that by attempting to deprive us of personality in all matters of thought, Miss Olivia would be incurring the risk of depriving us of the few things that we really and thoroughly study; depriving us, in the desire of something more absolute in the way of truth, of an invaluable subject of scientific research and aid thereunto. Take, for an instance, the sphere of intellectual activity with which I am myself best acquainted: that of criticism. The new school of criticism, like the new school of history, is altogether personal; it purports to show how certain works of art, or philosophical schemes, or men or historical periods, affect the mind of the individual critic; instead, as was formerly the case, of pretending to judge of all such things according to certain abstract rules. Now, if a critic is content to give you his impressions, you may, by being shown at once what manner of mind is his, and what manner of impression that mind is likely to receive—you may, I say, make allowance for the action and reaction, strike an average, and thus get for yourself an idea of the absolute potentiality, say, of the book he is writing about. But if, on the contrary, the critic measures the book according to a standard, you have first to verify that standard, to find out whence he got it, and whether it coincides with your own; and then, beneath all this remains the inevitable conviction that the adoption of the standard or the particular application thereof in the present case, is merely an expression of the nature and limits of the critic's personality. The question may be tested by examining who are the people (not Miss Olivia, for her aversion to personality is quite of another sort) that are most violently in favour of the old and against the new school of criticism. You will find that they are nearly always people either with a constitutional aversion to any sort of intrusiveness and meddlesomeness; or with a magisterial or slavish fear of presumptuousness, of want of deference from the unknown towards the consecrated. Myself, the longer I live, the more also do I feel how completely this world is made up of relative appreciations; how useless and absurd it is to attempt to get at a positive one. We must think according to our mind's organization; we must continually select the judgments of others and balance them against each other and our own; and other folk must do the same with ours. We are bound, by our constitution, to feel, each and all of us, the centre of that great system of circles, whose centre, as Miss Olivia remarked, is nowhere. Hence it seems to me that it were a great step in the direction of seeing the value of opinions, let alone their genesis and filiation, if personality could be reinstated in our books of criticism and philosophy. Is it nothing to have learned the secret of such characters as Renan and Michelet, as your Carlyle and Ruskin? And is it not far easier for us to calculate what may be the actual value of these men's opinions, by knowing the characteristics in which they originate?"

Carlo, who was consumed with the desire to be modern, and therefore to be personal, let go his oar and clapped his hands.

"Long live personal criticism!" he cried, "and long live Marcel! And allow his abject admirer to sum up the matter in a more or less brutal formula: Shall we not gain immensely by having the pseudo-scientific, or rather pseudo-religious, impersonal dogmatism of judgment according to standards, or supposed standards, replaced: in the æsthetic world, by men's impressions; in the intellectual world by their opinions; in the moral world by their enthusiasms and indignations? Shall we not gain by human beings showing themselves to be human beings, instead of abstract entities, clothed in paper and printer's ink?"

They were turning the corner of one of the outlying islands, and making straight for Venice, when the sun disappeared, leaving behind it at first but a palest yellow, against which the jagged line of the Cadore Alps, the egg-shaped Euganean hills, became with every moment greyer and more distinct. Little by little the luminous amber band enlarged and grew more vivid in colour; turning into a mist of rosy copper, which met the tender blue overhead, and sent delicate cobwebs of rosy cloud far above in the sky, the little waves turning rosy also, with crests of shining silver. Until, as they turned aside, and shot straight towards the back of the Giudecca, the copper colour deepened and deepened into red and orange, till at last the western sky became like a gigantic dome lined with burnished gold, embrowned and purpled with vapours below, and brilliant with clear yellow lights above, like the domes of St. Mark's: an immense vault of mellowed gold, to which corresponded a floor made of the jasper and alabaster, and onyx, the gold and silver tesseræ of the sea. Turning their eyes from the sunset they saw before them the towers of Venice rising in ghostly vividness from out of a steely blue sea into a sky of polished dark blue steel; and the whiteness of its houses, the glass of its windows, staring in an unearthly wintry glare, a ghostly city.

And Marcel, who had half forgotten the subject under discussion, murmured to himself, as he watched the yellow sailed boats, the black riggings of ships entering port, against that golden sky, the lines, like a picture by Claude or by Turner, of his favourite poet:

> " Ou les vaisseaux, glissant dans l'or et dans la moire,
> Ouvrent leur vastes bras pour embrasser la gloire
> D'un ciel pur où frémit l'éternelle chaleur."

But the words of Marcel and of Carlo seemed to have touched a particularly vibrating string in Baldwin's nature.

"You said, Marcel," he remarked, "that to see the character, as well as the mere opinions of men like Renan and Michelet, and Ruskin and Carlyle, is a scientific gain. Do you not go beyond the mere scientific interest? Does it not seem to you an even greater gain morally, a pleasure, an encouragement or a warning, to have come in a manner into contact with such personalities? It seems to me that one of the great benefits of literature is exactly its power of bringing us into the presence of a desirable friend, or even of an enemy, at all events of a human being, contact with whom will develop ourselves, will give us spiritual pleasure or profit, or, what is often equally necessary to us, disinterested spiritual pain; the power of preventing the waste and multiplying the use, of that essential thing (I beg Olivia's pardon), human individuality. Science is necessary for the practical welfare of our life, and art is valuable as its amusement; but the life itself, that to which science and art are but conducive, what is it, save commerce with individuals? Our work, our play, are after all only a small part of our life; they are its basis or its ornamental superstructure. The life itself, what in the spiritual corresponds to the constant processes, as of respiration and assimilation, of the body, is this constant reaction of one creature upon another; and as the acutest pains and acutest pleasures of the body being only exceptional and momentary things, the most permeating and constant sense of bodily well-being or the reverse depends upon the condition of these perpetual bodily functions, rather than upon those of our eyes and ears, &c. ; so also, I think, does the enormous bulk of vague overallish pleasure or pain constituting happiness or unhappiness, depend not upon the intermittent functions which we associate with science and art, but upon that constant action and reaction of personalities—action and reaction which, I am inclined to conceive, constitutes life. Hence, in my opinion, there is nothing more important to a person than personality, and nothing more precious than such personality as will by its contact do us good, nothing more important than the rendering of such personality accessible."

"When I say *do good*," pursued Baldwin, " I don't mean in any direct or practical way : a creature may do us good, in the sense of making us happy, by redoubling certain better energies of our nature, and improving us in any particular way ; it may do us good also merely by heightening our degree of life, by turning a partial into a complete, or less incomplete, existence. To this literature can conduce. Indeed, literature is the only thing that can save from continual waste, that can distribute so as to bring to fullest use, the thing we call a soul. Neither art nor science can do this : we may enjoy a work of art, we may follow a scientific demonstration ; but we can live, be acted on by, and react towards, only a human being, real or imaginary. And we must remember that the circumstances of life are such that we can but rarely come fully in contact with a real, complete personality : it is only our few most absolutely intimate friends that we know otherwise than piecemeal ; and then, in this extremely small number of individuals, brought by accident within our thorough familiarity, how small is not the proportion of such with whom contact is rather more than an indifferent matter ? Here literature steps in. What do we not owe for the companionship of so many creatures, never actually of this world, but who seem nevertheless to have lived by our side, better known to us than the living creatures all round, more living than they, and forming more absolutely a part of ourselves ? How much more even do we not owe, therefore, to those men and women who have actually lived, or do actually live, but separated from us by time or space, who come near us, draw us out, ask for our sympathy, and, in the highest cases (as, for instance, I felt once while reading 'Sartor Resartus'), give us theirs ? Creatures often not merely separated from us by impassable barriers, but placed in a way above us, and who yet draw near, feel with us and let us feel with them ; in whom we recognize, dead as they may be, what the finest creations of the imagination can never give us, what we feel in the touch of a man or a woman, and miss for ever in the presence of a statue or a picture, the power of being something more, the possession of something further, the quality for which all living things for ever yearn—life."

While Baldwin was speaking, they had been skirting the lagoon side of the Giudecca island, past the grey-ribbed cupola and minarets, the greyish pink masonry of the Redentore, an exquisitely delicate and fantastic lilac pattern upon the bluish lilac sky; past the red wall overtopped by the mulberry trees and pomegranates of some orchard, whence the shrilling of crickets came over the water; gliding gently over the shallow waters, lilac with a pale rosy sheen, towards the sunset; green on the other side, and fretted by the moon with innumerable green facets. As Baldwin finished the gondola drew in under a garden wall on the westernmost extremity of the Giudecca. Lights were shining from the windows of the old white villa house built into the water, and from it issued the notes of a piano and the hum of voices.

"Father and mother must have been waiting for us for dinner," said the practical Carlo.

Marcel, in his half dreamy way, got out of the gondola, and would have offered his assistance to Olivia in climbing the slippery, sea-washed wooden steps. But the poetess had already taken the arm of her old friend and playfellow, and said to him, as they entered the house—

"I don't know what it is about you, Baldwin, but somehow you always make me feel inclined to contradict you; and yet I agree with you. I'm not a pessimist like Monsieur Marcel, I don't really think he's in the right; but feel it's easy to agree with him. I think it is that you're too cut and dried. You have no sympathy for people's doubts, and I am full of doubts. Do you never have doubts yourself?"

Baldwin laughed.

"Constantly. But I usually work them out for myself, and give other folk only my certainties. But it is a bad habit, I allow."

II.

After dinner, while Marcel and Carlo were still seated with the elder folk in the dining-room of the old villa, or rather garden house, Baldwin and his former playfellow, the poetess, strolled down into the garden.

"You complained, as we came here, of my being cut and dried, having no sympathy with doubt— never feeling doubt myself," said Baldwin, as they crossed the court, carpeted smooth and white by the moonlight, where the orange trees glistered in every leaf like glass cut in facets, and an invisible choir of crickets and frogs mingled with the dripping sounds of a fountain hidden in the dark foliage. "The fact is, that the doubt which you mean, the doubt of which you have a fit upon you just now, Olivia, is not of the sort about which one can ask people for advice, for logical assistance. It isn't doubt about any particular idea or dogma, about anything that other folk can understand; it is doubt about oneself, about the reality of one's feelings, about the reality, in a way, of oneself. Religious people bring it into connection with God; we, who are not religious, remain sufficiently wide awake to see that it is about our own selves; and this very perception of its, so to speak, subjective nature, makes us all the more sceptical. It's a thing that comes over one when one has just enough experience of life to perceive that one's feelings are not always the same, that one's ego varies, and is made to vary by a hundred external causes; and when one has too little experience of life to take this as a matter of course. We all begin by being mysteries to ourselves, solid, concrete like the people outside us, indeed almost outside the reach of our own analysis. Then we gradually get to understand the mechanism, we cease to be mysteries; but we also begin to feel that we are shams. Then we get into a semi-mystical state, as you are, we perceive ourselves as mere phenomena; and having discovered, as you said, that we are *not* the centre of anything, we strive to understand something that is; we see that we are after all (what children and servants never see) very relative concerns, fluctuating, elusory, often unreal, and we hanker in consequence after the absolute, the real ; trying to leave all our shams behind and become united with something which can't be a sham—which isn't one, because it doesn't exist at all. At least we do so if we are poets or metaphysicians. Doubt, doubt ; or rather certainty of change. To what extent is any of my feelings real, what is their relative weight by the side of the feelings of others ? Are they mere pieces of cardboard painted to look like metal, but which bend and twist, and which every wind blows away? Your brother, because he is five years younger than you, because, perhaps, he is an Italian in part, doesn't ask himself these questions : you do, Olivia, because you are no longer a child. Is it not so ?"

"Oh, thank Heaven that you force me to say it, Baldwin," exclaimed Olivia, with a sigh of relief. "Somehow one cannot say these things except to people who do not need to be told them. With others—with my brother, because he is a child, and with Marcel, because he is a stranger, I feel forced, since I can't keep it altogether to myself, to speak of such things under false names, to put myself and others on to false tracks ; I pretend to myself that I wish to get at the absolute in God, because I can't tell them that I wish to fly from the doubtful and elusory in myself, and I feel as if I must say something, because it worries me so constantly."

Baldwin smiled.

"So you talk mystical metaphysics. You say you hate personality, because you are not comfortably sure about your own and that of others?"

Olivia nodded.

"How long," she said, almost as much to herself as to Baldwin, "will any of it last? How long shall I want, care for, the same thing? Is it a reality to-day; and if it is, will it be a reality to-morrow? The habit of seeing one feeling replaced by another does not prevent my feeling. But while feeling, it makes me see the mechanism, the accident by which all has arisen, the mechanism by which all will disappear. And the sense of understanding the machinery, of seeing the strings which pull my puppet self, brings with it a sense also of insincerity: the past and the future give the lie to the present. All this," added Olivia, half angrily, "doubtless seems very ridiculous to you, Baldwin; the pseudo-inner life of a pseudo-poet—of a poetess, that is! You have somehow, I suppose by some horrid process of horrid abstract logic, got to know that people do feel in this way, but you have never felt it."

"You consider me, that is to say, as a machine that grinds out logic—so much of wood, so much steel, carefully labelled 'to be kept perfectly dry,' laughed Baldwin. "Do you remember once last spring, a conversation we had about poor Agatha Stuart?"

"We have had so many conversations about her, Baldwin. And I don't see what that has to do with the question of such doubts."

"Doubts—that is not exactly the word either," mused Baldwin. "I should like to call what we are talking about after a line of Whitman's—'of the terrible doubt of appearances.' Well, the conversation I allude to was one late evening last March: it was stormy, and you had on a white teagown—the white teagown impressed itself on my memory, and may serve to recall the occasion to you, as I suspect it was the first time you had put that dress on. You had been reading me a poem of yours about your cousin Agatha. I told you what my feelings about her were—how we had formerly quarrelled over religious subjects, and I had thought she was merely interfering and presumptuous, and had often been rough and sharp with her while she was alive; then, when she was dead, and I re-read her letters and heard a great many things I had not known about her, and remembered many I had forgotten, how I had seemed suddenly to understand it all, and how I had felt miserably ungrateful for her interest in me, and how it had seemed as if my best friend had been wasted and lost in her. Do you remember my telling you that, one evening last spring, my dear Olivia?"

The poetess nodded.

"Quite well, now. It was a rainy evening, and we

were looking into the garden after dinner, while Charlie was playing the piano. I told you, as the person who had known poor cousin Agatha best, that you had been mistaken; that Agatha never really cared much for any one, except perhaps me; that she was interested in you, not because she wanted your friendship, but because it seemed to her that God was being cheated of you, and you were being cheated of God."

"Exactly," answered Baldwin, slowly. "That evening left me, has left me, with a fit of the 'terrible doubt of appearances.' I was disconcerted much less by what you have told me than by my own way of taking it. It seemed to me as if I were so constituted that nothing could be really painful to me so long as it was still exciting, that I enjoyed the drama too much to feel the blows I got in it. It impressed me very much, I mean this unreality of myself, at the very time. Certainly, with the exception of literally one or two minutes at most, I distinctly enjoyed that talk when we leaned out of the window, you in your white brocade dress, looking out into the rain and darkness among the leafless trees; and the fact that I was being robbed of a long petted belief, that I was being deprived of a friend who had walked faithfully by my side this year and more (often consoling me, poor non-existence, with the certainty of its non-existent affection) added merely an excitement in which the beauty of the woman by my side, the shimmer of her dress, the spring storm and rain and darkness, the vague strong pleasure of talking about poor Agatha, of finding myself in presence of your feeling for her, seemed to acquire a greater poignancy, almost a greater pleasureableness. And I wondered at myself. But I went away cruelly dashed. For the thing which resulted from all this talk was, or seemed to be, that I had been mistaken, that I had not been loved where I thought I had been; that, alas! this ghost which for months had walked by my side, had taken my hand and looked into my eyes, was a mere phantom of my own imagination; that I had been mistaken when I had said to myself, 'Nothing can deprive me of this friend'—no, indeed, for I was being deprived of her then, being told I had never possessed her."

Olivia did not answer; she was simply amazed. They were standing by the little pond, where the bay trees shimmered, each leaf a metal blade, and the big cypress seemed to wait silently, as if holding its breath, its black plume motionless against the metallic moonlit sky.

"Had it all been an unreality?" went on Baldwin; "had I been imagining myself a dupe of my own stupidity and suspiciousness, spurning and then regretting bitterly a proffered invaluable friendship, while in reality there had been no affection to spurn or to regret, while I was a dupe when I repented of my indifference, not when I felt it? Was it so? I turned the matter round and round, I ransacked my own consciousness, and the only answer that came, indeed that comes, always the same, 'I cannot tell.' The real Agatha—what was she, and how did she feel? Strange to say, I felt easy on that point. It seemed to me as if I had lost nothing or but little in the possible loss of the real Agatha; for did there not remain, does there not remain, unchanged and unchangeable, the imagined one? Do I not know that one; have I not lived by her side, leaned upon her in my trouble, looked into her face in my isolation? The dead—yes, even the dead may be lost to one, I grant it you; but the creature born of one's fancy and one's desires, the unreal, cannot be lost. She remains, and remains a certainty."

Olivia looked at him in surprise.

"You unreal creature!" she exclaimed.

"It was not about Agatha that I began to doubt," interrupted Baldwin; "it was about myself. The whole incident was phantasmagoric: after it nothing concerning myself seemed real. When, just now, you described your own trouble with the 'terrible doubt of appearances,' you were describing a good portion of my life quite lately. *Always?* the way in which we express all that we feel strongly—*always?* But it was not there yesterday; and yesterday something else was in its place; so what shall we think of to-morrow? Unreal, everything is unreal, because it is passing. Yet, at the moment all seems so real,

Does it depend upon a particular condition of nerve? a fluid, a molecule, right or wrong at a given moment? And who can tell how that molecule may be to-morrow—nay, an hour hence? If we are changing continually, and feel ourselves changing, what is this *ourself?*"

There was a pause as they walked up and down the paved court, Olivia's tall, slender figure in the white vague dress, her pale face and pale blond hair, looking diaphanous, almost transparent, in the bluish moonlight, as if she were herself but the embodiment of one of these shifting moods, herself a mere momentary apparition. But as Baldwin spoke, any of that "terrible doubt of appearances" which might have been in her mind vanished entirely. She felt the shock of the sudden contact of reality. Her old friend, in this sudden manifestation, became for the first time absolutely real to her.

"You are very strange, Baldwin," she kept repeating—"very strange. Why, you are much worse than Marcel or I."

"Yes, for I can't make poems of it all."

"But then," she went on, with some hesitation, "if you are like that, why always show yourself cut and dried, a hard lump of opinions?"

Baldwin laughed.

"Because it's more sensible and useful. All these doubts, all that one feels on personal subjects, concerns only oneself, at most such others as may be in the same state. You poets can appeal to such others, give them your sympathy by showing them your feeling: it is one of your great uses in the world; one of the uses also of the great novelist. A mere logic chopper can't. But such things don't prevent one's having opinions. On the contrary, one's opinions come out of it, since all that constitutes one's life, one's experience: out of each vague and shimmering feeling comes an opinion, which is solid, and clear, and stable. I wished to show you how I had come to have a certain opinion, and I showed you myself. Now that I have done so, forget it; and consider me henceforth once more the man of cut and dried opinion, the desultory philosopher on the loose."

There was a certain banter in Baldwin's voice.

"I don't know whether you are serious or not," answered Olivia.

"Perhaps I don't know either. Let it remain a case of doubt—of the 'terrible doubt of appearances.'"

At this moment they were joined by the two other young men, lazily smoking in the moonlight.

"Look here, Baldwin," said Carlo, passing his arm through that of his friend, "I have been making grave reflections, while Marcel was talking with mother upstairs, and I have come to the conclusion that you have very seriously contradicted yourself."

"Well, 'and if I contradict myself, why, I contradict myself,' as Walt Whitman says," answered Baldwin, laughing.

"But I won't permit you to do so. You are my private philosopher, my Socrates, Virgil, Mephistopheles—everything you choose; and I can't afford to allow you any self-contradictions. Why, I should have to go over to Marcel! and Marcel is too depressing."

"And what is this self-contradiction for which I may be dismissed from your august service?" asked Baldwin.

They were walking underneath the pergola, whose woodwork made a black pattern, with its curved beams and twisting vines and pointed leafage, on the blue light of the sky: here a bunch of leaves in full light, floating in the blue, transparent luminous themselves; there the trellis drawn in white precision by the moon, or a mere fantastic writhing of branches; while under foot was a pavement of fretted moonlight, broken into patterns by the shadows of the woodwork and foliage.

"Why, thus." answered Carlo, "You made us, as we rowed from Chiaggia, a very fine speech about the value of personality, and the necessity of its being duly expressed in literature. Pray, how do you make that square with the opinion which you expressed last night, that as a whole a book like the 'Fleurs du Mal' is an abomination? If you think personality such an important thing, what right have you to object to such an expression of it as that?"

"Perfectly logically, my dear Charlie. I consider personality a most important item in literature; and I consider the personality of Baudelaire, for all his genius, as that of a vicious cad. I blackball such personality; and I therefore blackball the expression of it."

Marcel had been walking on with Olivia. At the name of his favourite poet he turned round towards Baldwin.

"It is extraordinary how some things are engrained in a race," he remarked, with his usual mildness: "here is Baldwin, a cosmopolitan if ever there was one, brought up in France and Italy, and who yet cannot rid himself of that essentially English habit of applying moral standards to artistic questions. How is it that you, as part of an utilitarian nation, as an utilitarian individually, can fail to recognize that a man must do what he can do best, that there is no greater waste in the world than forbidding genius to find its own aims and methods?"

"Am I an utilitarian?" answered Baldwin. "Well, perhaps I am. Perhaps to be utilitarian is to be narrow-minded; but I would rather err, or take my chance of erring, on this side. As to this question, I think that when you say, as you do, Marcel, that a writer ought merely to write sincerely and to the best of his powers, without asking himself what may be the result upon others, you are simply confusing two matters. You are arguing in reality not against the application of a moral standard to artistic questions, but against the application of a moral standard to what is distinctly a moral question."

"I am laying down a utilitarian principle, my dear Baldwin," interrupted Marcel: "namely, that it is every man's duty to do as well as he can do whatever he does best. You cannot dispute that principle."

"Certainly not, as long as the thing which your man can do is in itself a thing worth doing. I am just as much persuaded as you are that no man has a right to refuse to do his own business which he can do well, because the business of another man, which he can do less well, or not at all, strikes him as more worth doing. It is certainly his duty to do what he does best. But this presupposes that the choice lies entirely among things which are all of them desirable ; that these many and various sorts of work, some more, some less necessary, are all of them such that mankind will be the better for their being done. Now, when the question is : Shall a man like Shelley spend his time in writing lyrics finer than any other man's, or writing humanitarian essays no better than sixty other men could write, the answer is plainly : Shelley shall write what he writes best—namely, lyrics. But when you ask : Shall Baudelaire or Swinburne write, because he writes them well, morbid or obscene poems, such as only he can write equally powerfully, rather than poems neither morbid nor obscene, which may require less special endowment, the matter is shifted on to another ground. The choice is no longer between two things each of which is desirable, but between two things one of which is desirable, while the other is distinctly not. You might as well ask, Shall this man be a mediocre mechanic or a first-rate pickpocket? It is only of things that are useful, or at least harmless, in themselves, that we can say, Let them be done by those who do them best. When once we get into the region of things which are harmful, the desideratum is that they should be done by those who do them least well: success to useful undertakings, ill luck to harmful ones. This confusion," added Baldwin, "is due to the fact of considering literature as a mere art, and the choice of a topic or attitude as something *within* the artistic jurisdiction; as already within the bounds of the legitimate and desirable, and therefore liable only to the condition of being well done. But inasmuch as a writer deals with results which are practical, and practically concern the moral health of mankind, he is still, in the choice of his work, outside the merely artistic domain. The question is not yet, 'How can it best be done,' but, Ought it to be done at all."

"At that rate," answered Marcel, "you strike at the root of literary sincerity. A book like Rousseau's 'Confessions,' which is of incalculable interest to the pyschologist, goes into the fire along with the 'Fleurs du Mal.'"

"Are you sure, Marcel," put in Carlo, with his Italian suspiciousness of anything like pose—"are you sure that Baudelaire was a sincere man in the same sense as Rousseau?"

Marcel took no notice of this interruption.

"At all events," he went on, "you are for forbidding a man saying what is, or what appears to be, true about himself. And that is discouraging sincerity."

"Not at all," answered Baldwin. "A man may be perfectly sincere without blurting out what concerns only himself; it is no part of an honest man's duty to wash his dirty consciousness in public. As to physiological specialists, they must seek their knowledge in some more private fashion, even as their psychological brethren: moral pathology need not be investigated in the open thoroughfare; and I certainly consider a book like the 'Confessions' as a remarkably nasty pathological exhibition."

"There you are, contradicting yourself again, Baldwin," exclaimed Carlo: "you approve of such wholesale showing up of vice as we have had from the *Pall Mall Gazette*; and you condemn Rousseau for displaying his individual weaknesses."

"The cases are absolutely different, Charlie," replied Baldwin. "To shed light, the greatest amount of light, on the organization of vice, is to help in its repression; it is, what is even more important, to show the full responsibility to all those who, from thoughtlessness or moral slackness, are in danger of joining the fearful unconscious conspiracy of evil. But a book like Rousseau's helps neither to repress nor to warn. It merely shows mediocre people that a very great man, and in many respects a very admirable man, may be morally unclean; and thus teaches them to condone and tolerate in themselves what has become, in their eyes, excused or even ennobled by the solidarity with his greatness. Such an example, like the example of Napoleon, and the example of Machiavelli's successful political scoundrels, is profoundly dangerous to the moral health of the mass of mankind."

Olivia had remained silent during this conversation. Fond of speculation, with a poet's fondness for the distant and unattainable, she had, on the other hand, a vague aversion to discussion, which brought subjects into their practical prosaic reality, and hacked them, as it seemed to her, out of all intellectual shape; a sort of semi-æsthetic sensitiveness of fibre which also made, sometimes to her own shame, the thought of concrete evil as intolerable as a series of false notes or a disgusting smell. She was one of those exquisite beings who are unfit for the rough work of the world; and who do the world good merely by setting before it, in their own delicate and immaculate selves, an ideal and a consolation. But she felt that this attitude of mind did not satisfy her own conscience; and she made an effort to join the conversation, which, as a result, immediately resumed a certain abstract character.

"But, Baldwin," she said, "does progress depend upon what you call the mass of mankind and upon its moral healthiness? Is it not the work of the individuals, the exceptions, of those who do not participate in what you call moral health—that is to say, a balance of faculties which means mediocrity? It comes home to me more and more every day how little mankind at large has to do with human improvement, how utterly all that is the business of a small minority. Merely looking at the types that meet one in the streets, even among so intelligent a race as this, I am struck by the utter dulness of mankind. You will object that many of these people, of these seeming incapables, carry on some trade or business of a by no means easy sort. But they have not invented nor even developed this trade or business: they have been taught it throughout generations by others who had gradually learned it from the men who did invent or develop it. These incapables have been forced into a kind of capability much as a top is lashed into spinning; and one is astonished at the seeming ingenuity of an artisan or a peasant whose face seems to show utter incapacity. Similarly even in what may be called the thinking classes, one is astonished at the power of discussion, of appreciation of certain people whose face, whose whole nature, is stamped with this same incapacity:

here, again, they are thinking, as the others are acting, in the way invented and taught by their betters. It is curious to think over one's own acquaintances, the people whom one treats as intelligent, with whom one speaks, for whom one writes, and to imagine the attitude which such folk would have assumed, had they lived in some past time, on the promulgation of any of those facts or principles on which they are now almost automatically basing their mental and moral decisions. It is curious to reflect how, even among these superior beings, one would have found, when intellectual movement was less general (and perhaps one would find even nowadays were any new intellectual or moral effort suddenly required), nothing but inert or active obstacle ; curious to reflect how, in the course of civilization, at least nine-tenths of mankind have been employing whatever mental or moral force they might have in wasting the time of the other tenth."

"What you say is perfectly true," answered Baldwin, "but that does not go against the fact that this mass of mankind, these various people who strike us as incompetent with regard to any higher and more original work, have yet a most important share in all progress. These creatures who could never invent, nor even accept (for there is an intermediate class for that) any new thing, material or intellectual or moral, are those who preserve and hand on the material and intellectual and moral things invented and gained by previous generations. Mediocrity, so to speak, is the old stocking in which civilization is hoarded ; of course as long as all the money is always in the old stocking it does not increase, and thus the old stocking may often be in the way of any such employment of capital as may lead to increase. But it remains equally true that the stupids, at least the mediocre, are those upon whom the moral and physical security of the world rests; the clever folk, the innovators, would not carry on the business of life, they would often deliberately check it. Now, in all moral matters, to carry on the traditions, even the prejudices, of mankind, is of the very highest importance ; to prevent their waste and destruction in a moment of sudden new-fangled enthusiasm. Personally, for instance, I am for making divorce sufficiently easy to put an end to all such unions as have become false positions, impediments to development, mere holding in social and spiritual mortmain ; but I am very glad that there should be people to defend the indissolubility of marriage ; just as, although I am on the whole a Liberal, perhaps even a Radical, I would on no account do without a sufficient number of obstructive Tories. Well, to return to what I am saying. The mass of mankind ought to be a sort of moral filter, through which everything new has to be passed, with this difference, that in the moral filter what is valuable remains, what is worthless passes out. And such a moral filter they most distinctly are, mediocre and even vicious as they may be, the stupidity and perversity of each individual being compensated in the mass. Therefore I stick most decidedly to my opinion, that the moral healthiness of the mediocrity is a thing most jealously to be guarded. The mass can always reduce the individual, or the individual's doctrine, to the condition of healthiness or innocuousness, but only if the mass is itself in proper condition. The filter must be clean, if what passes through it is to be cleansed. Now if you allow a superior individual, a moral or intellectual reformer, to make a whining and helpless display of his moral diseases (which he must deal with himself, or carry to a moral specialist) before the multitude, as was the case with Rousseau, you are striking a blow at the moral health of the mass, even as a man like Machiavelli may be said to have done so. Progress requires that popular imagination should not learn to condone or admire evil because it exists among the superior few: if the king is a leper, he must cover his leprosy."

Neither Olivia nor Marcel made any answer: Olivia, because she was thinking of the curious suffering personality revealed to her but half an hour before by this man who spoke, it seemed to her, always in a manner so impersonal, always so harsh; Marcel, because this kind of thought jarred upon his theories and his practice, and that any such jar was intensely painful to him. But Carlo, who boldly asserted that he had no opinions, and intended tasting all before deciding on any, burst out with an objection.

"But supposing I say to you, Baldwin," he began, "that I don't care for progress; supposing I prove to you that progress does not mean greater happiness? Happiness depends upon a balance between our activities; above all, upon the existence of a certain surplus energy: we can't be happy if we are always uncertain in our minds, and always weary and hurried and worried, can we? Well, what you call progress, which is increasing complexity, must inevitably disturb the harmony of our faculties and deprive us of all that margin of feeling which is required for happiness. We are becoming daily more critical, more self-conscious; our emotions and our activities will soon be eaten up by our consciousness——"

"There's for you, Baldwin," whispered Olivia.

"Moreover," went on Carlo, "we shall lose all force of deciding from being shown too many alternatives, all force of willing from examining too much how we will——"

"Quite true, quite true," murmured Marcel, whose whole pessimistic philosophy this lad, boiling over with energy, was thus cheerfully summing up. "In this way, progress, which means complexity, will make us less, not more, fit to live and enjoy ourselves."

Baldwin laughed.

"We shall grow old, we have grown old, as that Italian foretold Goethe—'perchè pensa? pensando s'invecchia'—which prophecy, by the way, was not carried out, certainly, in Goethe's self. No; I don't think we need be afraid of becoming too highly organized, of our civilization reaching too high a point, my dear boy. Remember, in the first place, that we are in an evident age of transition, and have no right to suppose that in a hundred or two hundred years things will be exactly as they are. All these new habits of thought, which are so painfully obvious to us, which, allow me to add, we take a pleasure in making so painfully obvious to ourselves, will gradually be integrated in our nature; will become, little by little, automatic. We shall do the new things: give a share to mankind in our judgments, understand complex mental states, make allowance for difference of time and race, enjoy new kinds of art, as we do so many things which at first required a strain of attention almost preventing real mental action, such as reading a foreign language, playing the piano, nay, even riding or smoking. There will be nothing half so marvellously complicated in the process by which, with reference to an utilitarian standard of duty, in consideration of exotic standards, in cognisance of complex states of mind, our descendants will rapidly decide how to act towards a given individual, as there is in the process by which our friend Carlo plays at first sight a piece scored for many instruments and noted in many clefs. No, no, the human mind does not give way so easily as you are pleased to suppose: it merely eliminates from consciousness, strides across what it once wearily toddled over. I can quite imagine a pessimist of pre-railway days prophesying that we should all go crazy from seeing too many things whirl past us; whereas experience has shown that we see only just the same amount as if we were in a postchaise: the mind adapts itself, and, having to see things over a greater number of miles, sees less in each."

"I shut up," answered Carlo, quite satisfied. "By the way, Baldwin, you mustn't think that when I raise objections to your views I necessarily go against you and believe in those objections. But I like to see what can be said on both sides; I like to draw people out; I assert because I want my assertions to be demolished."

Baldwin laughed.

"I know you do. I don't think you are cut out for a pessimist, Charlie."

"No," answered the young man, very simply; "how can one feel bad about a world in which there are such quantities of interesting questions?"

Carlo's answer provoked a general laugh, as they walked in the long trellised avenue, where the roses shone out a wan pink, and the moonlight made pools and runnels and water-like drippings among the trees and bushes. At the extremity of one of these walks they stopped, and, pushing aside the tall stems of the bay trees, leaned on the low wall, and looked out on to the pale sea, hung with mists and paved with moonbeams, the realm of the Fata Morgana, which seems to recede the more you pursue.

Marcel was the first to break the silence, made more silent by the dim voice of Olivia, who was singing to herself some fragment of an old Venetian song.

"You speak of progress, of happiness, of moral health and moral sickness," he said : "but what are all these ? Words, words of which no one of us can so much as determine the meaning. Let us take progress in one of its nobler senses : not merely the progress which ministers to our bodily comfort, but the progress that means more light, a clearer comprehension, a wider power of sympathy. How does this affect what you call happiness, and what you call moral health and moral sickness? It teaches us that, in the first place, no standard is unchangeable, that no standard is divine ; that those laws which we once believed were from God, are the adaptations, shifting and momentary, to the shifting and momentary conditions of man ; that what is now vice was once virtue, that what is now virtue may in time become vice."

"Nay," interrupted Olivia ; "science may teach us that what was once virtuous, as being the lesser of two evils, may become vicious when it becomes the greater; or when the alternative ceases entirely, as, for instance, in the case of slavery. But all science goes to confirm that he is acting for the good of society, that he is virtuous and to be venerated, who, whatever the case, chooses the alternative which implies the lesser evil, the greater good; all science shows us that, however much the conditions of mankind may have changed, there were always courses which were good and courses which were evil, and men and women, therefore, who were good and bad."

Marcel smiled bitterly.

"I grant you that," he said; "but science, and when I say science I mean thought, has shown us something else besides. It has shown us that a man or a woman is sent into the world with a definite moral constitution, with definite powers of resisting or necessities of succumbing; and is then placed, by the mere accident of birth or education, in such a situation that he must resist or must succumb. Science shows us that, instead of a criminal, there exists only a victim; science teaches the old lesson of religion, that we must not judge, but only mourn; it says to us, like Christ, that we must not throw the stone; nay, more, it says what even Christ never said, that, in the presence of such as the world calls wicked, those others whom the world calls good must cast down their eyes, must sink on their knees, and, as the hero of that great novel of Dostoïevsky does to the fallen woman, kiss the hem of their garment, and cry out that this reverence is for all suffering and all sin."

Marcel, as always, spoke very low, and, as he slowly uttered the last words, his voice dropped to a scarce audible whisper. Instinctively the eyes of Baldwin sought those of Olivia. She was still gazing out at the moonlit lagoon, but the tears had gathered in her eyes; such appeals as this shook her delicately strung nature like some harrowing melody.

"No," he said, "that is not the lesson of science, not the lesson of what you call thought. It is, on the contrary, the result of a revulsion against science, as the similar doctrine of early Christianity expressed a revulsion against paganism. For science has merely replaced by a definite formula the allegories in which paganism taught the great fact of the necessity of evil and pain, and submission of the weak to the strong; both paganism and science opposing to our desires of how things should be the reality of how they are. Paganism had shown the superiority of strength. Christianity did not deny it—nay, it accepted but too well the demonstration, and to it made but one answer—'Blessed are the weak.' Science has demonstrated the fatality of sin; and to this new crushing of our desires by our reason a new sentimentalism has answered—'Blessed are the sinful.' Nay, do not deny it; that is the meaning of that magnificent scene between Raskolnikoff and Sonia in the Russian novel; that is the meaning of your own answer, Marcel, whenever I have ventured to suggest that you have not branded in your books some thoroughly vile and noxious creature: the poor creature could not help being that; it is his or her misfortune—'c'est un pauvre être qui souffre.'"

"I do not deny it, and never would do so," answered Marcel, passionately. "I see that society requires to be reminded that it makes individuals sinful, and then punishes them."

"Society," replied Baldwin, "requires to be reminded of no such thing. Society requires to have recalled to it, if anything, that the distinction between good and evil has its origin, not in the conscience of the individual, but in the interests of the community. Responsibility can enter into the estimate only of him who forbids our being free agents; and society is not an omnipotent creator who chastises the creatures whom he has made sinful, that we should say to society, 'You are unjust.' Society does not create; it struggles: the fatality of evil is not made by, but imposed upon, it. The question of free-will in the theological sense in which we are using it now, of original individual responsibility, is one entirely outside the jurisdiction of mankind. The frame of mind, the constitutional peculiarities which caused his crime, is important to society only as a practical guide in judging whether the creature who has done this mischief may yet be able to do good sufficient to render his existence valuable, in judging whether the creature is or is not such as must be unhesitatingly exterminated by death, or prison, or obloquy; whether, in short, it is a case for radical or palliative action. If an injury to society is the result of dire distress or mental sickness, it is worth while to consider whether the causes of that dire distress being removed, the mental sickness being healed, the person or class to which such an injury is due may not become harmless or even useful. But whether the injurious action is committed with pain or with rejoicing, whether the criminal is happy or unhappy, except in so far as this happiness or unhappiness affects, as I have said, his future capabilities for good or ill, is no concern of society's. Evil is probably more often accompanied by circumstances distressing to the evildoer; but this does not in the least diminish its power of injuring the other members of the community, and of such injury spreading. The one aim of society is to diminish the doing and spreading of such injury. Now the fact of one crime being the result of another crime does not interfere with the fact that, unless repressed, it will engender yet a third crime; quite the contrary."

"You forget," put in Marcel, reproachfully, "or you do not perhaps know, that about all suffering, whether innocent or guilty, there is a kind of holiness."

"I know, on the contrary, that nothing can be more false or more pernicious than to bestow the glory of holiness upon suffering. Holiness means moral value; and suffering, as such, has no moral value whatsoever."

"Oh, Baldwin!" exclaimed Olivia, "you go against all human instinct there. You know perfectly that suffering has a kind of poetic value, that it attracts our veneration, and places an aureole round the head of the sufferer."

"Suffering, my dear Olivia, attracts us to the sufferer because we are attracted to free him from it; it places an aureole round his head upon the supposition—in many cases false—that it is supported magnanimously: the air of holiness depends upon the intuition, 'If this man, in his condition, is as good as we, he is much better'; the apparent dignity, what you call the poetic value, of suffering, means merely that we recognize it as something odious which ought to be removed, as something often degrading which, when it does not degrade, testifies to an unusual nobility. This does not alter the fact that, in itself, suffering has no moral value, therefore no holiness. It is merely a great destroyer. That some natures pass through suffering without injury and even with profit, is merely saying that a sieve is a sieve, that there is such a thing as survival of the fittest. But there are all the natures which have not profited by suffering, whose nobility, instead of being increased, has been irremediably damaged or utterly lost—natures which might yet have been, in normal circumstances, useful in their way and excellent."

"But suffering," persisted Olivia, "adds to our power of understanding and sympathizing; and is that not a moral value?"

"It does not imply that suffering is good or holy. That to have suffered gives additional powers of comprehension and sympathy to some natures, means merely that as there is an immense amount of suffering in the world, no person's experience and power of helping can be complete without a knowledge of it— a knowledge obtainable only by participation. A person who should never have seen sickness could not be completely sympathizing and useful as regards it; but that is not saying that sickness is a good thing. On the contrary, the experience of suffering in A. is useful only in proportion as it can diminish or forestall the sufferings of C. and D. and E. It is the enemy, whom we must know if we would vanquish; but the enemy Suffering is no more holy than the enemy Satan. Therefore I say, that the fact of crime being the result of suffering, does not diminish by a tittle the necessity of exterminating crime, and, if necessary thereunto, exterminating the criminal."

Olivia did not answer. Such questions sickened her soul, and almost prevented her thinking. But Carlo, to whom, in reality, suffering was not much more than a word, a pawn in the metaphysical game that delighted him, burst out against his friend—

"You are very hard-hearted, Baldwin," he said, "or

pretend to be so. You have no repugnance for the suffering of the guilty."

"I have repugnance, my dear boy," answered Baldwin, with that readiness which the metaphysical Olivia particularly alluded to when she said that this materialist ought to have been a priest, "I have repugnance for the suffering of the innocent. In so far as the evildoer is a victim, I pity and desire to avenge him; in so far as he makes victims of others, I desire to exterminate him on the spot."

"We were talking," said Marcel, as they slowly walked towards the garden house, where the gondola awaited them once more to take them home—"we were talking not of the measures which society may take for the suppression of evildoers—a subject that afflicts me profoundly—but of the effect which science must have on our own views of good and evil by showing us the fatality of each. You had been singing hymns to progress. Myself, as a pessimist, I asked you, after all, what does all this progress come to? Progress, among other things, brings with it—at least so it seems to my mind—the belief in determinism; and determinism, by removing responsibility, puts an end to all idea of right and wrong."

"Not at all," answered Baldwin; "and thereunto belongs our previous discussion about the sufferings of evildoers. Determinism shows why one man is destined to have a will, and another to have none—why one man is destined to be a nuisance, and another a benefit to society; but determinism cannot tell us that the man with the will is not more useful than the man without the will; determinism cannot remove the fact that the nuisance *is* a nuisance, and the benefit a benefit. Now our ideas of right and wrong depend not upon the consideration of cause, but upon the consideration of effect. A thing is wrong which leads to a balance of suffering, a thing is right that leads to a balance of happiness; and the question why a creature is noxious, or whether it is so from fatality or otherwise, does not interfere with the fact that all noxious things must be stamped out. Now right and wrong, morality, is the question of what should be abetted and what should be stamped out: it is the question of the result of a certain action, not of its cause. Your determinism merely explains why some people are good and some bad; it does not diminish the fact that good people are to be encouraged, and bad ones to be discouraged. I deny, therefore, that progress, in the sense of greater knowledge and wisdom, can at all interfere with our notions of right and wrong."

"I have nothing to do with right and wrong," answered Marcel, somewhat peevishly; "they seem to me mere fluctuating unrealities. I see happiness and unhappiness; or rather, I see unhappiness mainly. Progress means development, greater complexity, and sensitiveness. The modern man is much more difficult to deal with than the man of former days. He has, in virtue of his greater complexity, a far greater number of desires, and desires which are conflicting ; while, at the same time, increased sensitiveness implies greater lassitude. The power of extracting pleasure is diminishing with familiarity with all such things as might yield it; and yet the demand for satisfaction is growing more and more imperious with every fresh complexity of our nature. The world, all that which ministers to man's desires, bodily and spiritual, remains the same, and man is changing; and thence that want of adaptation between the inner constitution and the surroundings which we call disease. Look at the two men who have perhaps—amongst us French at least—done most to form the younger generation, Baudelaire and Renan. What is the secret of their pessimism—rebellious and murderous in the one, sceptical and resigned in the other? It is that they have outstripped their contemporaries, and that, being more highly developed, more complex, more sensitive than other men, they are also more exacting and more impotent, tormented already by the double disease of the future, satiety of the possible, hunger for the impossible. These men are but the elder brothers of all mankind to come: Baudelaire has found the limit to all possible satisfaction of the senses; Renan the limit of all satisfaction of the intellect. The one has felt till he has found only pain instead of pleasure; the other has thought till he has found that thinking leads only to eternal doubt. We can enjoy no longer. This is the secret of the pessimism which lies at the bottom of all our hearts, a gnawing worm in the present, a devouring monster in the future."

Marcel sighed as he stood in the moonlight, slowly crushing in his hand the aromatic leaf of a laurel, and fixing his curious clairvoyant glance on Olivia.

But Olivia did not respond to that look. To Baldwin's surprise, the poetess flushed with indignation.

"No, no!" she exclaimed, in a quick, low voice; "you are mistaken, Monsieur Marcel. We have not all of us such pessimism in our hearts. This pessimism which you describe is not the pessimism of a man like Carlyle, nor even of a man like Schopenhauer. It is not the pessimism, which only the noblest can feel, when it comes to them that every day and hour and half-hour of their own peace and happiness is filled brimful with the suffering of a million others. This pessimism of yours comes merely from the concentration of all interest upon oneself and one's own self's powers of enjoyment; measuring all good and evil by the standard of one creature's pleasure or pain or lassitude. This pessimism is mere selfishness. The secret of the ignoble misery of a man like Baudelaire is simply that, having lived exclusively for his own gratification, and having exhausted, not indeed the enjoyable things of this world, but his own faculty for enjoying; having overtaxed and perverted his nature till it can vibrate only to the abnormal, he is devoured by the *ennui* and despair of his impotence and depravity. This is the pessimism of the voluptuary; the pessimism of intellectual selfishness is cleaner, less revolting, but it is not much nobler: he finds himself deprived of certain higher pleasures like religion; and thought, pursued only for its own sake, leads only to uncertainty: he, too, is sterilized by selfishness. No, no; we have not all of us such pessimism as this to make us wretched; and indeed, indeed, Monsieur Marcel, I do not believe you have it either, for you are good and honest and kind."

Marcel passed his hand wearily over his brow. "I may be good and honest and kind," he answered—"or rather I may have been it. But I am weary, tired, tired—I am sick, and with the sickness of our days."

"But you must not let yourself be that," exclaimed Olivia; "indeed you must not, you——" and she stopped; for the thought of what seemed to her the shipwreck of this noble soul in the gulf of selfish pessimism made her feel dizzy and faint.

"Olivia is quite right," said Baldwin, as the three walked slowly up and down the trellised walk. "All this pessimism is due to selfishness. It is the attitude of men who, having refused to feel or think or act, save for their own gratification, come to the end of all feeling or thought or action, and sit down in weariness, like a child crying after too long a holiday. This pessimism, to begin with, in so far as it is represented by a man like Baudelaire, is mainly founded upon the mere beastliest debauchery. It is no use glossing it over with fine phrases, but the misery of the 'Fleurs du Mal' is much more akin to that of the old rake so wonderfully described in the 'Suicide Club,' who says that fear is more delicious than love, than with the Faust who says, 'Habe nun, ach, Philosophie.' Moreover, allow me to say that I think it is all twaddle about our intellectual work coming to an end. No greater lie was ever penned than La Bruyère's 'Tout est dit,' which you Frenchmen are echoing in all tones. I am not a scientific man, but I know sufficient of science to see that there is no chance of our remaining twiddling our thumbs in a universe whence we have dislodged God only to instate the Unknowable. Every branch of science, like every branch of practical work, implies far too many all-absorbing details and applications for the scientific mind ever to feel as if it had nowhere to expend its energies. Further, there is the equally absurd twaddle about over-much thought and feeling weakening the body and breaking down the nerves. To begin with, feeling, in the case of Baudelaire, means merely debauchery. But, my good man, why should life consist only of the activity of the feelings and the intellect? Have we not got a body, and can't we exercise that also and take pleasure in its exercise? Above all, can't we think a little less of our own condition, and a little more of that of others?"

Marcel sighed.

"Ah," he answered, "you are English, you belong to an exceptional nationality. You can't understand these things."

"You have put your finger upon it, Marcel, only that your argument turns to my advantage. I am English, as you say; but I am sufficient of a cosmopolitan—nay, rather, of a Frenchman—to see and to be able to say without disrespect to your great country, which, you know, is in a measure also my country, that this sort of pessimism is due mainly to the miserable restrictedness of continental life. The French, you must admit, pay little attention at present to such things as do not touch their pocket or their vanity: the three questions, political, religious, and economic, absorb their practical efforts and one half of their speculation; whereas we English, inferior as we are in many respects, are distracted by a hundred different questions not dependent upon vanity or interest: agrarian reform, poor law, workmen's dwellings, penny dinners, diminution of vice, teetotalism, vivisection, &c., which do not practically affect the well-to-do classes, not to speak of dozens of various religious and humanitarian agitations; fads all these, in our neighbours' eyes, which make us disagreeable and ridiculous, but which are the proof of our greater vitality and health. Believe me, if your French pessimists would give a little of their attention to the miseries of others, they would soon find out that the limit of all feeling and activity had not been reached."

Marcel shook his head.

"Your time has not yet come," he said: "you are exceptional people, you English; you talk of pessimism being optimists; you judge of spiritual exhaustion while you have still a surplus of energy. We, who have hastened along the path before you, are weak, ill; do not talk to us of the wants of others; they merely add to the paralyzing weight of our own."

They were in the little court paved by the moonlight, where the statues shone forth, modelled by the moonbeams as with a brush full of white paint; or stood out, among the shimmering laurels, the pale roses, dark against the luminous blue; where the cypress moved scarce perceptibly its plumy tip, as if, by that faintest of motions, to make but more apparent the stillness of the night; while the blue light, the vague scent of autumn flowers and fallen leaves, the quaver of the insects and frogs, seemed to unite as a sort of general effluvium of sleeping things.

"Do not say that, Monsieur Marcel," intreated Olivia. "It is not true that the thought of others can make one but the more selfish and selfishly miserable. Does it not strike you this condition of being sated with some things and starving for others, is due, like the *ennui* and impotence of rich people, to a distribution of good and bad, of activity and idleness, which requires rearrangement, and which we can all do our microscopic something to rearrange? Does it not strike you that opposite to this Baudelaire, sated to sickness with pleasure, is the man whose whole life is a struggle with pain; that opposite this Renan, sated with thought and sensitiveness, is the man for whom thought and sensitiveness do not exist; that opposite the epicure, who cannot awaken appetite because he has eaten too much and fed on too highly seasoned food, is the beggar who has not a crust to put into his stomach? Oh, if there is anything in the world that can make us despair," continued Olivia, with excitement, but excitement which was solemn, "it is that, when there is so much misery for which to think and feel and act, there yet exists a number of men with noble gifts and sensibilities, who sit and moan that they have exhausted all subject of thought and feeling and effort."

As Olivia was finishing her sentence, there came from the garden house, staring out white and ghostly in the moonlight, the sound of Carlo's piano, of the young man's clear and guttural voice, with the swinging rhythm, the wide vigorous intervals of old Carissimi's song, "Vittoria."

The very first notes made Marcel start as if he had been rudely shoved or struck.

"Ah!" he exclaimed, with a pained contraction of his face, "how I hate that song! It is brutality put into music."

"And I," answered Baldwin, raising his eyes to the lit window—"I love it. It is the song of energy."

www.ingramcontent.com/pod-product-compliance
Lightning Source LLC
Chambersburg PA
CBHW030349230426
43664CB00007BB/590